STRIKING POWER

HOW CYBER, ROBOTS, AND SPACE WEAPONS CHANGE THE RULES FOR WAR

JEREMY RABKIN AND JOHN YOO

Encounter Books
New York • London

First American edition published in 2017 by Encounter Books,
an activity of Encounter for Culture and Education, Inc.,
a nonprofit, tax exempt corporation.
Encounter Books website address: www.encounterbooks.com

Manufactured in the United States and printed on
acid-free paper. The paper used in this publication meets
the minimum requirements of ANSI/NISO Z39.48-1992
(R 1997) (*Permanence of Paper*).

FIRST AMERICAN EDITION

LIBRARY OF CONGRESS CATALOGING-IN-PUBLICATION DATA IS AVAILABLE
Names: Rabkin, Jeremy A., author. | Yoo, John, author.
Title: Striking power : how cyber, robots, and space weapons change the
rules for war / by Jeremy Rabkin and John Yoo.
Description: New York : Encounter Books, 2017. | Includes bibliographical
references and index. | Description based on print version record and
CIP data provided by publisher; resource not viewed.
Identifiers: LCCN 2017006243 (print) | LCCN 2017012162 (ebook) |
ISBN 9781594038884 (Ebook) | ISBN 9781594038877 (hardcover : alk. paper)
Subjects: LCSH: War (International law) | Military weapons
(International law) | Technological innovations—Law and legislation.
Classification: LCC KZ6385 (ebook) | LCC KZ6385 .R336 2017 (print) |
DDC 341.6/3—dc23
LC record available at https://lccn.loc.gov/2017006243

Interior page design and composition: BooksByBruce.com

Contents

Preface

In his 2017 inaugural address, President Donald Trump protested that for decades the American people had "subsidized the armies of other countries while allowing for the very sad depletion of our military...spent trillions of dollars overseas while America's infrastructure has fallen into disrepair and decay."[1] No longer would the United States waste its blood and treasure fighting abroad for the interests of others. "From this moment on," Trump declared, "it's going to be America first." During his campaign, Trump had launched even sharper critiques of U.S. foreign policy. Paying attention to the interests of foreigners had led the United States into disastrous wars, most lamentably in Iraq. "We shouldn't have been there, we shouldn't have destroyed the country, and Saddam Hussein was a bad guy but he was good at one thing: killing terrorists," Trump said during the campaign.[2]

Despite such rhetoric, the administration did not pursue a foreign policy of isolationism or even non-interventionism. In the Middle East, the United States has not only continued fighting foes from its recent wars but gone beyond them. In April 2017, the Trump administration set aside the passivity of its predecessor and launched 59 Tomahawk cruise missiles against a Syrian air base in response to the Assad regime's use of chemical weapons. It expanded the American deployment of ground troops in the Syrian civil war, provided arms to Kurdish militias, and lent air and tactical support to Iraqi forces fighting the Islamic State terrorist group. U.S. troops continued to fight in Afghanistan against a resurgent Taliban, even going so far as to use a massive ordinance bomb against insurgent tunnels. Promising to "bomb the hell out of ISIS" during his campaign, Trump has authorized a significant increase in drone strikes and special operations by both the CIA and the U.S. armed forces.[3]

In Asia, the Trump administration did not send U.S. forces into direct combat, but it resorted to the threat of force to support its foreign policy. To pressure the North Korean regime to halt its nuclear weapons program, Trump dispatched the USS *Vinson* aircraft carrier strike group and a nuclear submarine to the area. "There is a chance that we could end up having a major, major conflict with North Korea," he said. "Absolutely."[4] His administration proposed a more aggressive response to China's building of artificial islands in the South China Seas. "Building islands and then putting military assets on those islands is akin to Russia's taking of Crimea. It's taking of territory that others lay claim to," Secretary of State Rex Tillerson said in his confirmation hearing.[5] "We're going to have to send China a clear signal that, first, the island-building stops, and second, your access to those islands also is not going to be allowed."[6] To enforce such demands would require more frequent freedom of navigation patrols and could even call for naval blockades.

For all that, President Trump shows little sign of reversing the Obama administration's caution on risking American lives. He continues to criticize the U.S. interventions in Iraq and Afghanistan as "costly"—by which he seems to mean costly in American lives but also in budget allocations. The Trump administration faces a quandary. Restoring a muscular American foreign policy will demand a higher rate of operations and deployments, increasing costs and risking greater casualties. Though the administration has proposed increases in military spending, it remains cautious about costly foreign commitments.

Technology can help resolve this looming impasse. Robotics, the Internet, and space-based communications have increased productivity across the economy. These same advances may have a comparably transformative impact on military affairs. Unmanned aerial vehicles (UAVs) allow pilots to strike targets more precisely at reduced costs, with less harm to bystanders and less threat to themselves. Cyber weapons permit nations to impose disruptions on an adversary in more precisely targeted attacks and without physical destruction. Space-based networks enable militaries to locate their forces exactly, lead their troops more effectively, and target their enemies more precisely.

These new advances are turning military development away from the twentieth century's reliance on draft armies equipped with simple, yet lethal, mass-produced weapons. As nations use force that becomes more precise and discrete, they can change the rules developed in the era of mass armies and attrition warfare. The laws of war need not fuss over the line between targetable military and immune civilian assets when UAVs can deliver precision-guided munitions on particular targets.

Reluctance to use force has led western nations to rely on economic sanctions, which punish entire populations. Drones and cyber attacks could provide a more effective alternative by inflicting harm on the target state's economy, but in a more precise manner. Such an approach may avoid the unintended effects of sanctions and operate much more quickly and reliably, and leave adversaries less time to adapt. To make the most of those new capacities, we should rethink current legal formulas purporting to regulate when military force is lawful against what targets it is used.

New weapons technologies could help the United States and its allies protect international stability. WMD proliferation, international terrorism, human rights catastrophes, and rising regional powers are threatening the liberal post-WWII international order constructed by the U.S. and its allies. Nations will be discouraged from confronting these problems with conventional force. But if new technology reduces the costs of war, while improving its effectiveness, nations may turn to force more often to promote desirable ends. International stability remains a global public good, in that peace benefits all nations regardless of who pays for it. This gives nations a strong incentive to free-ride off the efforts of others to maintain international peace and security. If using force becomes less expensive and more effective, nations may turn to force more readily when the times require it. New weapons may be particularly helpful in situations where a large-scale military response might be excessive, but mere words are insufficient.

New weapons technologies may produce the welcome benefit of limiting the destructiveness of conflict. While the United States, among others, is rapidly developing new means of fighting, these innovations may limit war. Robotics can reduce harm to combatants and civilians by making attacks more precise and deadly. Cyber can more effectively target enemy military and civilian resources without risking direct injury to human beings or the destruction of physical structures. Space satellites will provide the sensors and communications that make possible the rapid, real-time marriage of intelligence and force, and future orbital weapons may create a viable defense to nuclear missiles.

This book proceeds in three main parts. The first two chapters provide a historical overview of war, weapons, and the rules of warfare. We argue in chapters 1 and 2 that expectations about war and force, which may have prevailed some decades ago, do not fit the challenges of our time. Over the course of history, nations have adapted varied notions about the appropriate use of force as wider changes in technology and social organization generated new challenges and opportunities. Chapters 3 and 4 show that the law of war, in particular, has changed over time and the most recent efforts to codify restraints on armed conflict are ill-suited to our present challenges.

Chapters 5, 6, and 7 apply these insights to the new technologies of robotics, cyber, and space. They argue that new technologies give nations the ability to use force more precisely, and thus to exert force with lower harm. Greater precision will allow nations to settle their own disputes with less resort to full-scale hostilities. They will also give nations greater freedom to combat the current challenges to international peace and stability, such as WMD proliferation, regional aggression, and human rights catastrophes.

We have accumulated many debts in the writing of this book. First, we are grateful for comments on portions of this manuscript from Jianlin Chen, Dan Farber, Andrew Guzman, William Hubbard, Richard Johnson, Laurent Mayali, Eric Posner, and Ivana Stradner. Our work also benefitted from workshops at the University of Chicago Law School and the University of California at Berkeley Law School, and presentations at the American Enterprise Institute, the National War College, and the International Symposium on Security and Military Law. Our work was much improved thanks to the assistance of law students Benjamin Bright, Daniel Chen, Sohan Dasgupta, Gabriela Gonzalez-Araiza, Leah Hamlin, Allen Huang, Jonathan Sidhu, Joe Spence, Jon Spiro, and Mark Zambarda.

The authors also wish to thank their literary agent, Lynn Chu, of Writers Representatives, for shepherding this book from its first ideas to the final product. Her keen eye and rigorous thinking helped sharpen and focus this book. We also appreciate the editing of Katherine Wong and are grateful for the support of Roger Kimball, the publisher of Encounter Books.

The authors thank their respective deans for support: Henry Butler at GMU's Scalia Law School and Berkeley Law School Dean Christopher Edley (and interim deans Gillian Lester and Melissa Murray). Thanks are also due to our colleagues at the American Enterprise Institute, particularly Arthur Brooks, David Gerson, Danielle Pletka, and Gary Schmitt, as well as to James Piereson, president of the Thomas W. Smith Foundation.

Jeremy Rabkin thanks Ariel Rabkin for ongoing technical advice about cyber capacities, Nathaniel Rabkin for insights on contemporary conflicts in the Middle East, and Rhoda Rabkin for keeping all of us grounded.

John Yoo gives thanks to his wife, Elsa Arnett; he feels as lucky today as he has every day for the last three decades to enjoy her love and support. He also thanks his mother, Dr. Sook Hee Yoo, and his brother Chris Yoo. Our family came to the United States because of the wars of its past; this book is an effort to help us understand war better in the future.

CHAPTER 1

We Must Think Anew

Economists call it "creative destruction."[1] Robots are replacing factory workers. Online news sites are displacing newspapers. Passengers are abandoning taxis and summoning part-time drivers with cell phones. Household appliances and security systems are operating on home networks.

New technologies are having an impact beyond the workplace and household. Presidents George W. Bush, Barack Obama, and Donald J. Trump, for example, have ordered robots to kill individuals with precision-guided missiles from the sky. Unmanned aerial vehicles (UAVs) are leading the way for even greater technological innovations in war. The same high-speed computer systems can accelerate financial markets or disrupt national economies. Robotics and precision mapping can automate transportation, even passenger cars. They can also control pilotless aircraft that strike specific buildings or individuals. The same technologies that can assemble and deliver a book, a piece of furniture, or a sophisticated appliance to a customer within days are also enhancing military "productivity," which means fewer soldiers can kill or incapacitate more of the enemy at lower cost.

Technologies often transcend their original purpose. The cell phone initially freed people to make voice calls without the physical tether of telephone wires. Engineers next added cameras and data communications to the handheld phone. Users could now record and send pictures of controversial police actions, repressive crowd-control measures, or riots. Phones can now distribute these pictures to millions of strangers, before a journalist on the scene could write an eyewitness account. Users can also receive, as well as transmit, a stream of text, data, and information that is rearranging social relationships, consumer activity, travel, and entertainment. A world that is wired allows a vastly wider and more consequential range of communication than telephone calls.

So it is with war. Instead of ending armed conflict, technological advances have expanded it. World War II came to an abrupt end shortly after the United States dropped two atomic bombs on Japan. Many concluded that science had created a weapon so devastating, rational statecraft could never use war as a tool again. "Military alliances, balances of power, Leagues of Nations, all in turn failed, leaving the only path to be by way of the crucible of war. The utter destructiveness of war now blocks out this alternative," said even General Douglas MacArthur, no pacifist he, on the deck of the USS *Missouri* during the Japanese surrender. "We have had our last chance. If we will not devise some greater and more equitable system, Armageddon will be at our door."[2] Surely the United Nations would ensure that nations never again looked to settle their differences by resorting to war. It was not to be. Responding to those who hoped that the end of monarchy spelled the end of tyranny, Edmund Burke warned: "Wickedness is a little more inventive."[3] So it has proven in the decades after 1945. The major powers have not waged an all-out conflict, thanks, perhaps, to the very awfulness of the nuclear weapons that ended the last one. But, in the meantime, smaller armed conflicts and civil wars have together taken millions of lives.[4]

During the Cold War, many of these conflicts were viewed as "proxy wars." In the 1950s, the United States led an international action against North Korea's invasion of South Korea, because the Soviet Union and then Communist China supported Pyongyang. Starting in the early 1960s, the United States began committing troops to defend South Vietnam from North Vietnamese infiltration on the same theory. In the 1980s, the United States supported Afghan guerillas resisting the Soviet-backed government. Proxy wars allowed the great powers to continue their competition, but at less risk of nuclear war.

Even as the Cold War thawed, conflicts continued to break out. In 1991, the United States and its allies mobilized 600,000 troops to drive

Saddam Hussein's forces from Kuwait. By 2003, another American-led coalition toppled Saddam's regime in Baghdad with a little over a third of that force. In 2001, an even smaller fraction of that force, working with local insurgents, removed the Taliban from power in Afghanistan. In 2010, the United States, Britain, and France helped overthrow Libyan dictator Muammar Gaddafi without any ground troops at all, simply by providing focused air support to Libyan rebel forces. This was the same strategy that NATO had used a decade earlier, when it ran an intense bombing campaign to stop Serbian dictator Slobodan Milosevic's ethnic cleansing in Kosovo.

Most of these interventions did not produce permanent peace. Air attacks cannot control territory. Yet nations may still want to deploy force, whether for self-defense, to defend allies, to prevent human rights catastrophes, or to gain advantage. After almost two decades of inconclusive war in the Middle East, however, pessimists say that western states confront a choice between committing massive ground forces or standing on the sidelines. Smaller conventional forces have met with frustration in achieving the aims of strategy.

New technologies promise an alternative. Robotics, cyber, and space weapons can reduce the size of ground forces needed to wage war. They can withdraw human soldiers from the battlefield while making attacks more precise and deadly. They can allow nations to coerce each other without inflicting the same level of casualties and destruction as in the past. They can reach far beyond borders to pick out terrorists or selectively destroy WMD sites. They can reduce the costs that discourage western nations from stopping humanitarian disasters or civil wars. While armed conflict will continue as a feature of the human condition, it might now come at lower cost, for a shorter time, and with less violence.

Some critics do not share this optimism. They fear that because these new technologies will reduce the costs of military intervention, force will become a more attractive option in international relations. Philip Alston, a United Nations special human rights expert, argues against drones because "they make it easier to kill without risk to a State's forces."[5] U.S. practice may further violate international law because it uses robotic weapons to attack terrorists off of any recognized battlefield, which Alston believes is tantamount to killing civilians in peacetime. Even if this analysis is correct, it is no reason to reject new technologies. Nations that are able to deploy advanced technologies will not see the virtue in risking the lives of more of their troops as an alternative. Nations are unlikely to agree to treaties to limit these technologies until they are more certain of their impact on war and the balance of power. Moreover, these new methods of warfare may serve wider humanitarian concerns that are more significant than the legality of killing off-battlefield terrorists. Because drone strikes and cyber attacks can strike with more precision, they reduce death and destruction among civilians and even among combatants. If advanced technology can disrupt the financial or transportation networks of their rivals, they may achieve the goal of war—coercion of the enemy—with far less bloodshed than a focus only on military targets.

Meanwhile, new capacities may actually lead to less destructive wars by giving nations more options to resolve their disputes, or, better yet, more information that prevents conflicts from occurring in the first place. Armed conflict often results from miscalculation. Sometimes, aggressors doubt the resolve of potential opponents to commit force against them. Saddam Hussein, for example, seems to have assumed his seizure of neighboring Kuwait would trigger no serious opposition.[6] States may also resort to force because they do not trust the resolve of potential allies to protect them. In part, Israel launched its preemptive war on its Arab neighbors in 1967 for this reason. Robotic and cyber weapons provide nations with signals to convey information about their resolve or their trustworthiness. Reducing uncertainty in war will help nations to negotiate their differences with less need for armed conflict. New weapons offer more opportunity to reach settlements with less death and destruction.

In this chapter, we will briefly describe the military revolution in technology and its benefits. We will describe the current framework of the laws of war and its refusal to accommodate new forms of combat. History shows that technological improvements produce advances in warfare just as they bring economic development. Law has proven ill-equipped to slow military progress until well after weapons are first used and better understood. We conclude by explaining that the security demands of the twenty-first century will create even more demand for the deployment of new military technologies, which can help respond to threats to international stability with reduced costs and harms. Those who would prohibit or limit new weapons may well encourage conflict that is far more brutal and destructive.

The Revolution in Military Affairs

Unmanned Predator and Reaper drones rove the skies above the Middle East and Africa. They hover over a target for days and launch Hellfire missiles on a moment's notice. Robots on the battlefield below breach doors in house-to-house searches and explode improvised explosive devices commonly used by terrorists and guerrillas. UAVs take off and land on aircraft carriers while others perform reconnaissance and strike missions. Future advances will bring armed sentry robots, autonomous armored vehicles, and automatic missile and artillery fire. Soon, unmanned surface vessels may deploy on the high seas, close to shore, and others beneath the waves.

Combat is not just moving toward the robotic, it is also becoming ethereal. During its 2008 Georgia incursion, Russia became the first nation to deploy cyber attacks on enemy command, control, and communications systems to augment a ground invasion.[7] To delay the Iranian nuclear program, the United States and Israel allegedly launched the Stuxnet virus to damage centrifuges engaged in uranium enrichment.[8] China has stolen large databases of U.S. government personnel information in addition to penetrating the networks of U.S. defense contractors, airlines, and technology companies.[9] Russia has allegedly hacked into databases and email systems of the U.S. Departments of Defense and State, as well as those of the Democratic National Committee and the 2016 campaign of presidential candidate Hillary Clinton.[10]

These examples illustrate the dramatic advances in weapons technology over the last two decades, which observers sometimes refer to as the "revolution in military affairs."[11] The United States now fields thousands of UAVs for both reconnaissance and attack. Armed with stealth technology, these robots gather intelligence around the clock and launch immediate attacks in trouble spots around the world. In the future, the most advanced ground- and sea-based armed forces will employ remote-controlled units, such as sentries, light armor, and littoral naval vessels. Advances in missile technology and precision targeting will allow the United States to field a conventional global-strike capability that can hit any target in the world within an hour. Some experts even predict that autonomous weapons systems will soon be able to act free of direct human control.[12]

Some hope the revolution in military affairs will reduce the destruction of war. A nation will place fewer soldiers in harm's way when remote-controlled combatants are available. Precision-guided weapons, directed by clearer real-time intelligence, will inflict less death and destruction on soldiers and military assets. With drones available, for example, nations will no longer need to resort to World War II- or Vietnam-era bombing runs to destroy arms factories or oil installations. Precision-strike technology may also shorten war by targeting an opponent's leadership and strategic vulnerabilities, as the U.S. did in the 1991 Persian Gulf War and the 2003 Iraq invasion. Future technology could also reduce harm to civilians—one of the central aims of the law of war—by tightly concentrating the use of force on its intended targets.

Critics, however, worry that advances in weapons could increase conflict by making war easier to begin. If a nation can simply press a button and destroy a target without risking its own personnel, it will choose a military response more often. United Nations officials give voice to these growing worries. "The expansive use of armed drones by the first States to acquire them, if not challenged, can do structural damage to the cornerstones of international security and set precedents that undermine the protection of life across the globe in the longer term," declares Christof Heyns, the U.N.'s Special Rapporteur on Extrajudicial, Summary or Arbitrary Executions.[13] States can use drones and other technology to launch attacks far from conventional battlefields in ways that escape immediate detection, and perhaps even responsibility. Ultimately, pinpoint strikes will continue to blur any clear line between war and peace.

Whether outside observers applaud or deplore it, technology has driven an evolution of "war" from a clash of national armies on a battlefield to its current, multifaceted, and decentralized forms of conflict. Technology has played a role both in the rise of non-state actors and in helping states formulate responses to these non-conventional security threats. The September 11, 2001 attacks and the evolving sophistication of the Islamic State of Iraq and Syria (ISIS) show that states no longer have a monopoly on armed conflict. These groups have used modern communications, transportation, financial, and social networks to operate across state borders and carry out attacks in the home cities of the West, from Paris and Nice to San Bernardino and Boston. In formulating strategic responses, states have also relied on advanced technology, using high-tech surveillance and strike systems to gain better intelligence and effect precision attacks without the need for large conventional forces. In contrast to the wars of the twentieth century, which concentrated highly destructive forces on discrete battlefields, technology is now dispersing less acutely destructive forces over a broader span. Though technology has contributed to the reach of non-state terrorist groups, it can also assist nations in fighting them.

Cyber warfare, which is even easier to begin and more difficult to prevent, presents yet another form of unconventional conflict driven by technology. Internet attacks can cause real-world destruction and harm, or they can simply interfere with another nation's communications, financial, or information networks. A cyber attack, for example, could cause a flood by disabling the control mechanisms for a dam or could trigger an explosion by causing a power plant to malfunction. As Russia demonstrated in its invasions of Georgia in 2008 and Ukraine in 2014, nations can also use cyber weapons to support a conventional armed attack.[14] Cyber weapons can replace conventional weapons to commit sabotage, as was done through the Stuxnet virus aimed at the Iranian nuclear program. Or governments can use the Internet to steal significant military or intelligence information, such as weapons designs or strategic plans, which appears to be occurring with increasing frequency between the United States and China. "China is using its cyber capabilities to support intelligence collection against the U.S. diplomatic, economic, and defense industrial base sectors that support U.S. national defense programs," the U.S. Defense Department stated in a 2016 report to Congress.[15] "The accesses and skills required for these intrusions are similar to those necessary to conduct cyberattacks."

In this way, robotics and cyber weapons can exert force that does not necessarily kill or destroy tangible objects, but nonetheless is overtly hostile. Governments and scholars are not always clear about when such attacks meet the legal standards for an armed attack. For example, the new United States Law of War Manual, issued by the Department of Defense in 2015, declares that the existing laws of war *should* apply to what it calls "cyber operations."[16] But it then concedes that the rules here are "not well-settled" and are "likely to continue to develop." The United States even takes the position that it may not have a position. The Manual declares that it does not "preclude the [Defense] Department from sub-sequently changing its interpretation of the law."[17]

Indeed, the uncertainty as to how to classify these attacks has played itself out in nations' inconsistent responses to acts of robotic and cyber warfare. States have sometimes treated them as a form of espionage or covert action, refusing to consider the resulting damage as an act of war. China's theft of the U.S. Office of Personnel Management database did not prompt U.S. force in response, nor did North Korea's hacking of Sony's electronic files. Iran took no overt military action in response to the Stuxnet virus. American drones execute dozens of strikes in coun-tries—such as Yemen, Somalia, Afghanistan, and Pakistan—without sparking any military reaction. And yet, it seems clear that an armed response to such attacks would be appropriate in at least some contexts. Cyber attacks that disable key military command structures or critical civilian networks might very well be regarded as acts of war, along with attacks by robots and drones that kill or injure human beings or destroy property on a large scale.

The rules of war must evolve to keep pace with technology. Some nations demand an inflexible approach to the law of armed conflict because they hope that law can suppress war. Nations with minimal armed forces or weak strategic positions may support legal rules that inhibit other states from asserting potential advantages. Other states may oppose new technologies in the hope of preserving the advantages derived from their current forces. Still others may want to preserve mili-tary opportunities for low-tech, asymmetric tactics—those favored by guerrillas, insurgents, and terrorists. Many scholars and international officials may support an inflexible approach to the rules of war from intel-lectual comfort with the old way of doing things. It is to these problems that we now turn.

Frozen Law in a Changing World

Even as technology advances, legal and political leaders remain reluctant to embrace the use of new weapons. Despite their advantages, these new weapons have become the subject of a broad campaign to limit or even prohibit them. The claim is that these military advances violate the rules governing civilized warfare. Advocates for today's law of war, known as

International Humanitarian Law (IHL) to specialists,[18] have used multilateral treaties to construct a set of rules that depart from the realities of modern war. They now hope to freeze into place this new IHL, which tends to favor guerrillas, terrorists, and insurgents over western nations, and conventional ground combat over technology and innovation.

The law of war, however, more appropriately changes through natural evolution rather than artificial codification. They have long depended on the customs and traditions followed by states at war, which have usually decided on regulation after experience with weapons, not before. An evolutionary approach concedes that we do not currently know all the implications of these new weapons. We do not have full information on their characteristics and consequences, or the factual circumstances of their use. Rather than imposing rigid rules, the customary laws of war have usually adopted flexible standards—such as reasonableness in the selection of targets—that allow future decision-makers to judge the legality of force in their own circumstances. They place more faith in future leaders, commanders, and judges to come to better conclusions in reviewing the use of force after the fact than in the prescience of today's treatymakers. An approach built on flexible standards allows nations to gather more knowledge about the effects of new weapons, under conditions of deep uncertainty, before reaching fundamental decisions of policy.

In this respect, customary rules on the use of force resemble a common-law *standard*, such as the classic legal norm of reasonableness. A standard such as reasonableness allows judges to consider the totality of the circumstances before ruling on whether a defendant's actions were legal. A strict *rule*, however, such as contributory negligence, imposes a clear norm that reduces liability to a single factor and precludes the influence of later circumstances. Rules reduce decision costs because they are clear and easy to apply, they create legal certainty and predictability, and they require less gathering of information. Rules, however, prevent a nuanced application of law to facts and so often result in inequitable outcomes. Standards demand higher decision costs because of the need for more information and time for consideration. Standards produce greater uncertainty and unpredictability, but they more often produce the better answer. A rule gives more power to the legislators who write the norm earlier and narrow the discretion of future officials, while a standard places more trust in the competence and knowledge of later decisionmakers.[19] By following custom, the law of war accepts that the lawfulness of the use of force depends far more on the circumstances, that later officials will have greater access to information and experience, and that it is more important to get right answers than fast answers.

Many international leaders and scholars would replace the millennial-old, customary approach to the rules of war with instant law—with strict rules rather than standards. Nations launched an ambitious movement to codify new rules of military operations in 1977 with Additional Protocol I to the Geneva Conventions (AP I).[20] Controversially, AP I promoted two significant changes to the laws of war. First, it elevated non-state actors, such as independence movements and guerrillas, to the same status as nations with conventional armed forces. Second, it attempted to reduce the discretion of combatants to use force by expanding the definition of civilian targets that were to be off limits to combat. Because of these policies, the United States defied the majority of other nations and refused to ratify the treaty. In his message to the Senate withdrawing AP I, President Ronald Reagan declared that the Protocol was "fundamentally and irreconcilably flawed," and that its problems were "so fundamental in character that they cannot be remedied through reservations." He therefore had "decided not to submit the Protocol to the Senate in any form."[21] Chief among these flaws, President Reagan observed, was AP I's "grant [of] combatant status to irregular forces even if they do not satisfy the traditional requirements to distinguish themselves from the civilian population and otherwise comply with the laws of war." Reagan recognized the political symbolism of his action, characterizing it as "one additional step, at the ideological level so important to terrorist organizations, to deny these groups legitimacy as international actors."

AP I demonstrates the pitfalls of replacing the evolutionary approach to war with instant, inflexible legislation. AP I took form before the advent of desktop computers, the Internet, cell phones, global positioning satellites, and cruise missiles. That era's political circumstances were equally different. Nations were still drafting the text of AP I when North Vietnam conquered South Vietnam. The U.S. and U.S.S.R. dominated world politics and economics, half of Europe was forced into the Warsaw Pact, and the Third World, as it was then known, was still emerging from the throes of decolonization. The collapse of the Soviet Empire, the rise of China, the advent of Islamic extremism, and the spread of global terrorism were yet to come.

Given these significant changes in the world since the mid-1970s, AP I's provisions are growing hopelessly out of touch with the practice of the states that actually fight wars. Nations themselves realize this. In 1998, for example, a conference in Rome negotiated a treaty to establish the International Criminal Court (ICC).[22] Its drafters drew extensively on AP I to define the "war crimes" subject to prosecution. Neither the United States nor other major powers, including Russia, China, India, Turkey, Indonesia, Egypt, Iran, Israel, and Syria, ratified that treaty either. The ICC has so far reached convictions in only a handful of cases, none of them dealing with actions by western armies or with forces outside of Africa.

Nevertheless, AP I remains influential. Even at the time, the United States conceded that much of the treaty merely restated accepted practices.[23] It remains the most comprehensive statement of rules for the conduct of military operations. Commentaries on the law of armed conflict, including those by American scholars, assume that provisions of AP I are solid evidence of what the law of war now requires—if not by treaty, then as a matter of "customary law," which is binding on all states.[24]

It is important to understand what a significant break AP I is with the history and practice of the law of war. Historically, the laws of war represented customary law, which was established by the actual practice of states over long periods of time. Nations, for example, have long followed a principle of discriminating between combatants and civilians on the battlefield, but had never declared the rule in a general treaty before. States established the rule over centuries through the norms that they consistently followed in wartime. Their applications of the standard of discrimination in different factual circumstances provided guidance for future cases. AP I represents a wholly different approach. It assumes that interested nations can simply legislate the rules of armed conflict by treaty, rather than practice. It assumes that the treatymakers in 1977 could determine the best application of the rules to future circumstances, as opposed to those who fight the wars then.

This view attempts to transform treaty language into instant "custom." If many states have ratified a treaty, it must represent customary law just as much as, if not more than, universal conduct. Many advocates claim the promises of nations create law more firmly than the practices of nations.[25] This is not just an academic exercise, but has become the opinion of international tribunals. For example, the International Court of Justice (ICJ) stated in its 1996 advisory opinion on nuclear weapons, "Extensive codification of humanitarian law and the extent of the accession of the resultant treaties...have provided the international community with a corpus of treaty rules the great majority of which...reflected the most universally recognized humanitarian principles." It concluded that IHL treaties, as solidified into custom, "indicate the normal conduct and behaviour expected of States," presumably whether they had ratified the agreements or not.[26] Under this view, the United States can be bound by the rules set out in a treaty it has never ratified because its provisions can be regarded as customary law.[27] But those rules remain what they were in the mid-1970s because "customary law" is impervious to contrary practice, even though much military action over the last four decades has not followed AP I.

Domestic analogies reveal the peculiarity of this approach. On domestic statutory questions, courts and executive branch agencies regularly adapt legal principles to fit new factual circumstances. Some of these exercises, of course, can stoke controversy when the application of old legal rules to new technologies is disputed (and disputable). In 2015, for example, the Federal Communications Commission (FCC) prohibited Internet service providers from imposing different charges for carrying different types of content. The FCC subjected Internet service to the same regulatory framework as long-distance telephone service, even though Congress could never have imagined the Internet at the time it enacted the 1934 Federal Communications Act. To be sure, the Commission was divided, as was the U.S. Court of Appeals for the D.C. Circuit, which ultimately upheld the FCC regulation.[28] A new majority on the FCC has announced its intention to repudiate the Obama effort to regulate twenty-first century technology with an 80-year-old law.

The tension between adaptation and innovation becomes even more acute when cases turn on the meaning of constitutional provisions now centuries old. The framers of the Bill of Rights could not have envisaged modern technology. It was left to the Supreme Court to decide that First Amendment guarantees of free speech and press did not apply to television broadcasters as to newpapers. Yet the Supreme Court later concluded that the Fourth Amendment's protection against unreasonable searches and seizures prohibited police from using thermal imaging detectors to identify drug-growing operations and GPS tracking devices to track suspect movements without a warrant.[29] Even though there may be disagreement among both tribunals and society about the application of a particular law to new circumstances, legislators often deliberately write laws with generality so that future judges and lawyers can adapt the law's purpose to new circumstances.

Clinging to 1970s understandings of the law of war presents much greater difficulties than waiting for Congress or the constitutional amendment process to update legal rules. Unlike domestic law, which enjoys the enforcement of the judicial and executive branches, international law has no central institution capable of applying a uniform understanding of the law throughout the world. Because international law cannot punish rule breakers, states that violate the civilized laws of war will seize an advantage in armed conflict. States, for example, may keep to earlier understandings of the laws of war, others to a 1970s understanding, and still others may choose to skirt, subvert, or defy the rules outright. Those who honor the old rules will be at a disadvantage when fighting those who do not. It is hard to see that as a gain for international law. As Winston Churchill protested, "I do not see why we should have all the disadvantages of being the gentleman while they have all the advantages of being the cad."[30] Disorder, tyranny, and intimidation will have greater sway if western nations shrink from defending the postwar system because old rules make it too hard for them to fight.

Yet many scholarly commentators and government officials still tend to view the laws of war in quite formalistic ways. They rely on textual provisions of AP I, U.N. resolutions, and even dicta found in ICJ rulings and advisory opinions. From a fabric of words, they stitch together a protective suit that will supposedly protect us from foreign attacks (now unlawful, so our enemies cannot penetrate our rhetorical armor) and against foreign condemnation (because we wear the protective armor of "law"). But this pick-and-choose approach cannot work when confronted by new circumstances. In the past few years, for example, major academic publishers have produced several books on the legal limits of cyber war.[31] Scholars have published dozens of long, scholarly articles on this subject.[32] As these works acknowledge, however, the world has never seen anything that could rightly be described as "cyber war." These works cannot describe the actual practice of states, which can then coalesce into "customary law," because no practice yet exists.

Instead, these commentators and officials simply imagine the way that existing rules might apply to new technologies. They have little of substance to work with. Scholarly studies on the laws of war, published in the second decade of the twenty-first century, are of little help. They assume that the relevant rules are those codified in AP I, before the emergence of the Internet, email, and the information revolution. Nations never reconvened to rewrite the treaty to address new technologies. These commentators believe that these rules should govern only because they are most familiar. Their views, however, will have little purchase because they do not arise from the strategic needs and military capacities that do so much to determine how nations behave in times of conflict.

We are not arguing for a world without law. It will not be easy to decide what rules should prevail or what applications would be most feasible and desirable. We are arguing for rules that respond to the circumstances of war in the twenty-first century and the opportunities presented by new technologies. To argue in this way is not radical or extreme. It is entirely traditional. The law of war as laid down in the 1970s was not the law as it was understood in the 1940s. The law of the 1940s was not the law of 1914. As law in all areas regularly does, the law of war has continually adapted to new technologies and new circumstances, when old means no longer serve necessary ends.

War, Law, and Weapons

War and law are inextricably intertwined. As mankind has discovered new technologies and developed more effective institutions, it has brought invention to war. But nations did not then develop legal codes to impose on armed conflict. Instead, their consistent behavior over time gave rise to general principles that could guide leaders and combatants in the next war. Wars come first and the law follows, rather than the other way around. Rules limited, but did not prevent, the use of force by nations to coerce other nations.

The direct relationship between innovation and war is nothing new. In the ancient world, the evolution from bronze to iron tools and the discovery of more productive means of agriculture allowed cities to deploy larger, trained armies. Economic surplus allowed states to support warriors who specialized in combat. Progress in animal breeding made possible first the chariot and then large cavalry formations. The emergence of market institutions and effective government allowed China in the East and the Romans in the West to manufacture iron weapons on a larger scale, train and deploy bigger armies, and administer larger territories.[33] Whereas Sparta and its allies fielded an army in the Peloponnesian Wars of no more than 30,000,[34] the Roman imperial army under Augustus reached 250,000 troops and hit a high of perhaps 450,000 under Caracalla—numbers that Europe would not see again for more than a millennium.

In the Middle Ages, advances in technology, though slow, still prompted changes in warfare. As armor improved, mounted knights supported by rural towns prevailed. A few hundred knights controlled southern Italy and Sicily; a few thousand in the First Crusade successfully invaded and held Jerusalem.[35] But the invention of the crossbow in the eleventh century (along with improvements in the longbow) led to the weakening of knightly superiority in Europe; in China, where these weapons came into existence much earlier, mounted knights never held the upper hand. Progress in shipbuilding and navigation led to the replacement of human-powered triremes with wind-powered men-of-war. The invention of gunpowder made possible artillery and siege weapons, and professional militaries equipped with small arms. Military historian Victor Davis Hanson has argued that the Western nations became dominant because their innovative societies, capitalist and proto-democratic at the beginning of the modern world, more quickly adapted and deployed new technologies to war.[36]

Nevertheless, the relatively slow development of human societies kept military affairs relatively static. Despite the evolution of weaponry from the ancient and medieval worlds to the Renaissance, tactics and strategy did not significantly change. Horses still provided mobility on land and wind drove ships at sea. Armies and navies still fought at close quarters within eyesight of each other. Generals could move their forces only short distances because of the limits of transportation technology and logistics.

Firearms and artillery increased the casualties in these confrontations, but not their distance or speed. Alexander the Great would have recognized the formations, tactics, and strategies of Napoleon Bonaparte or even Robert E. Lee.

As military technology evolved at this slow pace, the rules of warfare did not change much. In the ancient world, law imposed few limits on combat, and those that prevailed seemed to hinge more on fidelity to the gods, rather than to man. It is not recorded whether the victims of the first iron weapons or the first war chariots demanded an international convention to outlaw their use. But if there were demands for a ban on such weapons, they did not succeed. In medieval times, there were repeated efforts to ban the crossbow. Pope Urban II, better known for urging knights to embark on the First Crusade, also urged the repudiation of this weapon. A Byzantine princess denounced it as "a truly diabolical machine." A few decades later in 1139, the Second Lateran Council urged a formal ban. The Holy Roman Emperor Conrad III decreed that use of the weapon should be punished as a capital crime.[37]

These protestations went unheeded because the law could not prevent armies from seizing the battlefield advantages offered by these new weapons. In a world where mounted nobles were the decisive military force, the crossbow was a disruptive weapon. It could launch arrows with sufficient force to burst through armor. It threatened to displace the lifelong training and valor of knights and nobles with a devastating mechanism, typically wielded by artisans or peasants (who were otherwise prohibited from carrying arms). The ban failed simply because the crossbow proved too valuable in winning battles.[38] With the right training, companies equipped with the longbow—a weapon already mentioned in the Bible— could devastate mounted nobles, as English kings and their well-trained peasants proved repeatedly in the Hundred Years War. Efforts to ban the longbow also failed; so too with the arquebus, forerunner of the musket, which appeared in the sixteenth century.[39] Some commanders treated wielders of this new weapon as, in effect, war criminals who should be killed at once.[40] But advanced nations would not stop deploying soldiers trained to use the new weapons because they so effectively altered the balance of power in their favor. Too many commanders insisted on retaining the advantages offered by these new weapons.

War's nature only began to shift significantly with the profound economic changes that occurred in the nineteenth century. Before the

Industrial Revolution, mankind made no significant gains in productivity. The distribution of wealth in the world depended more on the size of a nation's population. In 1000, for example, Western European GDP was $11 billion (in 1990 dollars), in 1500 it had risen to only $44 billion (less than doubling every century), and in 1700 it reached $81 billion. But the Industrial Revolution and the emergence of market capitalism in the nineteenth century broke humanity out of this Malthusian trap. Advances in agricultural and industrial productivity, due to technology, management, and political and legal systems, allowed for stunning increases in wealth and economic growth. In 1870, Western European GDP, estimated at $11 billion in 1500 (in 1990 dollars), exploded to $367 billion by 1870 and $840 billion by 1913.[41] The United States grew even faster. Its economy started at only $527 million in 1700. By 1870, the U.S. economy had reached $98 billion, and in 1913 it quintupled to $500 billion. China's economy, which did not experience a nineteenth-century Industrial Revolution, actually shrunk for most of that period.

The innovations that made these steep gains in economic growth possible also enabled far more lethal armed forces. Combat during the U.S. Civil War from 1861 through 1865 gave a hint of what was to come. Industrial production permitted larger, better-equipped armies. Union and Confederate armies could throw much larger weights of bullets and bombs with more precise accuracy over greater distances than ever before. Railroads allowed for the swift movement of men and supplies. The telegraph permitted faster, clearer communications. Wooden naval vessels, which had depended on the winds for more than two thousand years, evolved into warships protected by armor and driven by steam.

War's exponential growth in size and destructiveness triggered the first efforts at regulation. During the Civil War, President Lincoln issued General Orders No. 100, the Instructions for the Government of Armies of the United States in the Field—the first official public code of the laws of war. Article 15 of the Code set out the wide means available to nations at war:

> Military necessity admits of all direct destruction of life or limb of armed enemies, and of other persons whose destruction is incidentally unavoidable in the armed contests of the war; it allows of the capturing of every armed enemy, and every enemy of importance to the hostile government, or of peculiar danger to the captor; it allows of all destruction of property, and obstruction

of the ways and channels of traffic, travel, or communication, and of all with-
holding of sustenance or means of life from the enemy; of the appropriation
of whatever an enemy's country affords necessary for the subsistence and
safety of the army, and of such deception as does not involve the breaking of
good faith either positively pledged, regarding agreements entered into during the war, or supposed by the modern law of war to exist. Men who take up
arms against one another in public war do not cease on this account to be
moral beings, responsible to one another and to God.[42]

Following this logic, an army at war could impose blockades and
sieges and even bombard a city, so long as its reduction had military
value. Still, Lincoln's General Orders No. 100 also put into written terms
the need to shield civilians, where possible, from the harshness of war.
Article 22 declared that the Union armies would respect a distinction
between "the private individual belonging to a hostile country and the
hostile country itself, with its men in arms." But civilian immunity from
hostilities would run only as far as military necessity allowed. "The
unarmed citizen is to be spared in person, property, and honor as much
as the exigencies of war will admit."

Francis Lieber, a Prussian immigrant and advisor to the Lincoln
administration, drafted the rules. He believed that the modern age had
made war into a contest between mass armies rather than individuals.[43]
Lieber did not think that the customs of international law should ban
most methods of war, so long as the destruction was no "greater than
necessary." Accepting conflict as a permanent feature of international
affairs, Lieber believed that fiercer wars were more humane because they
were shorter, an idea shared by Clausewitz and Machiavelli. Therefore,
the laws of war allowed almost any destruction that advanced the goals
of the war, and the use of "those arms that do the quickest mischief in
the widest range and in the surest manner."[44]

The Industrial Revolution and the rise of mass production equipped
armies of draftees with highly lethal, yet relatively cheap, standardized
weapons. In World War I, rifles accurate over long distances became
commonplace. The British Lee-Enfield rifle could fire twelve rounds per
minute with accuracy at 600 meters from a ten-round magazine; the
British Vickers machine gun could fire 450-600 rounds per minute at
a range of 4,000 meters. Artillery became much more significant due

to the larger number of pieces, their range and accuracy, and the use of high-explosive shells. Airplanes and tanks made their first appearance in World War I. Dreadnoughts used oil engines, displaced 16,000 tons, and mounted fifteen-inch guns that could hit targets twenty miles away. Submarines entered into widespread use for the first time. Western armies unleashed the first weapons of mass destruction, chemical and biological agents that killed or incapacitated on the battlefield.

Modern industrial production, transportation, communication, and logistics produced even larger armies. By the end of World War I, Russia had mobilized about 12 million soldiers, Germany 11 million, Great Britain 8.9 million, France 8.4 million, Austria-Hungary 7.8 million, Italy 5.6 million, and the U.S. 4.35 million. Modern weaponry's longer range and destructiveness gave the advantage to defensive warfare in trenches, which inflicted staggering casualties on these new large armies. In the Battle of the Somme, from July 1 to November 18, 1916, both sides suffered more than 1 million killed or wounded—the British Army lost 57,470 on the first day alone, the worst day in its history. Overall casualties dwarfed any previous war in human history: the Allied Powers lost 5 million killed, 12.8 million wounded; the Central Powers lost 8.5 million killed, 21 million wounded. By comparison, in the Napoleonic Wars, France lost 371,000 killed, 800,000 wounded. Its allies lost similar numbers: the British, 312,000; Austria 376,000; Russia 289,000, and Prussia 134,000. Efficiency did not stop with the production of consumer goods; it extended even to the business of killing.

World War II exploited transportation advances to expand the use of air power and armored vehicles, which returned the combat advantage to the offense. Casualty levels climbed again, but within World War I ranges: the Soviet Union lost about 9 million in combat deaths, Germany 5 million, Japan about 2.5 million, the U.S. 407,000, the United Kingdom 384,000, with total worldwide combat deaths ranging from 21-25 million. But World War II witnessed a phenomenon that perhaps had not appeared since the Thirty Years War: massive civilian deaths (about 30 million) in numbers that exceeded military ones. The advent of the atomic bomb at the war's end raised the specter of even greater civilian casualties in the future.

International law could not stop the spread of technological progress to the machines of war. This has been the lesson of history. Lieber's

Code did not prohibit the Union blockade of the South, the burning of Atlanta, or Sherman's march to the sea, nor did it prevent the introduction of new weapons such as modern rifles, trenches, and artillery. In World War I, the Allies demanded that German submarines allow ships the opportunity to off-load civilians, which also gave up the element of surprise. Germany ultimately refused, which handed Woodrow Wilson the official rationale to bring the United States into World War I on the side of Great Britain and France. The Washington Naval Conference of 1922 sought to limit large battleships and maintain a rough balance of maritime power between the great powers, but Japan evaded the rules while the locus of sea power shifted instead to aircraft carriers. Nations used chemical weapons in World War I, signed a treaty to ban them in 1925, but have used them in conflicts since.

We are not arguing against all forms of cooperation during armed conflict. Nations have applied general custom to limit the use of weapons that cause unnecessary suffering or superfluous damage and destruction, depending on the factual context. The general principles of Lieber's Code still guide the conduct of war, even as new technologies transform weapons, tactics, and strategy. Nations have the freedom to use military force in ways that advance the objectives of the war, so long as they minimize harm to civilians as best they can.

Instead, we question the idea that nations should look to formal treaties and rules to produce lasting limits on war. Despite the recent deterioration in the Syrian civil war, nation-states have generally refrained from the use of chemical weapons against each other since the end of World War I. They have followed the Geneva Conventions on prisoners of war, though not consistently. Nations have observed others norms in the breach, chief among them the immunity of the civilian population and resources from attack. World War II not only saw the aerial bombing of cities and the nuclear attacks on Japan, but the years since have seen precision targeting of terrorists off the battlefield, attacks on urban infrastructure, and the acceptance of high levels of collateral damage among civilians. International lawyers and diplomats may proclaim that nations follow universal rules, either because of morality or a sense of legal obligation, but the record of practice tells a far different story. Efforts to impose more specific and demanding rules, such as limiting targeted drone attacks, banning cyber attacks, or requiring human control of robotic weapons, will similarly fail because they cannot take into account unforeseen circumstances, new weapons and military situations, and the immediate exigencies of war. Just as new technology led to increases in economic productivity, so too has it allowed nations to make war more effectively.

Nations will readily adhere to humanitarian standards when they gain a benefit that outweighs the cost, as when protecting enemy prisoners of war secures reciprocal protection for a nation's own soldiers taken captive by the enemy. Limitations on the use of weapons will follow a similar logic. Nations will be most inclined to respect legal restraints on new weapons when their use by both sides would leave no one better off or would provide little advantage. Cyber and robotic weapons do not bear the same features as the weapons where legal bans have succeeded, as with use of poison gas on the battlefield. Cyber and robotic weapons need not inflict unnecessary suffering out of proportion to their military advantages, as do poisoned bullets or blinding lasers. Rather, these weapons improve the precision of force and thereby reduce human death and destruction in war.

Nor have these new weapons technologies yet sparked a useless arms race. Nuclear weapons eventually became opportune for arms control because larger stockpiles provided marginal, if any, benefits due to the destructive potential of each weapon and the deterrence provided by even a modest arsenal. Mutual reductions could leave both sides in the same position as they were before the agreement. Today, the marginal cost of nuclear weapons for the U.S. and Russia so outweighs their marginal benefit that it is not even clear that a binding international agreement is needed to reduce their arsenals. Russia, for example, reduced its arsenal below New START's ceilings of 1,550 nuclear warheads and 700 strategic launchers even before the U.S. approved the deal.[45] The United States likely would have reduced its forces to those levels even if the Senate had refused to consent to the treaty, a position the executive branch also took in 2002 with the Treaty of Moscow's deep reduction in nuclear weapons. Today's new weapons do not yet bear these characteristics. The marginal gains in deploying these weapons will likely be asymmetric across nations insofar as some nations will experience much greater gains in military capability by developing cyber and drone technology. Put differently, prohibition or regulation of these new weapons will not have equal impacts on rival nations. Indeed, we do not even now have enough information to understand which nations will benefit and which will not, which makes any form of international ban even less likely.

Nuclear weapons are the exception that proves the rule. Their unique characteristics and deterrent value make them suitable for international cooperation to limit their use. But the twentieth century has otherwise shown that technological advances, and the increases in military effectiveness that have followed, have outpaced law. Efforts to prevent the introduction of new weapons have failed because the weapons themselves initially advantage early adopters. Legal regulation will not emerge until nations have gained significant information about how the technology and its constraints on its use may affect them. In the absence of specific agreements, nations will still follow the customary rules of war, which provide general principles of reasonableness to apply to new circumstances, such as traditional prohibitions against wanton destruction or unnecessary suffering. It is to the new world of war that we now turn.

Static Law for a Changing World?

The laws of war have not kept pace with the rapid change in weapons technology. Efforts to freeze war in place by adopting an inflexible legal approach may lead to a failure of the current framework of war or its rewriting by nations less friendly to the Western international order. Another set of changes in war, also spurred by changes in politics, economics, and technology, is placing further pressure on the idealized AP I and U.N. Charter vision of the international order. In this new century, the classic paradigm of war between nation-states with disciplined militaries has slowly given way to a more chaotic world in which terrorist organizations, regional guerrillas, and ethnic or religious groups conduct equally violent hostilities. The great majority of casualties now come from civil wars and disputes within states, rather than wars between states. Today, the great powers use their militaries to threaten or intervene against smaller states, rather than in direct battles against each other. To grapple with these problems, the laws of war should allow both the use of new weapons more widely and the use of force more often.

The geopolitical order of the nineteenth century was determined largely by the military and economic strength of nations, not international agreements. Though legal treatises at that time still embraced the traditional view that a just war requires a legitimate *causus belli*, many causes were regarded as "good" and there was little enforcement of the just war requirement. Nations often went to war to enlarge their territory, as the United States did in the Mexican War of 1846-48, or to prevent others from expanding their influence, as when Great Britain and France fought Russia in the Crimean War of 1853-56. European nations constructed a Concert of Europe to strike a balance between the great powers, with war as the final mechanism to ensure that no state grew too powerful. Even when a state invoked transparently contrived claims to justify war for other reasons, as Bismarck's Prussia did to unify Germany, no outside power helped the victims. Wars were brief in time and limited in scope.

The breadth of destruction wrought by World War I, however, prompted nations to attempt a rewrite of the international order. Rather than a balance of power and contending alliances, nations would guarantee their security in a peace treaty that established a scheme for "collective security" to guarantee every state its "political independence and territorial integrity" against aggression.[46] They established an international forum to help resolve disputes, the League of Nations, then tried to outlaw war in the Kellogg-Briand Pact, allowing (supposedly) a resort to force only in self-defense. But the League failed to take effective action in response to either Japanese aggression against China or Italian aggression against Ethiopia. It could not draw in the two most powerful nations in the world, the United States and the Soviet Union, to cooperate to maintain international order. When Britain and France declared war in response to Germany's aggression against Poland, no one even bothered to consult the League.

After the failure of the League to keep the peace, the victors renewed and extended their commitment to collective security. Maintaining the League's guarantee of political independence and self-determination for all member states, the United Nations Charter banned war except in cases of self-defense. Force would remain the province of the Security Council, along with coercive measures short of war, such as economic sanctions. Article 42 declares that the Security Council "may take such action by air, sea, or land forces as may be necessary to maintain or restore international peace and security. Such action may include demonstrations, blockade, and other operations by air, sea, or land forces of Members of the United Nations."[47] Article 51, however, contained the great exception for self-defense: "Nothing in the present Charter shall impair the inherent right of individual or collective self-defence if an armed attack occurs against a Member of the United Nations, until the Security Council has taken measures necessary to maintain international peace and security."[48]

Article 51 itself does not define self-defense. Nonetheless, well-regarded legal commentators insist that the U.N. Charter allows force only when the Security Council cannot intervene successfully to counter a cross-border invasion.[49] This logic mimics domestic criminal law, which allows victims to physically resist a threat of deadly harm only if the police cannot prevent the violence. This doctrine does not, however, reflect the practice of most U.N. states. States have used armed force against each other hundreds of times since 1945. The Security Council has authorized only a handful of them due to the veto power of any of the five permanent members of the Council (U.S., Russia, Britain, France, and China). Moreover, the U.N. Charter does not simply authorize the Security Council to respond to "aggression." It also authorizes the Council to act against "breaches of the peace" and "threats to the peace," which implicitly acknowledges that threats to a nation's security go beyond an actual cross-border "armed attack."[50]

Prior to 1945, international law recognized that nations could respond to lesser threats with measures short of all-out war. These measures might run from mere diplomatic protest to various coercive actions.[51] The U.N. Charter also recognizes this tool of traditional statecraft. It allows the Security Council to authorize "measures not involving the use of armed force" against threatening states. Such tactics include "complete or partial interruption of economic relations and of rail, sea, air, postal, telegraphic, radio ... communications."[52] The Charter also provides that the Security Council may deploy "air-force contingents for combined international enforcement action" when "urgent military measures" are required.[53] This provision evidently contemplates the deployment of such "contingents" in operations that are independent of a land invasion (which could rarely be organized on an "urgent" basis and is not provided for in the Charter).

For all of its peaceful aspiration, however, the U.N. Charter has been ineffective in constraining state military behavior as the political and technological circumstances of the world have evolved. The Security Council did not reach agreement on establishing an international bomber force. The Council has rarely invoked most of its other coercive powers. Of course, that is not because the world has experienced peace. Instead, the differing agendas of the permanent members of the Security Council have paralyzed the U.N., leaving it to nations to resolve disputes in other ways.[54] While disputes have sometimes erupted into war, they have not yet escalated into a World War III. Some scholars believe that the "Long Peace" of the postwar world emerged from the balance between the U.S. and the U.S.S.R., while others argue that nuclear weapons imposed caution on all the great powers.[55] We cannot be sure that even that reprieve will endure, now that Pakistan, North Korea, and, perhaps others have acquired nuclear weapons.

Even as the prospect of general war has receded, other forms of hostilities short of all-out war have emerged. Formal declarations of war have become rare—the U.S. Congress last enacted a formal declaration of war in 1942 (against Bulgaria). Perhaps that is partly because the U.N. Charter seems to prohibit resorting to "war." But formal "war" has also become less easy to define because hostilities often fall short of open armed conflict, and formal peace treaties rarely mark their end. While the Second World War ended with unconditional surrender, Cold War disagreements prevented any general or comprehensive peace treaties among all participants. In Korea, a "temporary" armistice remains in place to this day, as with Israel and its neighbors (except Egypt and Jordan). North Vietnam ended its war in a unilateral annexation without awaiting any other nation's approval.

The lines between war and peace (or conflict and trust) have become even more blurred in recent years, as major conflicts have involved non-state actors or states acting in disguised ways. If the Russian army had launched tank columns and regular infantry against the Baltic states, it would almost certainly have triggered a NATO military response and even a conventional interstate war. But the Russian invasion of Crimea in 2014 was much more ambiguous. Moscow sent special agents to seize strong points, enlisted local support, and disguised the underlying aggression with claims about local consent to what quickly became a *fait accompli.*[56] Russia has continued the challenge by supporting local "militia" in eastern Ukraine who resist the authorities in Kiev, ostensibly in the interests of regional autonomy. Military analysts call this mix of covert operations combined with limited conventional military force a hybrid war, which often does not provoke the sort of response that would meet a full-scale invasion.[57]

New forms of irregular warfare do not just benefit revisionist states such as Russia, even small groups can now wage hostilities that generate instability and even seize territory. ISIS emerged from terror groups that had challenged the government established in Baghdad after Saddam's overthrow. Terrorism has become another way to exert pressure without risking a direct trial of arms against an organized army. In the hands of ISIS, terrorism took on some of the characteristics of guerilla warfare, using surprise attacks and terrorizing civilians to take and hold land, people, and resources.[58] In Lebanon and Syria, outside states such as Iran have made the challenges even more difficult by supporting armed militias with arms, training, and even troops. A regular army can defeat guerillas, but that has usually required a long struggle. Great powers, like the French in Algeria by the late 1950s, often lose patience with a lengthy struggle.

Hybrid war and guerrilla or terrorist insurgencies present the same set of strategic challenges for nations. Hybrid war tactics discourage initial intervention of an outside power by making the challenge seem limited, partial, and small stakes. Terror and guerilla tactics discourage a major power from making a long-term commitment for fear of a slow drain in low-intensity combat. Terrorists and guerrillas disperse to prevent a government from focusing its forces in conventional battle, and they seek cover behind the civilian population. They target civilians, even their own supporters, to intimidate them into remaining on their side. They aim to goad a government's regular forces into making wider attacks on civilians, which may have the effect of driving civilians away from the state. The power with the greatest military muscle is not necessarily the most capable contestant. If the only answer to such irregular tactics is "war," then a major power may decide not to respond.

States have also developed their own means of coercing opponents with tactics short of conventional war, such as annoying or harassing adversaries through intermediaries, another accepted military tactic that the U.N. Charter does not apparently endorse. As early as the American

Revolutionary War, the British stirred up frontier Indians to attack American settlers. An independent United States winked at pirate attacks on Spanish commerce as a way of assisting independence movements in Latin America. In the nineteenth century, states deployed even more active measures. When small countries defaulted on loan agreements or seized or abused their nationals, major powers were often unwilling to declare war, either because the injuries were small or because they feared intervention by other powers. They instead resorted to "gunboat diplomacy." Demands for redress were backed by a show of naval force, sometimes by small-scale bombardment. Nineteenth-century scholars of international law called it "pacific reprisal."[59] It was not war but a form of retaliation for the sake of coercion.

The U.N. Charter authorizes states to use force in self-defense "if an armed attack occurs." But we have something close to pacific reprisals in the current policy of drone missile attacks on terrorists not only in Afghanistan but also in Pakistan, Yemen, and Libya. While the United States claims that it is acting in "self-defense" when conducting these strikes, it cannot credibly claim it is repelling an ongoing attack. Such strikes are consistent with the U.N. Charter only if we expand the concept of self-defense to include anticipation of an attack, even one that may not be imminent. In other words, the United States might claim that anticipatory self-defense allows preemptive strikes when the probability of an attack is small, but the potential for destruction is high. Or the United States and its allies must admit that they are engaging in preventive war designed to nip challenges to international security in the bud, even when there is no immediate claim to self-defense.

We are not arguing that war between states is disappearing, as some utopian writers do. Great power competitions continue to plague international politics, and those rivalries can still break out into conflict. Nuclear weapons may reduce the scope of hostilities, but the limits imposed by the superpower balance have eroded with the disappearance of the Soviet Union. The world is returning to a less orderly state of affairs. If the lines between war and peace blurred during the Cold War, they have become even less distinct today. Nations rely even more on measures short of full-blown armed conflict to coerce each other. New forms of international actors, such as terrorist groups, use force at a level that does not provoke a full-scale military response. Technological advances may provide western nations with a broader spectrum of coercion to respond. The rules imposed by the U.N. Charter and AP I cannot meaningfully govern these changes.

Responding to these new facts of war with new military technologies will provoke objections from international lawyers. They insist on highly restrictive rules for defining legitimate targets in war, such as AP I's prohibition on the targeting of civilian property.[60] Legalists can also invoke the AP I requirement that even attacks on otherwise legitimate "military objectives" are unlawful, if they "may be expected to cause incidental loss of civilian life, injury to civilians, damage to civilian objects...which would be excessive in relation to the concrete and direct military advantage anticipated."[61]

These requirements of distinction and proportionality may make sense in a conventional war in which the main aim is to defeat the enemy's army on the battlefield. But they make less sense if the aim is to affect the political calculus of enemy leaders. That was surely what the drafters of the U.N. Charter had in mind when they authorized interruption of sea or radio communication or even bombing as an "urgent military measure." These tools built upon the blockades and economic embargoes that the Allies had used to deadly effect in World Wars I and II. Such actions seek not to defeat an enemy's armed forces, but to increase the costs on its society and economy. Much of that pain would fall upon civilians. Intercepting all "postal, telegraphic, radio, and other means of communication" imposes a sense of isolation, which might undermine civilian confidence in the target country's leaders. If it seemed reasonable for the Council to undertake such measures, it seems reasonable for member states to have those options on their own.

By the 1990s, nations regularly resorted to economic sanctions, such as those against Haiti, Serbia, and Iraq. They were never confined to military objects, but included civilian goods and services, such as oil and banking. The resulting pain primarily struck civilians.[62] Sanctions on Serbia in the early 1990s, for example, produced an "economic meltdown," in which unemployment and extreme poverty engulfed half the population and average income actually dropped by fifty percent.[63] If the Council hoped to induce governments to change their positions, it was by threatening them with domestic disorder as food and other civilian necessities became more scarce and more costly.

U.N. Charter rules, however, may not justify even armed attacks on military targets if the purpose is coercion. AP I insists that "attacks" must be launched solely at "military objectives."[64] When there is no purpose to incapacitate the target state's military capacity, it may be the case that there is no "military objective." In the 1980s, the United States accused Libya of involvement in a terror attack on American soldiers in a Berlin nightclub. Libya had not invaded American territory. Its terrorism was not ongoing, though it might have been repeated. The Reagan administration retaliated by bombing Tripoli. It took care to say that the bombs were aimed at Libyan military installations, including a civilian site where the Libyan dictator Muammar Gaddafi was known to meet with top military commanders. Gaddafi "was not personally immune from the risks of exposure to a legitimate attack," stated Abraham Sofaer, legal advisor at the U.S. State Department. "He was and is personally responsible for Libya's policy of training, assisting, and utilizing terrorists in attacks on U.S. citizens, diplomats, troops, and facilities."[65] Nothing achieved by the bombing would have made it substantially more difficult for Libya to organize future terror attacks in Europe or elsewhere.

The U.S. attack on Libya also skirted the conventional understanding of discrimination and proportionality. One can see the point by thinking about "collateral damage." Close members of Gaddafi's family were killed in that attack. They were civilians who took no part in military affairs. AP I does not make clear how much incidental loss of life among civilians would have to occur before an attack would be "excessive" in relation to the "concrete and direct military advantage" achieved by attacking Gaddafi's meeting place. A critic of the U.S. attacks might argue that the military advantage was so remote and speculative that it could not justify any incidental harm to civilians. A defender of the strike could respond that the air attacks might deter Gaddafi from pursuing further terror attacks.[66] The U.S. gained a concrete and direct military advantage by deterring Libya from future international terrorist attacks on U.S. troops. Its limited strikes achieved an objective that otherwise might have demanded far greater attacks, with more loss of life and destruction. Again, they reveal the growing incompatibility between the formal rules of international humanitarian law, spun together out of the U.N. Charter and AP I, and the demands for coercive, limited uses of force in today's world.

Two trends now seem to be converging. On the one hand, the underlying architecture of international politics is becoming more disordered. Instability is spreading throughout the world, in Eastern Europe, East Asia and Central Asia, North Africa, and the Middle East. The European Union has not developed any military capacity of its own but NATO is under more internal stress than ever before. Meanwhile, insurgent or revanchist forces have found ways to project intimidating force without the risk of full-scale military invasion. We face hybrid war in Eastern Europe, terror campaigns in Western Europe, and the construction of new islands to extend maritime claims in the South China Sea.

Part of the response may be new weapons technologies, but only if they are accompanied with new thinking on how and where they can be used. The most important characteristic of new technologies, in cyber, drone, and robotic weapons, is the capacity for remarkable degrees of precision. It was once possible to claim that bombs aimed at "military objectives" were only incidentally working "collateral damage" on civilian objects. Now, military technology gives us the capacity to strike with precision, which means destroying relatively little beyond intended targets. New technologies may offer a compelling response to the challenges of our time by allowing western nations to respond to the provocations of authoritarian aggressors or reach out to strike terrorists far removed from a battlefield.

We are not claiming that new weapons will, by themselves, resolve every challenge and deliver us to a new era of stability and peace. Every weapon, even supposedly autonomous or robotic ones, requires human guidance and strategy in the background. We may misjudge our challenges or our opportunities. We may underestimate the resolve of enemies or overrate the immediate threats they pose. Technology does not make statecraft obsolete. It simply offers more tools and options.

Embracing new technologies does not require us to believe in literal magic bullets that will render confrontational opponents supine after one volley. Nor would relaxing current understandings of the laws of war. The point is to provide alternatives to avoid the choice between all-out war and fatalistic resignation. The aim of many interventions would not be so much to disable the military capacity of the opposing side as to indicate the Western capacity and willingness to impose costs.

Short of completely incapacitating the opposing side, even large-scale war is a tacit bargaining situation, as Thomas Schelling pointed out more than fifty years ago.[67] Part of the bargaining may involve inflicting harm on an opponent to signal readiness to do so on a larger scale. It may not be feasible to penetrate the delusions of the most crazed, megalomaniacal dictator—but even sobering those in his circle may be helpful. At any rate, most tyrants have concerns about preserving themselves. Signaling, as we will argue later on, is an important element of military exchanges. One might think of new technologies as providing us the capacity to communicate with more exclamation points, and to indicate that our enemies cannot rely on the protections afforded by highly restrictive interpretations of the laws of war.

Conclusions

By the end of 1862, Union armies had been struggling for almost two years against Confederate armies in the American Civil War. On December 1, President Lincoln offered a new strategy in his message to Congress. He proposed a constitutional amendment, authorizing federal compensation to states that abolished slavery over the next four decades. His message concluded with this memorable admonition: "The dogmas of the quiet past are inadequate to the stormy present.... As our case is new, so we must think anew and act anew. We must disenthrall ourselves, and then we shall save our country."[68]

It was an offer of peace through compromise. As Lincoln may have expected, the offer was not accepted. Perhaps that gave Lincoln the confidence—or the political support in the North—to proceed with an alternative approach. A month later, on his own authority as commander-in-chief, President Lincoln proclaimed the emancipation of all slaves in all states "in rebellion against the United States."[69]

Infuriating Southerners, the Emancipation Proclamation cut off hopes for a compromise peace. But it also meant that Southern states would have to retain more military units to guard the home front, thus depleting manpower available to the main Confederate armies. Many slaves were encouraged to escape, undermining agricultural production. Many escaped slaves then reinforced Union strength as laborers or soldiers. Those who remained often provided valuable intelligence to advancing Union armies. Making the war a battle over slavery helped deter European powers from offering support to the Confederacy. Though an extreme and risky measure, the Emancipation Proclamation proved to be a highly effective tactic.

Lincoln's Emancipation Proclamation should remind us of this fundamental truth: Conflict stimulates new thinking. To suppress the Southern rebellion, the North harnessed its industrial prowess to deploy a number of historic innovations, from ironclad ships to repeating rifles. President Lincoln was personally involved in promoting these technical innovations. But he remained mindful that war is, above all, a political, not a technical undertaking.

Lincoln's words describe the central argument of our book: "The dogmas of the quiet past are inadequate to the stormy present." We are living through a revolution in military affairs as fundamental as the emergence of vast armies and mass-produced arms in Lincoln's time. Military cyber units—the U.S. recently elevated its cyber command to a par with its regional combatant commanders—launch viruses to harm an enemy's military capacity and disrupt its economic and communications networks. Unmanned robots patrol the skies hunting for individual terrorist leaders with air-to-ground missiles. Massive computing power, instant communications, and precise satellite reconnaissance bring any location on earth within one hour of a global strike missile. Much discussion of military affairs is now constrained by anachronistic understandings of the "law of war," as much as Napoleonic approaches initially infected early thinking about the Civil War. We want to expand the debate over war today by rethinking the prevailing dogmas. As our case is new, we must think anew and act anew. We must disenthrall ourselves.

CHAPTER 2

Returning to Coercion

This chapter begins our analysis of war and technology with the changing nature of conflict in the twenty-first century. Even as technology in commerce and war is beginning to make revolutionary strides, the threat of major war is receding. The risks of great power conflict have declined since the massive destruction wrought by European nations in the nineteenth and twentieth centuries. Mankind is currently living through the longest period without a significant interstate war since the birth of the modern international system in 1648.[1] In the last seventy years, deaths from interstate wars have fallen by an entire order of magnitude from the rate of centuries before.[2]

But we are not entering utopia. Armed conflict remains a persistent feature of the human condition. Conventional or nuclear war between the great powers remains a considerable threat. After seizing part of Georgia in 2008 and annexing Crimea in 2014, Russia continues to destabilize Ukraine and harass NATO's eastern borders.[3] In the midst of a military modernization drive, China is building artificial islands to support its claims to all of the South China Sea, through which $5.3 trillion in trade passes every year. After eight years of retrenchment and withdrawal, the United States may well embark under President Donald Trump on a military buildup and a reinvigorated foreign policy.

In the past, some wars between great powers were almost amicable. Regular armies could settle the dispute on the battlefield, far from civilian population centers, almost in the manner of a duel. In 1866, for example, Prussia provoked a war with the neighboring Habsburg Empire. Prussian forces quickly prevailed at the Battle of Koniggratz. Chancellor Otto von Bismarck restrained Prussian generals from trying to capture Vienna, and instead negotiated peace terms that limited Austrian losses.[4] Within a dozen years, the two powers entered into an enduring alliance. When war was not absolute and surrender was not unconditional, conflict focused on disabling military capacities until one nation accepted the political goals of the other.

Of course, some conflicts followed a very different pattern. In the Second World War, Germany did not surrender until Allied armies had seized every one of its major cities, sometimes only after grinding urban combat. Allied armies had to prove beyond dispute that they could assert control over all parts of Germany. But victory does not always go to the side with more troops or better weapons. A guerrilla war can become a contest of willpower rather than weaponry. After eight years of struggle, the French abandoned Algeria in 1962, not because of the incapacity of the French army, but because the French public would no longer support the military effort.[5] Eight years of struggle was not too much for the leaders of the Arab National Liberation Front, but it was too much for France.

Other challenges to peace come not from Soviet tanks pouring into West Germany, but from regional revanchists, authoritarian regimes, and terrorist groups. In this new century, civil wars, such as the one that has killed or displaced millions in Syria and Iraq, or conflicts in lands where the West has few interests, such as those in Sudan or Congo, have caused enormous death and suffering. Future killing may come at the hands of rogue nations, such as North Korea or Iran, that come into possession of weapons of mass destruction. Or deaths will flow from terrorist groups, such as al-Qaeda or ISIS, which operate with global reach and can wield violence once only in the hands of nations.

In this new world of security threats, the great powers will not need agreements to ban their latest weapons. They are likely to deter each other from destructive attacks, just as mutually assured destruction kept the Cold War from turning hot. Instead, the greater threat is that the great nations will be loath to intervene against rogue nations or terrorist groups, who employ unconventional methods to coerce the West. The United States and its allies will never be able to match these enemies in their willingness to descend into barbarism. Instead, we must exploit our advantages in cyber and robotics, our control of the air, seas, and space, and our ability to integrate information processing, computers, and soldiers. Drones, cyber weapons, and precision-guided missiles could give the West the ability to kill terrorist leaders, cripple an authoritarian regime's infrastructure, or destroy clandestine WMD research facilities. These technologies and skills could allow the great powers to use force more precisely and swiftly to prevent the rising threats of the twenty-first century from upending the international order.

Critics worry that the spread of these new weapons will lower the barriers to war. If launching a drone or activating a cyber weapon becomes too cheap and easy, they warn, nations will resort to force far more readily than today. But this earlier, more precise use of force could prevent threats from metastasizing into far worse dangers. It could even have a salutary effect in further dampening the risks of great power war. As we will show, war often breaks out between nations because they cannot overcome the informational and commitment obstacles to bargaining. Because of the anarchic state of the world, nations in a dispute cannot gather credible information about the capabilities and desires of their rivals and they cannot trust them to keep their promises. Cyber and robotic weapons give nations not only greater ability to coerce each other, but also more means to communicate their intentions in war and their reliability in peace. With these weapons available, we should see nations settle more disputes by negotiation, rather than by escalation.

We do not mean to argue that more advanced technologies will now transform the battlefield and ensure that future conflicts will always be won by the side with the better weapons. In the early twentieth century, for example, air-power enthusiasts argued that bombing could replace ground assaults. Colonial powers used air attacks in the interwar period, notably the British in Iraq and Spanish forces in Morocco. But command of the air did not ensure French victory in Algeria in the 1950s, nor Soviet victory against Afghan guerrillas in the 1980s. War is unpredictable because, in the end, it is a contest between human hearts and brains, not a duel of gadgets. The side with the more advanced weapons may not be the side with the most commitment in a long struggle.

This chapter proceeds in three parts. Part I will describe the new security challenges of the twenty-first century. It will explain that the nature of these civil wars, rogue states, and terrorist groups requires more widespread, albeit less destructive, uses of force to police them. Part II will explore how new weapons technologies, and a modern understanding of the tactics and strategy to take advantage of them, can lead to less rather than more conflict between the major powers. Part III will criticize the current rules of the U.N. Charter, which might deter states from using new weapons to confront these new threats. While the twentieth century's threats are receding, the instability and disorder of the twenty-first may require the great powers to use force more often, not less.

New Security Challenges for the Twenty-First Century

In August of 2013, the White House acknowledged clear evidence that the Syrian army had used chemical weapons, despite firm warnings from President Barack Obama against using such munitions.[6] The White House tried to mobilize support for retaliatory military action by western countries, including France and Great Britain. In the ensuing debate, some critics warned against costly entanglement in the ongoing civil war in Syria. Others worried that outside intervention might allow rebel forces to install a dangerous Islamist government. Some believed that western strikes might escalate the conflict and spread the fighting beyond Syria to neighboring countries, such as Turkey, Lebanon, Iraq, and Israel.

Almost no one opposed retaliatory air strikes on the grounds that intervention, in itself, would run contrary to international norms. The Chemical Weapons Convention prohibits the production, stockpiling, and use of chemical weapons, such as sarin and VX nerve gas.[7] But it does not authorize the use of force against violators; it only empowers states to refer a situation to the U.N. Security Council. In any case, Syria never signed the CWC. The U.N. Charter empowers the Security Council to authorize the use of force to protect against threats to international peace and security, for which the Syrian civil war or the use of chemical weapons might qualify. Despite pressure from the United States, Britain, and France, however, the Security Council could not act because of the vetoes of Russia and China.[8]

It was hard to see the Obama administration's proposal as anything other than "punishment." The White House denied that intervention would aim at influencing the outcome of the civil war.[9] The announced goal was to "impose a price" for using such terrible weapons, or, in more direct terms, to "punish" the Assad regime. The administration did not propose air strikes to destroy the chemical weapons stockpiles or their production facilities. The aim was simply to impose some "cost" elsewhere to deter future use of the weapons. Critics warned that the tactic would prove ineffective or have unacceptable side effects, but not that it was, in itself, improper.[10] The Obama administration finally embraced an alternate policy, an agreement with the Syrian and Russian governments for the internationally supervised removal of the chemical weapons.[11] Administration spokesmen insisted, however, that this outcome had only been possible because it had previously threatened Syria with punitive strikes.[12]

The Obama administration's approach to Syria predictably failed. Syria continued its brutal civil war that has killed an estimated 470,000 people, most of them civilians.[13] The Assad regime continues to use chemical weapons, though perhaps not in the amounts that it would have without the agreement. The remaining Syrian population that could flee has left the country. According to some estimates, more than four million Syrians have become refugees, destabilizing the region and pressuring even NATO allies.[14] In the power vacuum left by withdrawing U.S. forces in Iraq, al-Qaeda transformed into ISIS and seized large swaths of territory in both countries. ISIS has imposed a draconian version of Sharia law on the people under its control and created a safe haven where it can train new fighters from around the world. Along with the United States, Turkey has declared that the Assad regime must go and has crossed the border in force to root out ISIS. Meanwhile, Russia and Iran have sent unconventional fighters, regular troops, and modern air power to prop up the Assad regime.

The Syrian civil war illustrates the threats to peace in the twenty-first century, which now come less from great power war and more from rogue nations, terrorist groups, and failing states. Though the threat of general war has receded, these new challenges may demand that states use force more often, but at lower levels of intensity. Civil wars and humanitarian crises, however, may deter intervention because of the possibility of high casualties in urban environments. Terrorists and guerrillas refuse to follow the laws of war by refusing to distinguish themselves from civilians, hiding among them, and launching terror attacks on them. WMD and rogue nations present further difficulties because of the covert nature of their weapons programs and their disregard for the lives of their own civilians. Left to fester, these challenges can grow into serious threats to international stability, whether from terrorist attacks, the deaths of thousands of civilians, or authoritarian regimes armed with nuclear weapons. New technologies can help the great powers address these threats by applying force with greater precision at less cost.

Preemption and WMD Threats

Weapons of mass destruction pose new challenges. Widespread destruction has always been a possibility in war. In ancient times, the civilized states of Greece and Rome sometimes massacred or deported all the inhabitants of an enemy city. But before the twentieth century, the possibility for casualties had not reached millions from a single strike. A hostile army also had to invade enemy territory before it could slay and destroy. Now nuclear weapons can wreak devastation in the first minutes of conflict and, if widely used, destroy most human life on earth. Even the detonation of a single nuclear weapon in the United States could kill vast numbers of people and severely disrupt our society. Nations have an interest in keeping these most destructive weapons out of the hands of the most reckless leaders, especially those who might use them impulsively or share them with terrorists.

It is not unusual for a sudden change in arms to generate a strategic threat. In such circumstances, western leaders once thought that they could act preemptively before such a threat had matured, even before an attack was "imminent." In 1807, for example, Great Britain feared that Denmark and Norway would transfer their fleets to France, which would have allowed France to challenge the Royal Navy's control of the seas. Instead, after the Danes refused to hand their fleet over to the British, a British fleet bombarded Copenhagen for three days. The Danes changed their minds and gave up their fleet. The British government defended this intervention against a neutral nation as an act of "self-defence."[15] Great Britain took similar action in July 1940, after France had signed an armistice with Germany. Churchill ordered an attack on the French fleet in North Africa to prevent its transfer to German control. Most observers did not condemn this vivid demonstration of Britain's determination to go on fighting.[16]

But modern weapons have multiplied the destructiveness of attacks while accelerating their speed and surprise. To be sure, it may still take weeks, or months, to put a conventional armed attack in motion. The United States required months to assemble the invasion forces in the Persian Gulf War of 1990 and the Iraq war of 2003. But stealth bombers, hypersonic cruise missiles, and ballistic missiles have reduced the time for an attack to be detected, not to mention stopped. A ballistic missile can drop a nuclear warhead on a city in thirty minutes.[17] Ballistic missile technology has even spread beyond the arsenals of the great powers to rogue nations like Iran and North Korea.

Nuclear weapons threaten a magnitude of destruction that goes well beyond the transfer of a fleet in the nineteenth or twentieth centuries. They could cause devastating and indiscriminate long-term damage to the civilian population and the environment. A single five-megaton nuclear blast, for example, would generate a 2.8-mile-wide fireball, heat of 14,000 degrees Fahrenheit (the sun is 11,000 degrees F), winds ten times stronger than a hurricane, a ground shock 250 times worse than any earthquake, and air overpressure of 500 pounds per square inch.[18] In 1996, the International Court of Justice observed that such weapons possess unique characteristics, "in particular their destructive capacity, their capacity to cause untold human suffering, and their ability to cause damage to generations to come."[19] The spread of ballistic missile technology and advances in miniaturization have allowed even Third World nations to develop the capacity to launch nuclear attacks with little warning. The magnitude of harm threatened by WMD has grown, their detection has become more difficult, and the time necessary for their launch has dropped.

The calculus of war must shift to meet these technological developments. In order to prevent the possible use of WMD, nations should resort to force earlier depending on the nature of the threat. As many scholars and international tribunals have read the U.N. Charter, nations are now prohibited from using force except in two situations: in response to "an armed attack" or by authorization of the U.N. Security Council. On the other hand, most scholars acknowledge that nations may launch attacks to preempt an imminent attack before an enemy has crossed the border.[20] In the famous case of the *Caroline*, in which British forces pursued Canadian rebels across the U.S. border, Daniel Webster argued a nation could use force in anticipation of an attack that is "instant, overwhelming, leaving no choice of means, and no moment for deliberation."[21] The *Caroline* test, which the Nuremburg tribunal and the ICJ *Nicaragua* decision attempted to elevate to the status of universal customary law, appears to create a high bar for the use of force. But it also contains the seeds of a broader understanding of war more appropriate to today's world.

Caroline's imminence test placed its emphasis on timing because of the nature of early nineteenth-century weaponry. Fleets and armies moved slowly, their weapons engaged at short range, and they relied on primitive munitions. An enemy nation could not inflict crippling losses in a surprise attack. Nations could afford to wait until an attack became more certain because the risk of destruction was not great. A large-scale invasion would reveal itself because of the preparations involved. Even by the time of World War I, the European great powers required several weeks to mobilize their massive armies, as Barbara Tuchman vividly described in *The Guns of August*.[22] The *Caroline* test seems much less compelling when the threat comes from a hostile state intent on acquiring WMD and the means to deliver them quickly. To wait for peaceful resolution may mean waiting until the target state has already passed the nuclear threshold. It would be vastly more dangerous to take preemptive action against a state that has already acquired nuclear weapons.

In the face of such change, self-defense must expand beyond temporal imminence. Technological advance has increased the destructiveness of modern weapons, while making them harder to detect, quicker to launch, and cheaper to build. Nations should have the ability to use force even earlier than in the *Caroline* test, which involved a dispute between two friendly nations with armies and navies propelled by horses and sail and armed with cannons and muskets. Even if the probability of an attack has declined, the increase in magnitude must mean that nations can use force earlier to forestall it.

The Cuban Missile Crisis demonstrates the workings of such an approach. Moscow's secret deployment of medium-range nuclear missiles only ninety miles from the U.S. posed a threat to American national security and would have upended the balance of power. While the Soviets were transporting missile components by ship, it appeared that they had neither fully assembled nor fueled the weapons. No attack was imminent in a temporal sense. Nonetheless, President John F. Kennedy ordered a naval "quarantine" on Soviet shipments to Cuba—a use of force that blocked navigation around Cuba and threatened the boarding and detention of Russian ships and crew. He argued that Nikita Khrushchev's dispatch of the missiles "add[ed] to an already clear and present danger" because "we no longer live in a world where only the actual firing of weapons represents a sufficient challenge to a nation's security to constitute maximum peril." He emphasized that the speed and harm of modern weaponry justified earlier action. "Nuclear weapons are so destructive and ballistic missiles are so swift, that any substantially increased possibility of their use...may well be regarded as a definite threat to peace."[23] While scholars at the time debated whether the quarantine violated the *Caroline* test,[24] Kennedy's measured use of force brought the crisis to an end and was JFK's finest moment in office.

The Cuban Missile Crisis also illustrates the promise of more precise uses of force that new weapons make possible. Khrushchev's deployment brought parts of the U.S. within fast striking range of Soviet nuclear missiles for the first time. The United States did not wait until an attack was imminent to destroy the missiles and launch sites, which could have produced an escalation that led to a broader war. Instead, the United States imposed a blockade that used force in a narrower, less destructive manner, but still rendered it difficult for the Soviets to complete and launch the missiles. The potential harm from a Soviet attack was lower at this earlier point in time, because even though the potential magnitude of destruction from a nuclear attack was still great, there was a much lower probability of it. That expected harm was still high enough—it might even be tantamount to an imminent threat of a less destructive conventional attack—to justify a resort to force. In order to act earlier, however, the United States employed less violent methods than that justified by an imminent attack. Because the expected harm of an attack was lower (due to its greater uncertainty), Kennedy appropriately used more precise, less harmful means to coerce the Soviet Union to withdraw its missiles.

Preemption looks different when the threat is not so much an immediate attack as a sudden, menacing advance in enemy capacity. That was the threat from Iraq's nuclear program in the early 1980s. Israel launched an air attack on the Osirak nuclear reactor in 1981 because it believed that Baghdad was creating the components for nuclear weapons. An Iraqi nuclear attack on Israel would have catastrophic consequences, but no such attack could occur until some years into the future. Iraq had not recently attacked Israel, though it maintained its opposition to Israel's existence.[25] Israel acted before the reactor became operational to take advantage of a window of opportunity that would soon close. A later attack could have released radioactive fallout over Baghdad. The U.N. Security Council condemned the attack as a "clear violation of the Charter of the United Nations and the norms of international conduct."[26] Even the United States, which had traditionally protected Israel with its Security Council veto, voted against Jerusalem and condemned the attack.

At the time, Iraq appeared to be complying with its international obligations for its civilian nuclear program, had not attacked Israel or Kuwait, and seemed preoccupied with its ongoing war against next-door Iran. Still, Israel had the better of the argument. Its ambassador to the U.N. responded that to "assert the applicability of the *Caroline* principles to a State confronted with the threat of nuclear destruction would be an emasculation of that State's inherent and natural right of self-defense."[27] Despite his assurances to the contrary, Saddam Hussein continued to pursue WMD and was on his way to a nuclear weapon by the time of the 1991 Persian Gulf War. He had a hostile intent not just against Israel, but Iran to the east and Kuwait to the south. If Saddam had developed nuclear weapons by the time of the 1991 war, U.S. forces would not have succeeded so easily in dislodging Iraqi forces from Kuwait.

New weapons can make such interventions safer or more feasible to pursue. Beginning in the late 1990s, the United States protested efforts by Iran to secure a reserve of weapons-grade uranium fuel that could be used for nuclear weapons. Successive administrations seem to have cautioned Israel not to launch its own air attack on Iranian nuclear facilities, lest this provoke a dangerous level of conflict in the Middle East at a time when Iran was already supporting Shia militia in Lebanon and, after 2003, in Iraq.[28] Instead, the United States launched an elaborate cyber attack on the Iranian nuclear program. Stuxnet may have set back the Iranian program for a few years without causing any direct injury to human beings. It is not certain that bombardment from the air could have done better, and it more likely would have caused more casualties. Iran no doubt would claim many of the deaths were civilian, since it has always insisted that its nuclear program was for peaceful purposes. Nevertheless, Stuxnet might have created the conditions for more favorable terms in subsequent negotiations. In its eagerness for a deal, however, the Obama administration seemed to have forfeited the leverage provided by the cyber attack.

The cyber attack might have worked longer-lasting harm to Iran's uranium processing equipment. The Iranians could see that centrifuges were malfunctioning and had to be replaced, but they did not learn the cause for some time.[29] The United States government did not acknowledge its role in developing or infiltrating the computer codes that caused the damage. Ambiguity about the source of the attacks may have made the intervention less provocative and confrontational compared with an air strike. The uncertainties made it easier for both sides to avoid immediate charges and countercharges and an escalation of hostilities. Officials in the Bush and Obama administrations understood that a stealthy cyber attack on the Iranian program would be less threatening to the Iranian regime.[30]

Critics will claim that these new weapons will make unilateral intervention too attractive. Their very ease, precision, and light impact will encourage nations to resort to force in lesser or more highly focused increments. Bombing a city or landing thousands of troops will challenge a nation's sovereignty and spark demands for a military response. But a highly focused attack with specialized technology, which does little direct injury to civilian life, may give nations the flexibility to respond with diplomatic protests and a peaceful resolution.

It may be that new technologies will encourage an overly complacent attitude toward preemptive or preventive attacks. Still, we must balance this risk against the risks involved when states remain passive while WMD fall into reckless or threatening hands. Western nations may best counter the ambitions of an Iran or North Korea with high-tech weapons, which might force rogue states to the negotiating table. There may be no easy way to prevent a state from acquiring WMD. We might slow down Iran with attacks on its research facilities or its supplies of uranium, but it could turn to new, even more covert avenues to seek WMD. Western nations must use their new weapons to send a clear political message that Iran, its nuclear facilities, and its scientists are vulnerable to both conventional and covert attacks.

Syria demonstrates the limits of military strikes, whether using conventional or new weapons. Even though the Obama administration threatened strikes against the Assad regime for its use of chemical weapons, it also worried that destroying the stockpiles might pose great risk to civilians. While the Obama administration accepted Russia's face-saving compromise to remove the Syrian stockpile, western intelligence agencies have reported that the Assad regime subsequently used poison gas in its campaign against rebels.[31] The U.S. seemed particularly helpless because it could not reasonably threaten force. President Obama vaguely threatened air attacks, but could not identify any targets while ruling out any ground troops.[32] A strike on WMD facilities might trigger a release on nearby civilians, while hitting Syrian military facilities might violate AP I, since the U.S. and Syria were not yet at war and the U.S. would have no right to destroy Syrian military capacity.

The problem goes beyond the immediate impact of a punitive strike on a rogue nation's WMD capabilities. The Syrian government denied, dissembled, and then returned to using its weapons on both rebels and civilians. A U.S. strike would need to carry the threat of significant destruction and future repetition to deter Syria, in order to intimidate rather than incapacitate. New weapons provide opportunities for imposing coercive pressure by destroying an enemy's WMD assets, but that may not always be feasible or sensible. It does not follow that every use of new technology must pass muster with psychological warfare experts or grand strategists. But new opportunities will reconfigure the terms of conflict. One of the best reasons for accepting the new risks of new weapons may be reducing the spread of even worse weapons. It is hardly the only application worth thinking about.

Humanitarian Intervention

In 1994, ethnic Hutus murdered nearly a million Tutsi civilians in Rwanda. The word genocide, much abused, was coined to describe horror on that scale. Due to past violence between Tutsis and Hutus, U.N. peacekeepers had already deployed to Rwanda before the murderous campaign. They were promptly withdrawn for fear that an attack on them might entangle their home states (Belgium and Canada) in the conflict. The carnage ended when a Tutsi army, mobilized in neighboring Uganda, invaded Rwanda and overthrew the Hutu government.

There was much soul-searching in the aftermath. President Clinton described the failure to act in Rwanda as the worst failing of his presidency.[33] But landlocked Rwanda was not within easy reach of significant western forces. Scholars have disputed how easily the United States or other outside powers could actually have sent ground forces to stop the genocide and whether they were prepared for a long-term commitment. Other African civil wars have yielded even higher death tolls without interference from outside; Sudan's wars have killed 2 million, while Congo has lost 1.75 million.[34]

Five years later, the Clinton administration took the lead in mobilizing a NATO intervention to protect the threatened ethnic Albanian population in the Kosovo province of the former Yugoslavia. It feared that an intensification of the conflict between Kosovars and Serbia could lead to genocide. Regrets about Rwanda may have strengthened calls for western intervention, but the terms of intervention also underscored the limits of western willingness to act for humanitarian reasons. To enforce its demands for the withdrawal of Serb military forces from Kosovo, NATO initiated a bombing campaign that lasted ten weeks. NATO planes operated above 15,000 feet to place them beyond the reach of Serbian anti-aircraft defenses. There were no NATO casualties. There was no evidence of genocide or mass murder when international investigators gathered evidence for war crimes charges after Serbia withdrew. A U.N.-sponsored occupation of Kosovo has encouraged claims for independence but has yet to secure international agreement on the division.

An intervening state may claim that it acts solely from "humanitarian" concerns while other states may reject that claim. A democratic state that insists that its intervention has purely good motives may still stir concerns among its own people about the risks and costs. There are always good reasons to be cautious about projecting force into a conflict zone without immediate strategic value. Nevertheless, Rwanda and Kosovo illustrate the challenge to international stability from conflict within, rather than between, states. Since the end of World War II, about two-thirds to three-quarters of all wars have occurred only within one state.[35] One study estimates that civil wars account for about 80 percent of all deaths from armed conflict since 1945.[36] Another study reports that about 90 percent of postwar casualties are civilians.[37] Civil wars cause far more casualties and last on average far longer (six years versus three months) than interstate wars.[38]

These deaths primarily occur today in failed states. While scholars disagree about the precise definition of a failed state, the concept first described the successor states of the former Yugoslavia and African nations beset by civil wars after the end of the Cold War. Superpower competition had kept some of these nations afloat, thanks to aid from the U.S. or the U.S.S.R., while autocratic governments had kept others from breaking out into ethnic conflict. Failed states arise where government institutions no longer exercise effective authority, the economy has collapsed, and private groups control resources and population and rival the government.[39] States without an effective government may provide terrorists or criminal groups with a safe haven from which to recruit and train fighters, organize their arms and finances, and ship money, personnel, and weapons. Somalia's collapse, for example, not only allowed tribal warlords to divide the country, but it also became a breeding ground for the al-Shabaab terrorist group and other militant extremists. Afghanistan allowed al-Qaeda to operate freely and to plan and launch the 9/11 attacks.

Western interventions often sought to end ethnic strife and create stable governments in areas of little strategic importance. In Somalia and Haiti, for example, the United States sent troops to stop mass suffering and to establish stable governments. From a realist perspective, these actions delivered little benefit to the United States. Somalia had little strategic importance, few resources, and had already suffered through years of civil war. A poor country with few economic resources, Haiti had greater significance because of the potential refugee flows to American shores. Unlike Somalia and more like Haiti, Kosovo involved some security interests, but those of America's NATO allies rather than those of the United States. The United States certainly faced no threat of attack from Serbia, nor did it have any important strategic or economic interests in the Balkans at the time. In these cases, war served as a tool to combat threats to regional stability rather than as a means for unchallenged control.

The 2011 Libyan conflict provides another example of the challenge posed by failed states. Libya posed little threat to the United States or its forces abroad. Dictator Muammar Gaddafi kept his military deliberately small, limited to about 50,000 troops despite Libya's large oil revenues, to avoid a military coup. After the U.S. invasion of Iraq in 2003, Libya had voluntarily given up its nuclear weapons program, compensated victims of its terrorism, and normalized relations with the West. In February 2011, the Arab spring movement reached Libya. Gaddafi ordered the Libyan military and security services to fire on demonstrators, sparking a civil war. Rebels quickly freed the eastern half of the country and established their headquarters in Benghazi, but suffered a turnabout in their fortunes. After several weeks of indecision, the United States and its allies intervened when Gaddafi's forces threatened to snuff out the rebellion. The West had no desire to seize Libya's oil or territory. Instead, as President Obama said in March 2010, "Gaddafi must go" for wantonly killing Libyan civilians.[40] The West resorted to force not because Libya posed any imminent threat to its neighbors, but because of a civil war against Gaddafi's rule.

There may have been more at stake in Libya than just humanitarian considerations. Before the conflict broke out, Libya pumped 1.6 million barrels of oil per day—2 percent of global consumption—making it the seventeenth largest oil producer in the world.[41] Libya exported 85 percent of its daily production to Europe. Notably, NATO did not send its troops to other conflicts, such as those raging in Africa where the loss of life was as high or higher than in Libya but where there is little oil. However, if securing Libya's oil were the only goal, the United States and its allies intervened at precisely the wrong moment. It is more likely that European nations were concerned about instability so close to their shores, which might generate a flood of refugees headed for the European Union. However, by waiting so long to intervene, and acting so ineffectively, European nations ended up setting off the very stream of refugees that they feared.

Instead, the Libyan war bears similarities in motive to earlier postwar interventions. Haiti, Somalia, Afghanistan, Iraq, and even the former Yugoslavia did not raise the prospect of nation-state war of the kind that characterized the nineteenth and twentieth centuries. Aside from Iraq in 1991, which posed a threat to Kuwait, Saudi Arabia, and perhaps Israel, these countries did not menace their neighbors with aggression. Instead, they threatened the international system because of the internal conduct of their regimes.

Quite a few legal commentators argued, in the wake of the Kosovo intervention, that international law does not authorize resorting to war, even for humanitarian purposes.[42] The U.N. Charter allows military force in "self-defense," which can include aiding another state under attack.[43] But, according to many commentators, the Charter does not authorize outside states to deploy force to protect a threatened minority population against its own government. That reading of international law will be less compelling, however, if intervention becomes less costly, both for the intervening power and the targeted state. Drones might identify and disable the military units, either on the side of the government or rebels, in a civil war. They could destroy transportation used to carry prisoners and their detention camps too. They could compile detailed views of relevant sites, which might then come under scrutiny by international inspections. Cyber attacks might be used to disable broadcasting and social media, such as the radio broadcasts that incited the massacres in Rwanda.

New technology will make it easier to intervene to stop humanitarian disasters, but these options will not always render intervention effective or wise. What is stopped at one point may resume at a later time. What does not happen may not have happened. Outside states cannot intervene every time civilians are at risk of terrible violence. Premature or ill-judged intervention may even trigger hostile responses from local populations or goad outside powers to intervene. Technology won't supplant the need for judgment, but it will make it much harder to claim an inability to use force.

Technology will also erode rules that seek to limit the focus of interventions. In the 1990s, some critics questioned why Britain or the United States had not bombed rail lines leading to Nazi death camps during the Second World War. A considerable debate ensued on whether such action was feasible and whether it would actually have saved many lives.[44] Yet, as a contemporary European scholar has noted, AP I would now prohibit such action, because interfering with the operations of a concentration camp would not offer a "definite military advantage" to the attacker (as required by AP I's definition of legitimate "military objectives").[45] When there is a chance to save lives by ignoring the AP I rules, responsible governments will find it easy to bend those rules.

A cramped view of the right of nations to intervene for humanitarian purposes will likely fail if new weapon systems prove their value in preventing catastrophes. Their primary value may not be physically disabling the instruments of mass persecution but in making clear that leading nations may intervene to prevent such horrors. Using force can be as important for its political or psychological impact as its immediate physical effects. If new weapons can act as a warning or a marker, nations will not limit their use to extreme humanitarian crises.

Terrorism

Terrorist groups unconnected with any one nation-state, but nurtured in the ungoverned territories of failed states, present yet another security threat. The defining characteristic of terrorists is their lack of allegiance to any nation. The September 11, 2001 hijackers, for example, launched their attacks as part of the al-Qaeda network of Islamic radicals. Several were from Saudi Arabia, one of the U.S.'s oldest allies in the Middle East. Though they operated from a safe haven in Afghanistan, the hijackers had no defined territory, cities, or people to defend. They received funds from private and religious charities and drew manpower from a pool of disaffected, alienated, or unemployed young men bitter over the Arab world's decline.

Instead of common ethnic or local origins, al-Qaeda members are unified by an Islamist-inspired desire to engineer fundamental political and social change in the Middle East. They seethe at the rise of the Christian West, the collapse of the historic caliphate, the presence of American troops in the region, and the corruption of Arab regimes. To them, the United States is the primary cause of the conflicts and reversals suffered by the Islamic world. They believe that attacks on the U.S. will convince it to withdraw from the Middle East and cease support of existing Arab governments. Victory for al-Qaeda does not involve defeating U.S. military forces and negotiating a peace settlement, but demoralizing an enemy's society and coercing it to follow its political goals.

Terrorism depends on unpredictable, sporadic, and quick strikes on civilians using unconventional methods. The 9/11 hijackers wore no uniforms, did not operate in regular units, nor did they carry their arms openly, as required by the customary rules of warfare. Terrorist networks organize their personnel, materials, and leadership into covert cells, which can operate overseas or within the United States itself. While these features may have been present with other groups for many decades, new channels of global commerce and transportation have given terrorists more effective means to organize, finance, and move operatives into positions for attack. These new technologies allow terrorist groups to strike from half the world away with a destructive power that only nations once could exert. Few nations could have duplicated the September 11, 2001 leveling of the World Trade Center in New York City and the attack on the Pentagon using conventional weapons alone.

ISIS's rise has expanded the terrorist threat beyond the high-casualty, spectacular attacks that were al-Qaeda's hallmark. ISIS enjoys some of the attributes of a state. It seized territory in Syria and Iraq in 2014, including the major city of Mosul. It controls population, at one time reaching to several million people, and considerable resources within that territory.[46] It performs some government functions, such as a justice system that enforces its interpretation of Sharia law (however barbaric), taxation, and welfare services. On the other hand, it does not conduct diplomatic relations, nor does it seem capable or interested in upholding its responsibilities under international law. One of those important duties is to prevent its territory from being used as a base for attacks on its neighbors. If anything, ISIS exists to spread a fundamentalist Islamic revolution that calls for the replacement of existing Arab regimes with a universal caliphate. It uses its territory as a training camp and staging ground for fighters who will remain in the region or travel to western nations to launch terrorist attacks covertly.

Terrorism places further demands on self-defense. Terrorist groups do not deploy large military forces. American intelligence cannot effectively use satellite reconnaissance to detect the deployment of terrorist units days or weeks in advance. Terrorists do not launch cross-border attacks with regular armed units to seize territory, rather, they seek to covertly infiltrate a country by blending into domestic society. Their goal is to launch surprise attacks primarily on civilian targets. A temporal imminence test loses its value if a nation cannot detect the enemy's preparations in anticipation for war. By the time the nation detects an attack, it may well be too late because the attack will already have occurred. As WMD technology becomes cheaper and more available, the difficulties posed by terrorism will only increase. Groups such as al-Qaeda, Hezbollah, and Hamas have the financial resources to acquire chemical, biological, and perhaps even nuclear weapons capable of killing tens of thousands of civilians indiscriminately. Imminence as a limiting rule on the use of force suffers because non-state enemies can launch attacks with greater speed, surprise, and destructiveness than ever before.

In order to fight terrorism effectively, nations will have to use force well before an attack becomes imminent. They will have to act when a terrorist leader or a collection of fighters becomes known to intelligence agencies, even though they may be weeks or months away from executing a possible plot. At the same time, because the odds of an attack are lower, it would be reasonable to resort only to less harmful methods of coercion. If a terrorist attack were imminent, a government could destroy camps, buildings, and units using less precise conventional artillery or missiles with high-yield warheads. But if an attack is less certain, it would be more justifiable to deploy precision-guided munitions against selected leadership or logistics targets that will cause less collateral harm. As the certainty of an attack falls, its expected harm falls too; nations should adjust their measures accordingly. A nation under threat of terrorist attack may resort to force more often, because it is heading off multiple plots long before they mature, but it will also employ more precise weapons that keep harm to the necessary minimum.

Maintaining International Order

The most important use of new weapons may involve preventing states from threatening their neighbors. Even as the Cold War's end reduced the threat of nuclear armageddon, it opened a Pandora's box of new threats to the peace by regional rivalries. Western nations have failed to contain these efforts to rewrite the international order because of the incremental, low-level nature of the hostilities conducted by regional powers. New technologies might provide a means to carefully calibrate a forceful response, beyond mere diplomatic protest, that could counter efforts to upset the U.S.-led liberal international order.

Russia has probably become the number one revanchist power in the world. Seeking to restore its influence in its "near abroad," Russia invaded Georgia in 2008 and annexed the Crimean peninsula in 2014—the first change in European borders by force since 1945. It has engaged in a covert military intervention and provocations to foment unrest in the rest of Ukraine. It has intervened in the Syrian civil war with bombers, cruise missiles, and small ground units, and has sparked tensions with Turkey while cooperating with Iran. It has launched a military buildup (increasing military spending by 7.5 percent to $66.4 billion in 2015),[47] despite its declining economy, and has adopted a muscular deployment of forces along its borders with E.U. states.

China's stunning economic rise has sparked a parallel increase in its military and diplomatic place in the world.[47] While China currently cannot challenge American superiority in the global commons of the air and sea, the trajectory of its economic and military growth foreshadows a day when it will be able to deny the U.S. access to the seas around East Asia and contest it for supremacy in the Pacific Ocean. China now boasts the second largest military budget in the world, at $215 billion per year, an increase of 132 percent in the last 10 years.[49] It has embarked on a military buildup that extends beyond territorial defense to power projection abroad. China has given strong signs of what it will do with new ballistic missiles and a sophisticated navy in its seizure of disputed islands in the midst of the South China Sea, declaration of air defense zones over the Senkaku island chain off of Japan, and its threats against Taiwan. Communist China does not naturally seek peace; since taking power in 1950, its leadership has launched wars against many of its neighbors, seized control in Tibet, and fought the United States over Korea.

Although one is declining while the other is rising, both Russia and China seek to revise the American-sponsored balance of power in their regions. To be sure, the United States remains the world's hegemonic power, one whose dominance in economic and military strength may be unprecedented in modern history. It deploys expeditionary forces from a network of bases around the world, it maintains a liberal trading and political system, and it keeps open the air and seas. Even though U.S. military expenditures fell during the Obama years, the $596 billion American defense budget dwarfs that of the other great powers and represents more than one-third of all global military spending.[50] These figures understate American control of the global commons—air, sea, space, and now cyber—necessary for the projection of power worldwide, and its ability to leverage its economic and technological advances into military ones.[51]

Nonetheless, the United States must stretch its forces globally to maintain order, while Russia or China need only achieve regional superiority. Large mechanized armies bent on territorial conquest may have become less relevant. The war to reverse Iraq's 1990 invasion of Kuwait may be the last such war we will see for some time. But that does not mean that regional powers will foreswear the use of force against the United States and its allies. Instead, they will exploit means of coercion that fall short of the level necessary to spark any serious conventional armed response. China, for example, has pressed its dubious maritime claims in the South China Sea by converting small shoals and rocks near the Philippines into bases.[52] Russia pressures Ukraine by sending weapons, air and artillery support, and even irregular troops to prop up a supposed independence movement along its border.[53] Both nations are conducting a low-intensity struggle with the United States in cyberspace, with China stealing the U.S. government personnel database in 2015 and Russia hacking into the electronic files of the Democratic National Committee and Clinton campaign leaders in 2016. Even if nuclear weapons and American hegemony render direct conventional war less likely, nations will still pursue their interests by coercing other states.

Rogue states, as the Clinton and Bush administrations called them, or "states of concern" in the Obama years, compound these threats to international peace and stability. Whatever their name, these autocratic states both oppress their own populations and threaten their neighbors. North Korea, for example, remains one of the most extreme dictatorships on earth, with a population deprived of basic services and subject to famine and starvation, an oppressive police state, with one of the world's smallest per capita GNP. At the same time, the Kim regime devotes the lion's share of its budget to its armed forces. North Korea maintains the fifth largest army in the world and it periodically launches attacks on South Korea, such as the 2010 sinking of a South Korean warship.

Iran has joined North Korea in challenging the regional status quo with a level of hostilities that fall short of outright war. Iran supports religious militias such as Hezbollah, which harasses Israel from southern Lebanon, and sends irregular troops to support the Assad regime in the Syrian civil war. It supported Shiite militia groups during the Iraq war. Both Iran and North Korea bolster their revisionist agendas with programs to develop nuclear weapons and ballistic missiles, which would allow them to pursue their unconventional attacks without fear of reprisal. Their programs could spark a nuclear arms race in the Middle East, where Saudi Arabia and Egypt might seek to match Iran, or in East Asia, where Japan and South Korea might develop nuclear deterrents. Rogue nations refuse to abide by the basic principles of the international system and may seek to export revolution or disrupt the existing order.

Yet, their autocratic natures and revolutionary worldviews make them less susceptible to diplomatic or political pressure.

Some nations may bear ill will toward the United States, such as Venezuela, but have few military means to inflict harm. Only very limited American force could be justified to forestall a threat from Caracas. Other nations, however, such as North Korea, present themselves as rivals and are acquiring the means to attack. Pyongyang still considers itself at war with the U.S. and South Korea and holds the national goal of expelling American troops and forcibly unifying the peninsula under its regime. While the Kim regime has held the capacity to attack American troops stationed in South Korea since 1953, it posed no military threat to the continental United States. In 2016, however, North Korea successfully tested a 10-kiloton nuclear weapon, and in 2012 it launched a satellite into low-Earth orbit—the technology necessary to develop a ballistic missile capable of striking North America.[54] As the magnitude of the harm posed by Pyongyang has increased dramatically (nuclear weapons), and the likelihood it could execute an attack is rising sharply (ballistic missiles), the United States could legitimately employ more destructive means to squelch the threat of a North Korean attack. More precise weapons may give the United States the means to degrade or eliminate a North Korean nuclear threat without causing the wider harm that might trigger a broader war.

The pace of today's most pressing international threats seems to be set by the disintegration of states and the rise of civil wars, the spread of terrorism, and the proliferation of WMD technology, as well as their negative spillover effects upon neighbors, or the international system as a whole. To be sure, the threat of conventional conflicts between states always exists, though the odds of a war between the great powers has receded since the end of World War II. While the chances of great power conflict have decreased, the capability to duplicate their destructiveness has expanded because of the spread of technology into less responsible hands. But technology may also present the means to curb these threats. New weapons technologies may provide western states with the ability to use more precise, focused force to punish oppressive regimes intent on genocide. They can allow nations to pursue terrorists into lands inaccessible by ground or sea units. They can raise the costs on rogue states seeking WMD or rising powers seeking to upend regional stability. To fully understand the reasons why new technology may succeed, we will now examine a useful theory to explain why force may help in keeping the peace.

Using Force to Commit to Peace

In order to control these threats, nations must return to the use of force as a means of coercion. Great powers have long used force to pressure each other. Even in the twenty-first century, nations will continue to advance their interests, at times with conflict, and at other times with cooperation. New military technologies will make it feasible for nations to use force more often, rather than less, because they will be able to achieve their aims without triggering broader war. In this section, we turn our attention to one possible theory that could help explain why expanding the methods of force could encourage greater peace between the great powers.

We do not adopt this approach as the sole foundation for our account of war, technology, and law, rather, we develop it as a possible theory that supports our intuition that advancing weapons technology can lead to less conflict. This theory sees war as the failure of rational nations to reach a settlement of their disputes. The anarchy of the international system undermines the bargaining process because nations have uncertain information about their opponents' capabilities and cannot trust them to keep their promises. More ways to use force could provide leaders with greater means of signaling their seriousness of will, military capabilities, and commitment to avoid war. That may justify the counterintuitive conclusion that new technology can bring more, rather than less, peace.

Our world might be safer if it were more actively policed, just as more active policing has reduced violent crime in American cities.[55] The international system, however, lacks an effective supranational government that can stop violence in the same way that domestic institutions maintain law and order at home. Not only must nations use force more broadly in self-defense, but in the absence of an effective government they must also intervene to prevent threats to global welfare from weapons of mass destruction, terrorism, and aggressive authoritarian nations. Rivals such as Russia and China pose a tough challenge for this mission. Both nations enjoy the resources and militaries to place them in the rank of great powers. Their ambitions clash with U.S. interests, from Eastern Europe to the seas of the western Pacific. While their intentions may make them rivals of the United States, however, their own economic status gives them a great deal to lose. American power likely deters them from any direct, widespread conflict.

Critics, on the other hand, believe that new weapons could make the use of force cheaper, and hence war more commonplace. But we believe this view is mistaken. The ability to use force more precisely will prove a benefit to the international system. The signaling of resolve and capability through less destructive attacks can help avoid the worldwide conflicts that caused such grave human suffering and death in the twentieth century. Ironically, the availability of new weapons technologies should reduce the chances of great power war and lead to more settlement of conflicts.

If there is a place for coercion (as opposed to merely repelling attacks), however, the scope for resort to force must be enlarged. It will no longer be obvious that retaliatory measures must actually be limited to attacks on "military objectives."[56] Keeping the peace today requires a return to earlier understandings of the use of force. International law should allow nations to use force against civilian targets, so long as they do not involve lethal means of coercion. Recent efforts to apply a broad definition of the principle of distinction to twenty-first century conflicts should be relaxed, because they will have the unintended and perverse consequence of rendering war more likely and more destructive.

Even if our approach were to allow the great powers to suppress WMD proliferation, humanitarian crises, and terrorism, critics will worry that it will encourage conflict. Wider discretion in the use of force will result in more violence, which could increase the risks of war. Close attention to a promising theory of international crises, however, suggests that new weapons may actually reduce, rather than increase, the chances of war. Great powers will go to war when they fail to reach a negotiated settlement of their differences. They can bargain with each other using diplomacy, but when words alone fail, they must resort to demonstrations or even applications of force. New weapons provide states with the means to exert pressure at lower levels of destruction and casualties, which provides great powers in a crisis more opportunities to divert from escalation to settlement.

Rivalries will still endure and nations will still have disputes. But a promising theory of conflict suggests that rational nations should settle their disputes when the gains from cooperation outweigh the benefits of conflict. As Thomas Schelling argued, "Conflict situations are essentially bargaining situations."[57] Situations involving the possibility of armed conflict produce high incentives to avoid the losses from going to war.[58] Nations can settle their disputes in a way that gives each side some benefit while foregoing the loss of life and resources due to armed conflict. This approach bears similarities to a law and economics analysis of litigation, where parties acting rationally and with full information should always prefer settlement to the great expense of going to court.[59] Similarly, nations that have full information about military resources and political will should prefer an agreement instead of a conflict that wastes resources and will probably produce the same outcome.

International agreements serve as a means to resolve disputes between nations. Treaties can resolve border disputes, formalize the transfer of territory, or promise favored treatment for citizens and goods and services. Peace treaties recognize the end of a war. Nations, however, encounter significant obstacles to the enforcement of treaties. At home, parties can rely on a legal system, backed up by courts and police, to enforce a settlement. International anarchy, however, interferes with the ability of states to enforce agreements, despite their obvious benefits to both parties. Without international courts or police with effective authority to elicit compliance, a nation-state can renege on a treaty without consequence other than retaliation from other states.

This produces a classic prisoner's dilemma.[60] Nations might not enter into treaties because they do not trust their partners. This problem will be particularly acute where one party must take a first step that bears high costs before the other party must act. For example, a nation that has strong offensive military capabilities, but weak defensive systems, may be reluctant to refrain from positioning troops in a disputed territory and lose its tactical advantages without a firm guarantee that the other side will do the same. Without institutional mechanisms for enforcement, the first nation cannot be sure that the second nation will not exploit its own commitment to demilitarize in order to seize the disputed territory.

Nations should agree to a deal which reflects their chances of prevailing in a conflict, which depends on the balance of forces between the two sides. Each nation will have an expected value that it places on winning a dispute. The expected value of a war equals its expected benefit minus its expected cost. The expected benefit will be a nation's probability of prevailing times the value of winning. The expected costs of the conflict will be the likely losses suffered from fighting. Before they launch a conflict, governments must estimate the probability of winning, the likely benefits from victory, and the costs of securing it. If both sides could know these things in advance, they should compromise accordingly. If one state is likely to win important benefits at a small cost, the potential opponent may see resistance as futile. If the attacker sees that conflict would entail large costs for no substantial gain, it does better by withdrawing or reducing its claims. In either case, war would be irrational.

Successful bargaining requires that nations act rationally. Leaders, however, may be delusional or motivated by incentives other than costs and benefits, such as a messianic religious vision. There will be less room to compromise with these regimes. They may hold little concern about the welfare of their people while giving much more attention to preserving their own hold on power. Such nations might still risk going to war, even though they have a low probability of winning and a high cost of casualties, because the odds are higher that the regime will remain in power. Compromise with authoritarian regimes will prove difficult, as with Saddam Hussein's Iraq during the first and second Persian Gulf Wars. Nations may also place such different values on the matter in dispute that there is no real overlap in the range of outcomes they will accept. If Beijing, for example, values Taiwan far more highly than Washington because of the symbolic and historical meaning of uniting China, the expected values of the two countries might not make a settlement possible.

Lack of a supranational government makes agreement even more difficult because nations cannot trust the information that they receive. If nations do not know important variables, such as the probabilities of winning a conflict, the value that their rivals place on a contested resource, or expected war costs, they will be unable to decide accurately whether to go to war or to settle. The most important factor in this calculus is a nation's probability of winning a conflict, which depends on military capabilities and political determination. Information in the public domain, such as military size, defense budgets, and economic growth, can provide some clues about a nation's military strength. But even these relevant public facts may prove difficult to collect and analyze. During the 1970s and

1980s, for example, the CIA badly mistook the size of the Soviet defense budget and underestimated Moscow's large amount of spending necessary to keep up with the U.S. The Soviet Union's quick collapse in 1989-90, therefore, came as a surprise to most of the American national security establishment.[61] Even if accurate figures are publicly available, economic growth may not directly translate into military effectiveness because of weakness in military equipment, training, or culture.

Other relevant information will fall primarily within the control of the opponent. The United States, for example, will have private information on the quality of its armed forces and the superiority of its strategies and tactics. Indeed, nations will go to great lengths to conceal military abilities in order to preserve tactical advantages or strategic surprise. The United States keeps performance data on many of its weapons systems classified, which makes it more difficult for the enemy to develop effective countermeasures. Imperial Japan concealed its advances in aircraft carrier operations, which allowed it to project force as far as Hawaii, well beyond American estimates at the time. Nations will also have private information on the political willingness of their leadership, elites, and people to fight. One nation may be willing to suffer vastly higher casualties than the other, which affects their probability of winning a conflict. While the United States suffered about 58,000 deaths in the Vietnam War, North Vietnam and the Viet Cong bore losses estimated at least ten times that number.[62]

Lack of knowledge of an opponent's military capabilities and political resolve creates an information asymmetry. Information asymmetries inhibit the reaching of agreements, whether they are domestic contracts or the settlement of international disputes. First, imperfect information will lead to mistakes in bargaining. If nations overestimate their probability of winning a conflict, and correspondingly underestimate their opponent's odds, they will not realize there is a broader range for agreement. This lack of information will result in less settlement and more war. Second, nations will also have an incentive to bluff. A nation might seek to hide its military abilities in order to gain a tactical or strategic advantage. Or a nation will exaggerate its resources in order to bluff its way to a better deal. Great Britain and France mistook Germany's capabilities in 1938 and 1939, which allowed Berlin to seize Czechoslovakia and invade Poland without response. Faced with possible bluffs, nations will have few means of gaining credible information about their opponents' true capabilities. Such uncertainty will undermine the ability to reach a deal.

Third, nations will have few ways to credibly reveal private information. In order to avoid the costs of war, a nation may wish to communicate information on its true capabilities to its opponent. This picture will allow parties to reach a more accurate prediction of a dispute's outcome, which should smooth the way to a settlement. In domestic litigation, for example, the parties to a lawsuit can reveal information through discovery in federal court that provides credibility. But under conditions of anarchy, nations will have difficulty revealing private information in a credible manner.

More precise, less destructive uses of force can help overcome the obstacles of imperfect information. Coercive measures can signal political will, the value placed on the resources at stake, or military capabilities that could influence the outcome of a broader armed conflict. The more costly the signal, the more credible the information becomes. A nation's leader can make a threat of war and send military forces near disputed territory or a potential conflict zone. Deployment eats up resources that would go to waste if the nation is bluffing. It also incurs "audience costs" domestically, because a leader will suffer politically if he aggressively deploys force but then backs down.[63] Escalating steps of force will provide the opportunity to send more precise signals that gradually consume more resources, reveal more military capability, and edge closer to war. More signaling should reduce the chances of bluffing and reveal more reliable private information.

A good example is the Cuban Missile Crisis. The U.S.S.R. sought a rapid change to the balance of power in its favor by stationing intermediate-range nuclear missiles in Cuba. At this time, the United States had an ample deterrent capable of striking Soviet territory, while Russian forces could not yet match U.S. levels—this would change after the crisis when Moscow embarked on a program to build a large arsenal of ICBMs. President Kennedy decided to prevent the deployment. But before launching an all-out attack on the missiles, the United States effectively sought to force Soviet premier Nikita Khrushchev to agree to cancel the move. Kennedy ordered a limited use of force, a naval blockade of Cuba, which sent a signal of his willingness to use force to remove the missiles, and the U.S.'s military capabilities. He reinforced these messages by placing U.S. nuclear forces on high alert. But using limited coercive means allowed Washington to reach a negotiated settlement with Moscow that avoided the costs of a direct conventional conflict.

As Schelling suggested, the Korean War may provide another example. The United States directly fought against North Korea, which was supported initially by the Soviet Union. After Chinese intervention in December 1950, the United States conducted hostilities directly against another great power. The conflict, however, remained limited both in geography and means. Hostilities never left the Korean peninsula, despite the proximity of U.S. forces in Japan and Chinese bases in Manchuria. Both sides only resorted to conventional weapons, despite a large advantage in U.S. nuclear weapons and delivery systems. After Chinese intervention, both nations engaged in grueling ground combat for two years, even though the front settled early around the original dividing line between North and South Korea. Acceptance of high casualties by both the U.S. and China signaled their unwillingness to accept a peace that deviated from the original 38th parallel. It also demonstrated their credibility in respecting an armistice or cease-fire, because the alternative would be a renewal of costly fighting for little benefit.

If nations engage in such signaling as part of the bargaining over a settlement of their disputes, means of exerting limited force will prove valuable as ways to demonstrate resolve without choosing between complete acquiescence to enemy demands or all-out war. Instead of a naval embargo, or costly ground tactics, the United States could bargain with Russia or China with new types of weapons, such as drones or cyber. New technologies might not prevent a conflict from breaking out, but they will provide more opportunities to reach a negotiated settlement to avoid full great power hostilities. Conversely, limiting the ability to use lower levels of force might have the unintended consequence of rendering war more harmful. A ban on new weapons, for example, could narrow the range of targets and the means of coercion to produce more destructive signaling and ultimately more lethal conflicts. One nation may want to send a signal during a crisis that inflicts a precise cost on its opponent. With a broader set of targets and more levels of harm, the nations can send more discrete signals. But if nations limit their signals to kinetic attacks on military targets, they will have to employ more destructive levels of force. They might develop even more devastating kinetic weapons to produce the same effects as the precision offered by cyber or robotic weapons. Limits on new weapons technology might even destabilize crises by encouraging nations to use offensive weapons early in a crisis which might themselves be vulnerable to attack.[64]

Take, for example, disabling an opponent's financial markets or transportation and communications networks. During the Kosovo War, the United States Air Force dropped graphite on Belgrade's electrical grid, which temporarily disabled power to Serbia's capital city. While NATO claimed that the disruption in electricity undermined Serbian military operations, the attack on the electricity grid also sought to pressure Serbian civilians against supporting the Milosevic regime.[65] While such an attack would violate the ban on targeting civilian objects set out in the Additional Protocol I of 1977 to the Geneva Conventions, it could send a signal that might yield less loss of life and destruction than an attack on a hardened military target using kinetic weapons.

New technologies present opportunities, and dangers too, to send a greater diversity and range of signals during interstate crises. Nations could use cyber attacks to target each other's armed forces more precisely, and hence reduce direct casualties to both military personnel and civilians. While sending that message would inflict harm, it could avoid the casualties and physical destruction of a kinetic attack. Cyber attacks might reduce the collateral harm to civilians by disrupting only military communications networks or stealing only classified intelligence. While cyber attacks certainly could cause widespread harm, such as cutting water and electricity services to civilian populations, they could also simply disrupt a government's command-and-control of its military assets. Even if deployed against civilian targets, cyber weapons could still offer more precise and controlled power than a kinetic weapon.

The anarchy of the international system creates a second obstacle to cooperation. Even with perfect information, nations may still refuse to reach a peaceful settlement because they lack confidence that their opponent will keep its promises. They may understand that they will both be better off by avoiding war, for example, but nations may not trust each other to obey the agreement in the future. This problem will prove particularly acute in situations where a settlement changes the status quo between states or where rapid changes are affecting the balance of power.[66] One nation will find it difficult to trust its opponent to keep a promise if the latter will become even more powerful as a result of the agreement. New weapons technologies might provide new ways to increase commitment to an agreement. It provides states with more measured ways to sanction nations to stop violations, short of terminating an agreement altogether. Precision cyber and drone attacks provide more steps of coercion beyond diplomacy and economic pressure but are short of conventional armed conflict.

A critic might argue that without international regulation of these new technologies, the risk to civilians will increase. Nations at war, however, will have an incentive to distinguish between military and civilian targets to the extent allowed by the capabilities of weapon systems. Rational nations should seek to contain the harms of war in order to maintain the conditions for peace and to preserve the value of the civilian economy in the postwar period.[67] Defenders in a war do not want to kill their fellow citizens or harm their own territory, although they might destroy civilian property to prevent it from falling into the hands of the enemy. Conversely, invaders will have no interest in ruining the object of their aggression. Reducing civilian casualties may also encourage an end to conflict. Targeting civilians and destroying non-military resources may harden nations at war and make a diplomatic compromise more difficult. The unexpected carnage of World War I, for example, made peace restoring the *status quo ante* politically impossible for both the Allied and Central Powers.

Nations have long pursued indirect coercion against civilian populations in war. As we will describe more fully in the next chapter, they have often turned to economic sanctions to conduct hostilities short of armed conflict, or in conjunction with active hostilities. These sanctions pursued the objective of weakening the support of the civilian population for a regime's military policies. In World Wars I and II, the Allies conducted economic warfare against Germany and its allies by levying a blockade of civilian shipping.[68] After the wars, the U.N. Charter even expressed a preference for such tactics by authorizing the Security Council to impose "complete or partial interruption of economic relations and of rail, sea, air, postal, telegraphic, radio, and other means of communication" in the case of a threat to international peace and security.[69]

Economic warfare serves the same objectives as the approach described here for cyber and robotic weapons. First, it provides nations with a way to send signals in international bargaining through the gradual escalation of coercion, just as western nations used sanctions to bring Iran to the negotiating table over its nuclear program. Second, embargoes pressure civilian populations to change the policies of their leaders, or even the leaders themselves. While nations such as Great Britain and the U.S. have argued that embargoes only blocked goods that might contribute to an enemy war effort, the complete embargoes that prevailed during the World Wars seemed equally, if not more, directed against civilians. Perhaps new technologies, when employed as steps in the escalation of force, will also be understood as more akin to economic warfare than conventional bombing.

Limiting the use of force in a war bargaining situation can have several harmful effects. First, narrowing the range of targets only to military objects could have the effect of escalating the damage of signaling. In a crisis, nation A may want to send a signal that inflicts a certain cost on nation B. With a broader base of civilian targets, nation A could choose a relatively low level of harm to produce the desired level of coercion. Temporarily knocking out the electricity supply to the capital city, for example, will cause inconvenience to a large number of civilians. To produce the same level of harm upon a smaller base of military personnel and assets will require a higher level of force. Attempting to coerce nation B—consistent with a broad approach to distinction—might require nation A to attack and potentially destroy nation B's military targets and kill military personnel. Limiting the universe of targets to purely military sites could even provoke extreme crises by encouraging nations to launch vulnerable offensive weapons first, before they themselves are attacked. This "use it or lose it" incentive could force early and extreme escalations of a crisis into a military conflict.[70]

A prohibition on certain targets could also raise the chances of miscommunications that might have the unintended consequence of leading to war. Barring attacks on civilian assets will reduce the number of possible targets; only military personnel, facilities, and assets would be fair game. This strategy will limit the means of coercion between states. Only military means will prove effective against military units. It may also prove impossible, even with highly precise guided munitions, to tailor non-lethal uses of force solely to strike military units. Disrupting electrical supplies or destroying fuel stocks may exert low-intensity coercion against an opposing military, but it may also hurt civilians and non-military installations equally, if not worse. Other types of non-lethal tactics, such as cutting off access to the international financial system, may not have any direct effect on military targets at all.

Limiting force only to military targets may encourage the development and use of more destructive munitions. If nations expect that coercion will only take the form of attacks on their militaries, they will make military targets more difficult to attack. They may improve their military defenses to the extent that the attacking nation must deploy a significantly greater level of force to prevail. A defending nation, for example, might place critical facilities underground or in bunkers. It might even disperse critical military assets among the civilian population. Attacking military targets may force a nation to undertake an act of greater force to seek resolution of a dispute, while using lower levels of non-lethal force involving civilian targets might have equally communicated its message.

Reducing the number and types of targets and limiting the means to pursue them would increase the odds of war. Imperfect information can lead rational states to miscalculate. If there are further steps to convey reliable information, nations will have more accurate information on the expected values of war. That information will allow them to consider settlements before making the fateful decision for war. The more steps up an escalatory ladder, the more opportunity nations have to jump off before they reach the stage of armed conflict. On the other hand, limiting the ability of nations to communicate will reduce their ability to reach settlements of their differences. If nations have less opportunity to credibly signal information to each other, the chances of miscalculation and war will increase.

The twenty-first century has brought new types of security challenges to the United States and its allies. Where the last century saw worldwide war between continent-spanning alliances, today the threats to peace come from regional powers, rogue nations, terrorist groups, and civil wars. The West should maintain international peace and stability by employing the full spectrum of force made available by technological progress. It should also use force to prevent looming threats posed by terrorism or the internal breakdown of states from maturing into catastrophes. Contrary to the concerns of some, broadening the use of force will not lead to more war. It should allow the international system to reduce the number of more harmful conflicts by allowing nations to communicate their intentions more clearly, which should produce more settlement of disputes without resorting to war.

The U.N. Charter Rules

As Syria shows, the world is returning to the idea that the international system allows punitive measures. This runs counter to the view, embraced by most specialists in international law, that the U.N. Charter banished the idea of punishing states for misconduct. In 2013, for example, Gabriella Blum concluded that "the moral rhetoric of state 'crime and punishment' has been excised from the lexicon of international law" so that "coercive action against states can no longer be justified by any punitive urge but instead must be couched in terms of regulatory or preventive action."[71] Blum questioned the value of this shift, even as a means of reducing resort to force in international affairs. But she still saw the renunciation of punishment as the culmination of long-developing trends, already visible before the establishment of the United Nations.

Recent efforts to purge the international system of punitive responses mistake the traditional principles of the laws of war. The older view acknowledged a much wider range of occasions for the use of force and a wider range of legitimate targets. Today, most scholars insist that the resort to force, under the U.N. Charter, can only be appropriate in response to an "armed attack,"[72] though most acknowledge that the rule is often disregarded. Many commentators have emphasized what seems the logical corollary—that force, when it is justified at all, must be limited to what is necessary for repelling attacks.[73] Further, some commentators argue that forcible defensive measures must be exclusively targeted at the actual attacking forces. Most commentary on the law of armed conflict concludes that lawful force must, at any rate, be aimed at "military objectives" and never at "civilian objects."[74]

The prevailing scholarly interpretation of the U.N. Charter, however, rests on faulty assumptions and has never reflected the reality of practice among the great powers. It borrows from notions of self-defense in domestic criminal law, which generally prohibits individuals from using force unless they are under imminent threat of deadly harm, force in response is necessary, and it is proportional.[75] Other than self-defense, the government enjoys a monopoly on violence. The U.N. Charter attempts to limit force in precisely the same manner. A nation can resort to force only to stop an imminent attack. The use of force must be necessary because all peaceful alternatives have failed. The use of force must be proportional to the threat. Writes philosopher David Rodin: "National-defense is conceived, within international law and in the just war tradition, in very much the way that self-defense is conceived in domestic law and morality."[76]

But there are fundamental differences between domestic crime and international affairs. Most obviously, states are not individuals and the U.N. is not a functioning supranational government. The U.N. does not enjoy a monopoly on violence within international society; in fact, it can muster no armed forces of its own. Private individuals are denied a legal right to use force against surrounding harms because it is assumed that the police have the power to intervene. But if nations do not use force to stop an evil, no international government will step in to do the job. Unlike domestic affairs, in international relations anarchy and self-help are the norms. In domestic affairs, the goal of the rules on self-defense is to drive the level of violence to zero. But in international affairs, without a true supranational government to police the conduct of nations, there may be a need for violence to prevent many of the harms that we have mentioned in this chapter: WMD proliferation, humanitarian disasters, terrorism, and regional instability. "War is an ugly thing, but not the ugliest of things," John Stuart Mill wrote.[77]

Nations have used force in the past for beneficial purposes beyond just self-defense. At great cost in men, ships, and money, Great Britain used its naval dominance in the nineteenth century to eradicate the slave trade and to enforce a *Pax Britannica* that encouraged free commerce and trade. In 1917, the United States intervened in World War I to prevent the victory of the Central Powers and maintain a balance of power in Europe. In 1941, the United States again intervened in Europe to stop the expansion of fascism, and then spent another fifty years containing the Soviet Union. In the postwar world, the United States Navy replaced the Royal Navy in keeping the seas open to free navigation. These actions were not wholly altruistic. Both Great Britain and the United States benefitted from free trade and a balance of power in Europe and Asia. But they also shouldered the costs for maintaining an international order out of proportion to their share of the benefits, while other nations free-rode off their efforts.

Economic theory would predict this to be the case. International peace and stability are public goods that benefit all nations, just as clean air or domestic law and order are public goods at home. But those who supply public goods cannot charge someone for receiving their benefits. A company cannot give clean air to some neighbors but not others. Low crime rates benefit all residents of a city or state. Similarly, a group of nations that provide international peace cannot charge other nations a price for enjoying its benefits. Some nations will simply free-ride, such as those European countries that benefit from NATO security but underfund their militaries. Without a centralized government to provide these services and collect general taxes, public goods will be underfunded and thus undersupplied.

Many of the security threats of the twenty-first century have these features. Most nations will fail to contribute to a campaign against WMD proliferation, stopping a humanitarian disaster, or ending a regional threat from terrorism or a rogue state. They may rely on more powerful nations to take up the crusade, or they may calculate that their costs of intervening outweigh the individual benefits. After the 9/11 attacks, the United States bore the main burden in invading Afghanistan and hunting down the al-Qaeda network, which benefitted many other nations that contributed little. Great powers such as the United States might not intervene because of the human costs of military action or because their own gains from maintaining international order do not outweigh the costs. In fact, in the nineteenth century, the United States contributed little to maintaining the freedom of the seas and free-rode off of the British Navy. Nations today will use force too little, not too much, to combat twenty-first century threats to security.

New weapons can help ease this dilemma. If the United States, for example, can intervene to stop these problems at a lower cost, it may provide more international peace and security. New weapons provide just such an option. If the U.S. can use cyber weapons to sabotage WMD facilities without risking its own personnel, it will be more likely to act to stop a rogue nation. If the U.S. can use drones without having to dispatch ground troops, it may be more likely to send bombers to target terrorist leaders or the leadership of a regional militia bent on genocide. Reducing the costs of intervention will allow the United States and its allies to provide more protection for the international order.

Current interpretation of the U.N. rules, however, directly counteracts the potential of new weapons to bolster the international system. Neither preventing WMD proliferation nor stopping humanitarian disasters, for example, would qualify as self-defense. In the eyes of many contemporary international legal scholars, launching a strike to prevent Iran from acquiring nuclear weapons would count as aggression, just as the members of the Security Council condemned Israel for the 1981 attack on the Osirak nuclear reactor.[78] Striking a nation that harbors terrorist groups, unless an imminent attack is in the offing, would interfere with that nation's territorial integrity in violation of the U.N. Charter. Intervening in Kosovo violated the U.N. Charter, as neither the U.S. nor NATO could legitimately fear an attack by Serbia. An identical problem will arise with any humanitarian crises that remain within one nation's borders.[79]

One might argue that the answer is to work through the U.N., rather than against it. The U.N. Charter, however, only allows exceptions from its no-force policy by authorization of the Security Council, which can call on members to use force to maintain or restore international peace and security.[80] Such permission slips are not readily forthcoming due to the veto power of the permanent five members. No matter how dire the threat, it is likely that a problem will fall within the sphere of interests of one of the permanent members, who will then veto U.N. action to keep its rivals outside of its region. From the end of the Korean War in 1953 to the start of the Gulf War crisis in 1990, the Security Council proved unable to authorize a single use of force. After a brief burst of activity after the end of the Cold War, the Security Council has returned to its traditional paralysis. Russia prevented Security Council authorization of the Kosovo War, France and Russia vetoed the 2003 invasion of Iraq, Russia has blocked action on the Syrian civil war, while China protects North Korea from military force.

Without a more accommodating interpretation of its prohibitions, the U.N. Charter system will discourage the deployment of new weapons to check rising threats to international order. When similar challenges have confronted the United States and its allies in the past, they have felt free to disregard overly restrictive interpretations of international law. The

Cuban Missile Crisis, in which President Kennedy used force to prevent the U.S.S.R. from expanding its deployment of nuclear weapons, only provides the most salient example. Israel's attack on the Osirak reactor met with Security Council criticism, but was in hindsight undeniably in the world's best interests. The U.S. strike on Libya in 1986 never received U.N. approval, but forced Tripoli to reduce its support for international terrorism. The U.S. invasion of Panama in 1989 removed a dictator, Manuel Noriega, from power, but without any true showing of the necessity of self-defense from an imminent attack. While it received authorization to pursue al-Qaeda in Afghanistan in 2001, the U.S. more controversially invaded Iraq in 2003 without the aid of a U.N. resolution.

When the formal rules conflict so consistently with practice, the norms will eventually shift. States will find it easier to use force because of the lower costs of new weapons technologies, to both the attacker and defender. As they use these weapons to address the new security challenges of the twenty-first century, nations will be better off. They will be able to devote more resources to prevent threats to peace and stability by coercing other nations to cease harmful or threatening conduct. At the same time, the lower levels of violence incurred by these weapons also provide more avenues for communication and commitment between great powers. Rather than producing more war, new technologies should help reduce the chances of general war in favor of more peaceful resolution of disputes. To take advantage of these benefits, U.N. Charter rules will have to be read in a more permissive way. It will also be necessary to restore a more permissive understanding of *jus in bello* once fighting begins. It is to that latter task that we now turn.

CHAPTER 3

Except a Few Things Regarded as Barbarous and Cruel: The Law of War Before the 1970s

Of all American statesmen, Abraham Lincoln thought most deeply about human justice and divine providence. If we had no other evidence—and there is much else from his earlier writing—we would know that from his second inaugural address. Lincoln also had to think hard about war. He presided over a conflict that killed and wounded more Americans than any other in our history. He directed the only war in which the national government directed military force against fellow Americans. His main aim was to coerce the rebels to rejoin the very republic that was fighting them.

Still, even in this context, Lincoln characterized the legal scope of military action in very broad terms:

> Civilized belligerents do all in their power to help themselves, or hurt the enemy, except a few things regarded as barbarous or cruel. Among the exceptions are the massacre of vanquished foes, and non-combatants, male and female.[1]

Lincoln did not hit on this formulation impulsively. He wrote these words in a letter defending his most controversial war measure, the freeing of the slaves. Only a very broad understanding of permissible measures in war could justify the Emancipation Proclamation. At a time when all blacks in the South were held as private property, emancipation without compensation struck at the very heart of southern society and raised difficult questions about constitutional authority for the nation. It remains the largest confiscation of private wealth in the history of the United States.

Lincoln was sufficiently serious about the law of war and his administration issued the world's first official manual on the subject. It became known as the Lieber Code for the Prussian émigré professor, Francis Lieber, who drafted it. European scholars recognized it as a foundational contribution to the development of the laws of war. Lincoln's Emancipation Proclamation not only met his own general principles but also the more detailed standards of the Lieber Code.[2] Under Lincoln's laws of war, the Union could seize or destroy civilian property used to support the Confederate war effort. Slaves provided the labor force for the South's economy and freed whites to fight in its armies. "Armies, the world over, destroy enemies' property when they cannot use it; and even destroy their own to keep it from the enemy," Lincoln wrote.[3]

Today, most commentators on the law of armed conflict would question a measure that took a vast amount of private property from civilian hands. Such a policy would violate AP I, which declares as a "Basic Rule" that "the Parties to the conflict shall at all times distinguish between the civilian population and [enemy] combatants and between civilian objects and military objectives and accordingly shall direct their operations only against military objectives."[4] AP I fortifies this principle of distinction with an additional restriction that attacks on lawful "military objectives" must be proportional. An attack will still be unlawful if "incidental" harm to civilians or "damage to civilian objects...would be excessive in relation to the concrete and direct military advantage anticipated."[5]

These provisions are far more restrictive than what earlier generations understood to be the rules of civilized warfare. They are not idiosyncratic or absurd on their face. Versions appear in many of today's military manuals. Some kinds of attacks on civilians, in some circumstances, have been condemned for centuries. AP I's sweeping prohibitions overlap in significant areas with practices that earlier generations condemned as "barbarous." But there are also important differences between the practices and customs developed over centuries and these new limits on war.

AP I's formulas, if rigorously applied, would prevent new weapons technologies from achieving their full potential. The latest technologies provide opportunities for highly precise targeting. With the most advanced weapons, an attack can disable equipment or damage infrastructure without directly harming humans. Taking down an electrical grid or disabling communications networks can raise the pressure on a government to negotiate a settlement. Drone strikes and cyber attacks might coerce nations into conceding in a crisis, but without the long-term or permanent destruction of full-scale conflict. Using force against "civilian objects" could lead to a faster, less harmful resolution of a dispute than limiting attacks solely to "military objectives."

For the same reasons, new technologies may blur sharp distinctions between war and peace. AP I assumes that armed conflict is entirely a contest between military forces. The Red Cross claims that this approach simply codifies understandings about war that have been accepted since the eighteenth century.[6] As this chapter will demonstrate, that claim is simply wrong. Previous generations of Anglo-American statesmen and jurists did not embrace such restrictive views on permissible war measures. They did not countenance deliberate massacre of noncombatants, but used bombardments and blockades against civilian infrastructure and property to pressure the enemy. They were prepared to invoke such tactics even in disputes that did not rise to all-out war. To reap the full benefit of new technologies, we will have to recover the older understandings.

We are not arguing against all limits. To argue that some restrictions are overreaching is not to deny that limits remain necessary. Nor is it reasonable to conclude that because a particular tactic is *legally* permissible, it is *tactically* appropriate in all circumstances. American military commanders sensibly impose special rules of engagement for particular missions, taking into account the circumstances. "Armed conflict" is a term that encompasses many different kinds of conflict. Deciding *how* to fight may require as much prudent judgment as deliberation on *whether* to fight. Pleas of necessity are more often an excuse than an argument. Our purpose is to reclaim space for debate and deliberation, rather than allow restrictive views about the law of war to foreclose opportunities offered by new technologies.

Reasoning about War

Some war practices were regarded as "barbaric" even in antiquity, indeed by the very Greeks who gave us the term "barbarian"—as an all-embracing, disdainful term for non-Greeks. In his chronicle of the Persian Wars, the

Greek historian Herodotus recounts the response of a victorious Spartan general, Pausanias. He was urged to cut off the head of the slain Persian commander and display it on a stake, since the Persian had done the same to a defeated Spartan king. Pausanias refused to "abuse a corpse," decrying that as a "sacrilege" and "a deed more appropriate to barbarians than to Hellenes, though we resent [the barbarians] for [this practice] all the same."[7]

In the early seventeenth century, the Dutch jurist Hugo Grotius claimed that the law of nations had come to embrace a right to bury the dead after battle. He attributed the practice to long-standing custom, citing Greek and Roman authors from classical antiquity. But he acknowledged that "the ancients...generally ascribed to the gods" those rules which they would have "seem more sacred."[8]

From antiquity to the modern world, western armies have recognized that some practices would be morally degrading or spiritually polluting to the perpetrators. For the Greeks that meant honoring religious shrines, affording safe conduct to heralds and ambassadors, as well as respecting the bodies of fallen soldiers.[9] Of course, such restraints did not always prevail, even among the Greeks. Rape has been a deplored but observed feature of war through the ages. U.S. Marines even practiced mutilation of enemy corpses in the Second World War.[10] But historical practice gradually expanded the scope of the laws of war to prohibit certain ways of waging hostilities.

It is tempting to think that where moral revulsion is not enough to restrain armies, a sense of self-interest could still induce restraint. That idea also has a long history, stretching back, at least, to the Greek city-states. In his history of the Peloponnesian War, Thucydides recounts the debate in the Athenian assembly about a proposal to massacre the people of Mytilene, a dependent city-state that had tried to break free from Athenian control. Agreeing that the relevant question was not the guilt of Mytilene but the interests of Athens, the Athenian assembly decided on clemency in order to avoid driving other cities to desperate resistance. Rather than slaughter all adult males on the island as originally proposed, Athens decided to kill only a thousand of the leading citizens.[11]

As the war dragged on, however, the Athenians became less calculating about consequences and less inhibited about resorting to extreme measures. After Melos attempted to defect from the alliance, Athens ordered the slaughter of all adult males on Melos and the sale of the women and children into slavery.[12] Melos was not a unique case, only the most notorious for the retort of Athenian commanders to Melian pleas for restraint: "The strong do what they can and the weak suffer what they must." In the culminating episode of Thucydides' narrative, all the Greek city-states of Sicily united against Athenian invaders and then committed the captured Athenian force to annihilation. In the course of that long war, earlier rules of restraint were regularly disregarded. Greeks fighting fellow Greeks often descended to Persian levels of barbarism, though not, it seems, to "the most ungodly practice" (as Herodotus calls it) of subjecting captive males to castration.[13]

Avoiding only those practices deemed "barbaric" or "ungodly" still left a vast scope for war. In antiquity, condemnations of barbarous practices were not, in general, aimed at nurturing regard for civilian life. In extreme cases, conquering armies embraced massacre as a tactic, or the enslavement of women and children. Plutarch calculated that Julius Caesar killed more than a million people in the conquest of Gaul—most of them, it seems, not engaged in combat but exposed to retaliation as relatives of the fighters.[14] Plutarch does not seem to have regarded this as a terrible blot on Caesar's reputation. He compared Caesar with Alexander the Great, who had annihilated entire cities to punish resistance or rebellion. A present-day historian describes the strategy as "terror."[15]

Christianity could not completely banish such ferocity. Medieval writers still recognized a category of extreme war—*Bellum Romanum*, as they aptly called it for extreme situations like the Crusades.[16] Such extreme tactics were employed by the Spanish conquerors of the Americas as well. We might like to believe that eighteenth-century Enlightenment theorists, who advocated universal natural rights and government by consent, condemned the most brutal tactics with greater resolve. But it was more complicated than that. Even if one thinks government should be focused on securing the rights of citizens, it may not always follow that restrained wars provide the most security.

The mid-eighteenth century treatise *Le Droit des Gens* ("Law of Nations") by the Swiss diplomat, Emer de Vattel, acknowledged that hard lesson. It was a work studied and cited by the American Founders and by statesmen across Europe down to the late nineteenth century. It was one of the principal sources for the Lieber Code. On the whole, Vattel expressed the complacent moral tone of the Enlightenment, where morality and self-interest were generally envisioned as mutually reinforcing— a posture that later provoked a disparaging dismissal of Vattel from Immanuel Kant.[17]

Vattel emphasized the exemption of women and children, the aged, and the sick from attack.[18] He rejected the idea of war as punishment for general "crimes" like impiety, insisting that each sovereign state has the right to decide for itself how it will be governed.[19] The rights of the conquered should be respected, he counseled, to avoid violent resistance. "In this case, as in every other, good policy is in complete accord with humane treatment."[20] Nevertheless, Vattel acknowledged that a nation might slaughter enemy prisoners who could not be safely held or released.[21] In extreme cases, a nation could order a section of a country "completely devastated, its towns and villages sacked, and everything delivered up to fire and sword" when facing "the necessity of punishing an unjust and barbarous Nation, of putting a stop to its cruelty, and preventing acts of depredation."[22]

Vattel implies that a nation may fight more fiercely against a more terrible enemy, because the causes of the war would justify the methods. Contemporary commentaries insist, to the contrary, that rules for the conduct of war are entirely separate from rules about resorting to war. They usually invoke technical terms to describe these supposedly distinct sets of rules: *jus ad bellum* (law governing the legality of resorting to war) and *jus in bello* (law governing the conduct of war). Vattel did not make such a sharp distinction, nor did earlier writers. Though the Latin terminology suggests that the terms derive from Grotius or perhaps Augustine or Cicero, these terms were actually coined in the 1930s and subsequently popularized by Red Cross commentators.[23]

The distinction is hard to maintain completely, even today. If defeat means the end of national existence, leaders might deploy much more extreme methods than in a conflict over navigation rights at sea. In 1996, when the International Court of Justice addressed nuclear weapons under the laws of war (*jus in bello*), the majority acknowledged that it might be lawful to threaten the use of such weapons to avoid national annihilation. Nuclear deterrence during the Cold War threatened to unleash "assured destruction" to deter the most extreme threats from the most powerful enemies. In lesser conflicts, however, both superpowers preferred to abandon their war aims (as America did in Vietnam and later the Soviets did in Afghanistan) rather than resort to nuclear weapons.

That was Vattel's view. "Right keeps pace with necessity, with the demands of the situation," he observed.[24] Methods of war that would be quite wrong in many situations might be acceptable in more extreme cases. Thinking about *how* we should fight cannot be entirely separated from the question of *why* we are fighting or *what* we are fighting against.

Rules for the conduct of war depend on the nature of the dispute, the type of enemy, and the consequences of defeat. Traditionally, nations and commentators assumed this basic truth. Some enemies pursued more extreme aims, which justified more extreme methods of resistance. Different wars seemed to justify different rules because different enemies would not accept the same rules.

Reciprocity and Limitations by Agreement

What Vattel set down as moral principle was already custom. Armies observed various rules, but the full range of restraint applied only in certain kinds of war, with certain enemies. One can see the point by glancing at America's founding era. The Declaration of Independence recites a list of British abuses that culminate in the claims that the King's forces have "plundered our seas, ravaged our Coasts, burnt our towns" and perpetrated other acts "scarcely paralleled in the most barbarous ages, and totally unworthy the Head of a civilized nation." "Civilized" nations should not follow the war tactics of "barbarous ages." But only a few years later, during the course of the same war, General Washington sent a military force to subdue Seneca Indians on the frontier in western New York. The main tactic was to "ravage" Seneca crops and see that their villages were "burnt."[25]

Washington did not believe that his armies could act without limit. He demanded, for example, the humane treatment of captured British soldiers and even Hessian mercenaries. But the rules that applied between civilized peoples did not apply in other conflicts. Americans were outraged when the British army accused the colonials of fighting like Indians and mutilating captured British soldiers. They were also outraged by the brutal treatment meted out to captured Americans by British authorities, treating them, in effect, as criminals rather than prisoners of war.[26] American opinion was again outraged when a British raid burned the public buildings in Washington, D.C., in 1814, though American forces had burned many more Indian villages by then. As Henry Adams remarked, British troops "burned the Capitol, the White House, and the Department buildings because they thought it proper, as they would have burned a negro kraal [i.e., an animal enclosure in an African village] or a den of pirates."[27]

Modern readers are apt to view such distinctions as "racist" but that is missing the point. Nations embraced restraints when they expected reciprocity and they tended to disregard them when there was none. Wars with irregular fighters knew few restraints. The most famous example is the war that gave us the term "guerrilla"—literally, small war. When Napoleon's armies captured the enemy capital—Milan, Berlin, or Vienna—the opposing rulers negotiated a peace agreement and the population remained quiescent. In Spain, the king's abdication to a Napoleonic successor was met with fierce resistance from local guerrilla fighters. Both sides engaged in atrocities to terrorize their opponents and seize dwindling food supplies. When British forces under the Duke of Wellington arrived in Spain, they gained the support of local peasants by bringing their own supplies or paying local farmers, rather than seizing provisions by force. When they crossed into France, Wellington carefully excluded Spanish guerrilla allies from the invasion, lest they stir up French counterparts.[28]

During the American Civil War, the Lieber Code prohibited personal looting by soldiers, along with violence to unresisting civilians. It did not prohibit the seizure of property by the Union army or retaliation for guerrilla attacks. The Confederate Secretary of War protested that Lieber's code would "justify...the warfare of the barbarous hordes who overran the Roman Empire," reflecting the notions of "a German professor...more familiar with the decrees of imperial despotisms of...Europe than with Magna Carta...and the Constitution of the United States."[29] When the Union army faced guerrilla resistance in Arkansas, which threatened operations in western Tennessee, it expelled Confederate sympathizers, seized or burned their houses, and devastated many miles of civilian infrastructure along the western shore of the Mississippi.[30] General Sherman, who commanded this activity in its early stages, treated such measures as a matter of course in his post-war memoirs. Lieber's Code was not seen as a barrier to any of these tactics.[31]

The experiences of the U.S. Civil War and the wars of German unification inspired European scholars to propose a convention that could be applied to future international conflicts. At the Hague Peace Conference of 1899, which was supposed to foster the general cause of peace rather than settle any particular conflict, nations adopted the first treaty on the laws of war, the "Convention with Respect to the Laws and Customs of War on Land."[32] Article 2 stipulated that it would bind "the Contracting Powers in case of war between two or more of them," but it did not apply to internal conflicts nor to conflicts with non-signatories. It added the further restriction that the rules would not apply to a war in which a non-Contracting Power joined with one of the belligerents, lest one side gain advantage from violations of the rules by its allies.

Adherents to the Hague Rules did not think they applied to colonial conflicts. Two years after the 1899 peace conference, British forces in South Africa used brutal methods to deprive Boer guerrillas of civilian support. They "concentrated" farm families in army-run "camps" while devastating their farms, which gave rise to a term that a later generation of Germans would knowingly redeploy. International law scholars endorsed the tactic at the time.[33] American forces adopted similar "village removal" tactics to suppress an insurrection in the newly acquired U.S. colony in the Philippines, again with scholarly approval.[34] German forces massacred some 80,000 Herero tribesmen in Southwest Africa, which prompted a later generation to describe the episode as "genocide."[35] In 1900, the great powers sent troops to China to rescue foreign embassies in Peking from Boxer rebels. The killing of many Chinese civilians did not concern Kaiser Wilhelm. He had urged German troops to prove themselves "Huns of the twentieth century"—lauching a derisive nickname that would be embraced by Germany's enemies in the ensuing world wars.[36]

These episodes passed without comment at the second Peace Conference in 1907 and left no mark on the minor revisions to the regulations on land warfare. Acknowledging that the agreed rules were "not a complete code," the Hague Conventions admonished that where the agreed rules did not apply, "the inhabitants and the belligerents [in warring nations] remain under the protection and the rule of the principles of the law of nations, as they result from the usages established among civilized peoples, from the laws of humanity, and the dictates of the public conscience."[37] Such very vague rhetoric did not, perhaps, require much commitment. Perhaps it reminded army officers that they were not free to resort to "barbarism," if they could still define the word. But as a British historian noted of the body of restraining rules in that era, "very little of it was concerned with 'civilians.'"[38]

The 1907 Hague Regulations tried to assure humane treatment for prisoners of war and for "inhabitants" in occupied territory in times of war. A prohibition on the "pillage" of conquered towns was repeated in two places. Among the few restrictions on the conduct of actual military operations was a prohibition on bombardment of "undefended" towns. The signatories evidently assumed that if a town were undefended, an invading force could simply walk in and seize it.[39] But the rule allowed bombardment of defended towns, and efforts to starve a town by denying all food and other essential supplies during a siege.

The Hague Regulations do not address enforcement. Commentators and governments understood this to mean that the written rules would be enforced as the unwritten customs always had been—by reprisal. Prisoners of war were supposed to be treated humanely. A state that abused enemy prisoners had to fear that the enemy would abuse its prisoners. Describing states that ratified the Hague Regulations as "contracting parties" made clear that if one side breached terms of the contract, others would feel entitled to respond in kind.[40]

Retaliation was not a mere theoretical possibility. The most famous case occurred near the start of the world war. The Hague Regulations had a specific prohibition against "poisoned weapons" and the 1899 Hague Peace Conference also produced a separate declaration against asphyxiating gases as weapons of war.[41] When the Germans deployed poison gas in 1915, the Allies quickly responded in kind. Gas attacks remained a standard combat tactic on the western front until the armistice in 1918.[42]

After the war, diplomats tried to reinforce the old prohibitions in the 1925 Geneva Protocol, prohibiting resort to "asphyxiating, poisonous gases" as a weapon of war. The convention's preamble appealed to the "conscience of nations" and noted that such weapons had been "justly condemned by the general opinions of the civilized world." But it also took the precaution of stipulating that the parties to this convention "agree to be bound *as between themselves*," so use of these weapons remained lawful against enemies that used them.[43] Fear that Germany would again resort to such weapons prompted the western Allies to equip themselves, in the next war, with a sizable stockpile of chemical weapons, which were actually deployed to Europe to be available as reprisal for German use.[44] With the real threat of retaliation in kind, both sides did respect the use of poison gas in the Second World War.

Reprisal would not have surprised officials or scholars of earlier times. They understood that abuses were unlikely to be deterred without the threat of reprisals. As the leading English language treatise put it: "Reprisals cannot be dispensed with, because without them illegitimate acts of warfare would be innumerable."[45]

Civilian Immunity Was Not the General Rule

But what were the worst abuses? Today, most commentators would see attacks on civilians as the worst abuse of the rules of civilized warfare. That was not quite the traditional view. Medieval and early modern treatises, down to the work of Grotius in the seventeenth century, urged that military commanders should try to spare "the innocent." They took for granted, however, that non-soldiers might share some responsibility for sustaining unjust wars. Grotius recorded, as the opinion of many centuries, that armies should take care to spare women, children, churchmen, and agricultural laborers because their activities were not likely to affect the outcome of a conflict. He did not urge a general immunity for all those not bearing arms.[46]

The underlying idea of "civilian" immunity is relatively new. Classical Latin did not have a word for "civilian" in the sense of non-military.[47] Neither did English. According to the Oxford English Dictionary, the first usages of the word in that sense do not appear in English until the late eighteenth century. Nor did Enlightenment doctrines immediately prompt a change in thinking. Neither the Lieber Code nor the Hague Conventions use the word "civilian" in this sense, though they certainly indicated general concern for bystanders with no direct connection to the operations of war.[48]

One of the most celebrated expressions of Enlightenment doctrine, the American Declaration of Independence, embraces the traditional view. At the end of its recital of complaints, it protests that "our British brethren" have been deaf to warnings and complaints, despite American appeals to "ties of our common kindred and consanguinity." So, says the climactic affirmation, "we hold *them*, as we hold the rest of mankind, enemies in war, in peace friends." "Them" clearly refers to the people of Britain and of other nations that challenge our rights, not merely to governments and military forces.

Fifty years later, the doctrine of the Declaration was reaffirmed, with legalistic precision, in *Commentaries on American Law* by James Kent, a jurist who started his law career as a protégé of Alexander Hamilton and John Jay. Kent explained the meaning of war in these terms:

> When war is duly declared, it is not merely a war between this and the adverse government in their political characters. Every man is, in judgment of law, a party to the acts of his own government, and a war between the governments of two nations, is a war between all the individuals of the one, and all the individuals of which the other nation is composed.[49]

A decade later, Henry Wheaton, former reporter of decisions for the U.S. Supreme Court, then U.S. ambassador to Prussia, published *Elements of International Law*—the first full-length treatise on the subject in English. It affirmed that "[a]ll the members of the enemy state may lawfully be treated as enemies in a public war." The point was not that all "members of the enemy state" would be eligible to be killed on sight, but that they would forfeit some of their rights, most especially their property rights to legitimate war measures. "From the moment one state is at war with another, it has, on general principles, a right to seize on all the enemy's property, of whatever kind and wheresover found."[50]

These "general principles" had many applications in different kinds of wars. Eighteenth-century commentators recognized a condition of hostilities called "imperfect war," in which some coercive measures might be appropriate but not invasion by land forces.[51] Most commonly, governments would authorize privateers to seize enemy commerce on the high seas. It was a kind of licensed piracy, though limited by the targets specified in a letter of marque, which shielded the bearer from punishment as a pirate. The Constitution authorized the practice, which the U.S. had already deployed during the War of Independence. It again used privateers during the undeclared naval war with France in the 1790s and in the War of 1812. The whole point was to seize civilian cargoes of whatever kind as an economic sanction.[52]

In 1856, European powers agreed to disavow privateering, but not naval seizures. Still, seizures of enemy ships on the high seas could only succeed against states that engaged in maritime commerce. So navies developed other tactics, such as bombarding facilities on land, to coerce smaller states. By the late nineteenth century, commentators recognized a category of "pacific reprisals," which commonly involved the naval bombardment of commercial sites, such as warehouses. In 1905, German naval forces launched attacks on sites in Venezuela as reprisal for attacks on German merchants. British commentators condemned the Germans for attacking a Venezuelan military fortification and other military sites, which was more appropriate to actual war than to peacetime reprisal.[53] Such peacetime measures continued after World War I, as by Italy against Greece in the 1920s, and by Britain against China in the 1930s.[54]

In full-scale war, nations seized private property far more systematically. During the American Revolution, states seized property from those who would not swear allegiance to the new government. During the Civil War, the Union naval blockade of the South not only stopped all imports, including civilian goods such as cloth and thread, but also exports of cotton (almost all privately owned).[55] President Lincoln's Emancipation Proclamation applied to all slaves in areas "in rebellion," whether particular owners were staunch supporters of the Confederate war effort or mere helpless bystanders. Even some opponents of slavery criticized the Emancipation Proclamation as sweeping too widely. Benjamin Curtis, a former U.S. Supreme Court justice who had dissented in *Dred Scott*, condemned Lincoln's policy for confiscating slaves from those who did not support the Confederate rebellion.[56] Wheaton's treatise had already supplied the justification: "All members of the enemy state may lawfully be treated as enemies in a public war." The United States was not following idiosyncratic doctrines. It was, as the U.S. Supreme Court ruled in the 1863 *Prize Cases*, applying practices generally accepted under international law.[57]

By the last decades of the nineteenth century, however, these doctrines were under challenge. Commentators in Continental Europe urged that private property, if not directly related to military uses, should not be subject to seizure, even on the seas. Civilian property should be immune from seizure in naval war, they argued, as the logical extension of long-accepted doctrines that private property on land should be respected in wartime.[58] Almost all English commentators defended the traditional doctrine that enemy commerce on the seas was subject to seizure as a reasonable war tactic, one much less violent or cruel than land warfare. Both sides in the debate were keenly aware that Britain's Royal Navy had preponderant strength on the seas. American commentators generally backed the British view. In the world wars of the twentieth century, neither Allied navies nor German U-boats granted civilian immunity to ocean commerce.

In the late nineteenth century, the Cambridge legal scholar John Westlake defended seizure of enemy property at sea as a legitimate war measure. Countering continental scholars, he noted that war measures do not simply aim to defeat an opposing army but to "compel the enemy State to accept such terms of peace as it is desired to impose on it." Even in military operations on land, he noted, an invading army would only respect civilian property "so far as it does not interfere with any operations deemed to be useful for putting pressure on the enemy."[59] He condemned German commentators who justified "the devastation of a whole region as an act of terrorism," though conceding it was "not to be greatly feared" that the German government would "ever give effect" to such an extreme, unacceptable "doctrine."[60] He proved too trusting. In 1914, German commanders adopted such tactics by bombarding cathedrals, burning libraries, and shooting Belgian civilians to enforce compliance with German demands. Allied commentators denounced such practices as a reversion to "barbarism."[61]

That does not mean there had been previous agreement that all civilian objects were exempt from attack or that permissible attacks must only focus on "military objectives." Slaves in the South did not contribute directly to Confederate arms. The Emancipation Proclamation aimed at undermining southern morale and diverting resources from Southern armies by encouraging slaves to run away. General Sherman's march through Georgia and the Carolinas did not aim to seize and hold territory. Towns and cities in the line of march were captured and then quickly abandoned, often after much destruction. All along the route, Sherman's army mangled rail lines, pillaged farms, and seized livestock in an extended, rolling raid. Sherman himself had justified the march in a frank admission about its aims:

> I attach more importance to these deep incisions into the enemy's country, because this war differs from European wars in this particular: we are not only fighting hostile armies, but a hostile people, and must make old and young, rich and poor, feel the hard hand of war, as well as their organized armies. I know that this recent movement of mine [marching from Atlanta to Savannah] has had a wonderful effect in this respect. Thousands who had been deceived by their lying newspapers to believe that we [i.e., the Union army] were being whipped all the time now realize the truth and have no appetite for a repetition of the same experience.[62]

Sherman took pains in his memoirs to insist that his army had not committed violence against civilian persons and that even the looting of personal effects, such as jewelry, was "exceptional and incidental" to approved measures.[63] General Grant's memoirs added the claim that such violence was likely committed by local convicts released from Georgia prisons "who took advantage of their country being invaded to commit crime."[64]

Presumably they thought that letting soldiers commit rape and murder would have been "barbarous." Sherman denounced the Confederate tactic of spreading unmarked land mines on a public road as "not war but murder."[65] Some Union commanders argued that devastation of farms was a far more effective tactic. In his postwar memoir, General Philip Sheridan touted the contribution of his own raids in the Shenandoah Valley in Virginia, which he pursued just as Sherman had completed his attack on Atlanta:

> Death is popularly considered the maximum punishment in war, but it is not; reduction to poverty brings prayers for peace more surely and more quickly than does the destruction of human life, as the selfishness of man has demonstrated in more than one great conflict.[66]

What was true in all-out war among modern states was, of course, readily accepted in frontier wars with irregular forces. Tactics deployed against Confederate farms in the Civil War were later directed against

Indians on the Western plains—sometimes by the same officers. Commanding army units on the Great Plains after the Civil War, Sheridan presided over a series of small conflicts with Plains Indians. His military raids were directed at tribal livestock and other possessions, rather than human life.[67] In the nineteenth century, the British army conducted punitive raids in the same way against tribes on the northwest frontier of India. The leading British manual on the conduct of such campaigns, Colonel C.E. Callwell's *Small Wars: Their Principles and Practice*, urged "raids on livestock" and attacks that "demolished villages" and "destroyed their granaries."[68] It did not distinguish "civilian objects" from "military objectives."

A young participant, a lieutenant of cavalry at the time, described one raid on Afghan tribes on the Indian frontier. He scoffed at the euphemistic or evasive accounts of what was done:

One member of the House of Commons asked the Secretary of State whether, in the punishment of villages, care was taken that only the houses of the guilty parties should be destroyed. He was gravely told that great care was taken. The spectacle of troops, who have perhaps carried a village with the bayonet and are holding it against a vigorous counter-attack, when every moment means loss of life and increase of danger, going round and carefully discriminating which houses are occupied by "guilty parties" and which by unoffending people, is sufficiently ridiculous. Another member asked, "Whether the villages were destroyed or only the fortifications." "Only the fortifications," replied the minister guilelessly. What is the actual fact? All along the Afghan border every man's house is his castle. The villages are the fortifications and the fortifications are the villages. . . . A third legislator . . . commented on the barbarity of such tactics. They were not only barbarous, he affirmed, but senseless. Where did the inhabitants of the villages go? To the enemy of course! This reveals, perhaps, the most remarkable misconception of the actual facts. The writer seemed to imagine that the tribesmen consisted of a regular army, who fought, and a peaceful, law-abiding population, who remained at their business, and perhaps protested against the excessive military expenditure from time to time. Whereas in reality, throughout these regions, every inhabitant is a soldier from the first day he is old enough to hurl a stone, till the last day he has strength to pull a trigger, after which he is probably murdered as an encumbrance to the community. . . . In official parlance the burning of villages is usually expressed euphemistically as "So many villages were visited and punished," or, again, "The fortifications were demolished." I do not believe in all this circumlocution . . . the people of our islands [i.e., Britain and Ireland] only require to have the matter put fairly before them to arrive at sound, practical conclusions.

The author had one more point, which he illustrated by the practice of the Prussian forces in their war against France in 1870. The "burning of mud hovels cannot . . . be condemned by nations whose customs of war justify the bombardment of the dwelling-houses of a city like Paris, to induce the garrison to surrender by the sufferings of the non-combatants."[69] He could have added that the Prussian army had knowingly followed the Union army's bombardment of Vicksburg to hasten its surrender.[70]

Much more would be heard from this author, Winston Churchill. A year later, he published a memoir of military operations in the Sudan, followed the next year by a personal account of the war in South Africa. Then he won a seat in Parliament. By 1919, Churchill was the first peacetime minister of the new Air Ministry. He remained quite interested in air power when he became Colonial Secretary the following year. "The first duty of the Royal Air Force," he told Parliament, "is to garrison the British Empire." He put an RAF commander in charge of the new British mandate in Iraq, then boasted about the great cost reductions achieved by assigning suppression of local revolts to the RAF.[71] He angrily rejected plans to bomb villages to force payment of taxes.[72] To shoot down unarmed, unresisting civilians still seemed "barbarous." To destroy civilian property as a military tactic against rebels in the field, not necessarily.

He had much occasion to think about proper rules in two world wars.

New Weapons Largely Displaced Old Rules

In January 1914, Winston Churchill was the naval minister in a liberal cabinet. A retired former admiral had warned him that in the event of war, Germany would use submarines to attack merchant shipping. He replied: "I do not believe this would ever be done by a civilized, scientific, Power," comparing submarine attacks to "the spreading of pestilence and the assassination of individuals" and other practices that "are frankly unthinkable."[73] He was disabused of these illusions by the ensuing war. His postwar memoir, *The World Crisis*, summed up the experience this way:

> The Great War differed . . . from all modern wars in the utter ruthlessness with which it was fought. . . . Germany, having let Hell loose, kept well in the van of terror; but she was followed step by step by the desperate and ultimately avenging nations she had assailed. . . . Merchant ships and neutral ships and hospital ships were sunk on the seas and all on board left to their fate or killed as they swam. Every effort was made to starve whole nations into submission without regard to age or sex . . . . Bombs from the air were cast down indiscriminately. Poison gas in many forms stifled or seared the soldiers. Liquid fire was projected upon their bodies. . . . When all was over, Torture and Cannibalism were the only two expedients that the civilized, Christian States had been able to deny themselves: and these were of doubtful utility.[74]

Most of what he lamented—the sinking of merchant ships at sea, the use of naval blockades "to starve whole nations," indiscriminate bombing from the air—continued on a larger scale in the next world war.

Technological advances not only generated new weapons, but also brought civilians more deeply into the waging of war. Nations could not field large armies and navies without the mass production of equipment, food, and fuel by millions of workers, nor could they coordinate their operations without vast transportation, energy, and communications networks. Nations used their new weapons not just for tactical advantage on the battlefield, but to degrade both military industries and civilian support for the war. Governments would not live up to a ban on new weapons until they had seen their effects in practice.

Here we will look at the disputes about war tactics that were most bitter during the First World War. On the one side, the Allies attempted to choke off seaborne supplies to Germany, ultimately including food shipments. On the other side, the Germans attempted to stop all shipping to Britain with submarine attacks. World War I shows that new legal prohibitions will not easily suppress weapons or tactics that seem to have war-winning potential.

At the outbreak of the Great War, Britain announced that it would interdict shipments of war supplies to Germany. By 1915, the blockade was no longer a method for restricting the flow of military supplies but evolved into a strategy described with a new term: "economic warfare."[75] Germany retaliated by declaring a shipping exclusion zone around the British Isles enforced by submarines with the freedom to torpedo both British and neutral merchant ships without warning.

Allied and neutral powers expressed indignation at the German tactic. Britain's attorney general, F.E. Smith, documented that German submarine attacks were unique in naval history in leaving merchant crews and civilian passengers to drown.[76] He acknowledged that a belligerent state might rightfully seek "to weaken the adversary by attacking his financial and commercial resources" even on the high seas. But Smith insisted that pursuit of that strategy "does not and cannot carry with it the right to take the lives of noncombatants."[77] Across the ocean, the United States had, from the outset of the war, protested against restrictions on neutral shipping imposed by Britain and France. But German submarine attacks were seen as a different category of tactics from diverting neutral ships to Allied ports. While Americans criticized Allied blockade policies as excessive, they denounced German submarine attacks as barbarous.[78] In 1916, President Wilson had criticized submarine attacks on merchant shipping as "incompatible with the principles of humanity" and with "the sacred immunities of noncombatants."[79] He expressed particular outrage at attacks on passenger ships, such as the Lusitania, carrying ordinary travelers from neutral states. Despite repeated American warnings, Germany announced in early 1917 that it would resume unrestricted submarine warfare. At Wilson's urging, the U.S. Congress responded with a declaration of war.

In the meantime, the Allies had gradually tightened their blockade to encompass food shipments to Germany and most shipping to neighboring neutral states to prevent cargo from reaching Germany on land.[80] The Germans argued that the "starvation blockade" clearly violated international law. Besides, they complained, Britain had taken to arming its merchant ships, making it impossible for lightly armed submarines to give them advance warning, as previous practice required. Armed ships in war zones could not expect peacetime courtesies. As it happens, the decision to arm British merchant ships was taken by naval minister Winston Churchill, who insisted that the ships carried only "defensive arms" so they should not be treated as warships.[81]

The legal issues were complicated and somewhat technical. Both sides appealed to pre-war understandings, few of which were grounded in established treaties. Both sides claimed the right to undertake more extreme measures in response to lawless conduct by the enemy.[82] Some years before the start of the war, conservative peers in the House of Lords had defeated a treaty that was supposed to limit wartime interference with merchant shipping, warning that in the event of war Germany might well use its naval forces to block food shipments to Britain.[83] The U-boat campaign would, in fact, have imposed severe food shortages on Britain, if the Royal Navy had not finally developed a naval convoy system to counter the German submarine fleet. Once the United States entered the war, its navy assisted the campaign against the U-boat menace while reinforcing the Allied blockade on German and neutral ports.

The Allied position might seem self-serving. Certainly the Allied blockade affected vastly more civilians than the German submarine campaign. The Allies could not credibly depict their blockade as merely obstructing the delivery of supplies to German armies in the field. After the armistice in November of 1918, the Allied blockade continued for another eight months to pressure the German government to accept the final terms of the Versailles Peace Conference.[84] After the war, British military commentators celebrated the blockade as the decisive strategic measure that had undermined civilian morale, ignited a rebellion in German cities, and forced the German government to abandon the war.[85]

The Anglo-American position, however, had a serious moral grounding. The blockade imposed much hardship and misery. By 1918, when an influenza epidemic swept across Europe, undernourished Germans were particularly vulnerable. German officials could claim that hundreds of thousands of people had died premature deaths in consequence.[86] But the effects of the blockade were long-term, cumulative, and indirect, leaving much room for the German government to organize civilian relief efforts, which it neglected to do on an adequate scale.[87] The effect of a U-boat attack was usually a quick death by drowning. With submarines in the vicinity, even nearby Allied ships could not stop to rescue survivors.

From the British perspective, the moral distinction was clear and obvious—even years later. In 1929, President Herbert Hoover, who had launched his public career distributing food aid to Europe at the end of the world war, proposed an international convention to exempt food shipments from wartime blockades. The British government rejected the proposal, though at that moment conducted by the Labour Party, which had long claimed to be an advocate for humanity. As a report to the cabinet from military leaders explained, "To tell a potential enemy that in all circumstances you will feed him is not to reduce the risk of an aggression."[88]

The British still insisted, however, that submarine warfare was an evil that must be repudiated. At the Washington Naval Conference in 1922, the British advocated a convention that would have reaffirmed the prewar understanding of permissible naval tactics. Civilian shipping should never be attacked without warning and never put in danger of destruction, the treaty stipulated, "unless the crew and passengers have been first placed in safety."[89] The treaty proposed to enforce these standards by imposing personal liability on non-compliant crews "as if for an act of piracy" (a crime for which the usual punishment was death).[90]

The 1922 Convention foundered, due to opposition from France and Italy. The British persisted. The fundamental provisions were included in the London Naval Treaty of 1930, then extended to Germany in the *Procés-Verbal* on Submarine Warfare in 1937.[91] But even at the time, there were doubts. "[T]he submarine is too useful and important an instrument of modern naval warfare to be restricted in this fashion," an American legal analyst predicted in 1934.[92] In 1939, on the very day Britain declared war, in fact, a U-boat struck without warning against a British passenger liner.

Britain wasted no time in announcing a food blockade, even during the so-called "phony war" that preceded the German invasion of France on May 10, 1940. That summer, the new prime minister, Winston Churchill, defended food blockade in an emphatic public speech. He declared that his government would be rightly condemned "if we were to prolong the agony of all Europe by allowing food to come in to nourish the Nazis and aid their war effort, or to allow food to go in to the subjugated peoples, which certainly would be pillaged off them by their Nazi conquerors."[93] After it entered the war at the end of 1941, the United States used its own navy to reinforce the British blockade.

In this war, however, the United States took a different position on submarine warfare. On the day the Japanese struck Pearl Harbor, the United States adopted its own policy of unrestricted submarine warfare against Japan. The new American policy was adopted so quickly, it could not have been a sudden impulse. As historians later discovered, the U.S. Navy had been contemplating this tactic for more than a year. It was clearly contrary to previous American claims about international law, including the main reason for declaring war against Germany in 1917. Staff advisors to the Chief of Naval Operations suggested that unrestricted submarine warfare could be justified as a reprisal against Japanese atrocities in China or some other Japanese misdeed. In the event, no public explanation was provided for the change in U.S. policy, nor is there even a document recording President Roosevelt's approval.[94] The resort to a new policy on submarine attacks must have been fully anticipated within the Navy, however. A local commander in the Philippines authorized submarine attacks even before the Navy Department wired approval in the hours after the Pearl Harbor attack.[95]

The United States Navy pursued the policy with relentless determination. It became, as a naval historian concludes, "the most successful practitioner of submarine warfare in history."[96] By 1943, shipments of oil to Japan, for example, had fallen to 29 percent of 1941 levels and by 1944 to less than 14 percent.[97] By the end of the war, U.S. submarines had sunk 1,300 Japanese merchant ships, nearly as many as Japan had on hand at the start of the war.[98] Lacking vital supplies, Japanese war industry dwindled to a standstill. The civilian population faced slow starvation.

At the Nuremberg trials, British prosecutors insisted on bringing war crimes charges against top German admirals for submarine warfare. Defense lawyers introduced an affidavit from Admiral Chester Nimitz, commander of U.S. naval forces in the Pacific, acknowledging that the U.S. Navy had pursued similar tactics against Japan to those adopted by U-boats in the Atlantic. The tribunal declined to convict on that charge, which legal commentators saw as a tacit admission that the Second World War had changed the prevailing rules.[99] Meanwhile, Article 42 of the U.N. Charter authorized the Security Council to impose a "blockade" of any state that resisted its directives—with no exception for food shipments.

There has been no serious proposal for a new convention to limit submarine attacks on civilian shipping as a war tactic. Less formal restatements of the relevant law imply that western states, particularly the United States, are prepared to embrace very severe blockade policies in a future war, so long as they acknowledge some humanitarian limits. Since no major power has implemented a long-term blockade since 1945, it is unclear how such a tactic would now be pursued, but we have some indications of what is now viewed as acceptable.

In 1994, experts from the Western naval powers agreed on a guide to applicable international law, the San Remo Manual. It offers a number of humanitarian restraints on behalf of hospital ships and ships devoted solely to the transport of civilian passengers, but still allows attacks on enemy merchant ships when they refuse to stop for inspection or sail under convoy of enemy warships.[100] It cautions that neutral merchant ships should not be struck without warning, unless the cargo may "make an effective contribution to the enemy's military action" and "circumstances do not permit" giving a warning.[101] It prohibits only blockade measures with "the *sole* purpose of starving the civilian population," but acknowledges that the blockading force may restrict food shipments if they do not conform to the supervision and conditions imposed by the blockading power.[102]

U.S. Navy manuals have indicated that merchant ships may be subject to attack if they contribute to the enemy's "war-sustaining effort," which includes not only relevant imports but also revenue generating exports (such as oil shipments).[103] That policy is affirmed in the 2015 Department of Defense Manual on the Law of War, which even cites Admiral Nimitz's Nuremberg affidavit to illustrate circumstances in which making provision for survivors of an attack may not be "feasible."[104]

These episodes and their aftermath do not prove that nations will always seize any new weapon or tactic that promises brief advantage. Poison gas, which caused so much misery in the First World War, was not used in the Second World War. Nuclear weapons have not been used since 1945. Experience in the First World War seems to have persuaded military commanders of all the major powers that poison gas was not a war-winning weapon.[105] The Germans did not draw that conclusion from their experience with submarine warfare in the First World War, nor did American naval planners. Germany was already trying to starve Britain in both world wars, while the United States was so much less vulnerable to Japanese counterattacks in the Pacific that it did not have to worry that its submarine campaign might prove a provocative strategy. Given the strategic situation of the U.S., with a preeminent navy but no great dependence on imports from abroad, American planners did not need to worry about setting a dangerous precedent for future wars.

As these episodes also illustrate, nations tend to interpret the rules or norms in their own interest. That does not mean moral arguments all reduce to bluster. Unlike the German U-boats, U.S. submarines did not attack neutral ships or ordinary passenger ships. And indignation against German submarine attacks in the First World War was probably colored by reports of German atrocities against civilians in Belgium, which inclined Allied opinion to see German tactics at sea as characteristically heedless of humanitarian concern.[106] The Allies did not see their own measures in that light. Nor did others. Certainly, no other states were moved to assist Germany after 1915 to counter Allied tactics. That was so even in regard to the most extreme Allied measures in the Second World War.

Attack from the Skies

Bombing of cities was the controversial new tactic in the Second World War, as submarine attacks had been in the previous world war. But even air attacks were not a complete novelty. Here, too, there was dispute about applicable rules, followed by a breakdown of inhibitions. In 1917, soon after it resumed U-boat attacks on Atlantic commerce, Germany embarked on another desperate tactic. It sent Zeppelin air ships to drop bombs on London and a few other English cities. The Allies denounced the Zeppelin raids as "terror" attacks since they seemed to have no purpose other than to terrorize civilians. In the meantime, British and French airplanes dropped bombs on German cities, but this was depicted as something quite different because the intended targets were arms depots or arms factories. Britain was so committed to this tactic that it organized the first independent air army in 1918, the Royal Air Force (RAF). German cities escaped the RAF's planned bombing campaign when a revolution in Berlin brought a new government, which hastily agreed to an armistice in November 1918.

The Versailles Treaty tried to spare the world from any threat of subsequent German air attack by prohibiting a German air force. That was not enough to make western states lose interest in air power. As noted earlier, the RAF was redeployed for service in colonial outposts, where it bombed villages to suppress rebellions. The U.S. Army Air Corps was deployed to Nicaragua to help the Marines suppress the Sandino rebels in the 1920s. Other colonial powers found similar uses for air attacks in the interwar period.[107]

Meanwhile, Hugh Trenchard, Air Marshal of the RAF, developed plans for an air assault on the enemy capital at the outset of the next war, which, in the early 1920s, he imagined as a war against France.[108] By the mid-1930s, other threats had come to the fore. Prominent military analysts, lamenting the years of slaughter inflicted by trench warfare in the previous war, urged entirely new tactics. Both British and American military leaders negotiated contracts for the construction of fleets of long-range bombers years before the outbreak of World War II. It is not true, however, that air power simply inspired naïve optimism. In Britain, senior officers in both the army and the navy protested Trenchard's loose talk of forcing the enemy's surrender by bombing civilians. The British navy saw it as analogous to German U-boat attacks on civilian shipping and likely to provoke at least as much condemnation and resistance.[109]

In 1923, a conference of western legal experts at The Hague tried to agree on rules to regulate air warfare. They agreed on a general prohibition on "aerial bombardment for the purpose of terrorizing the civilian population, of destroying or damaging private property not of a military character, or of injuring noncombatants."[110] The wording implied that "destroying or damaging private property" was not inherently subsumed by the ban on "terrorizing." A subsequent provision allowed aerial attack on towns or cities "in the immediate vicinity of the operations of the land forces" on the same wide terms allowed by the 1907 Hague Regulations for artillery bombardment.[111] It was plausible to hope that bombardment from the air as from artillery might force the surrender of a town or city already within reach by advancing infantry.

The 1907 Hague Regulations prohibited bombardment against places that were "undefended," meaning towns or installations that could be seized without resistance. By this reasoning, every town beyond the front lines might be regarded as "defended." That would mean, under the old rules, that aerial bombardment could be conducted without limit to force the surrender of the whole country. The Air Rules tried to impose limits by requiring that beyond the front lines, air attacks must be directed at a "military objective," which included not only troop centers and arms

depots but factories engaged in war production and "lines of communication or of transport used for military purposes."[112]

It is telling that western states attempted to negotiate limitations on
bombardment even in the early 1920s. It is equally telling that the governments never adopted these rules. The British government, with the largest
air force at the time, was persuaded by internal objections. Air Marshal
Trenchard, acknowledging that it would be wrong simply to pursue
indiscriminate bombing of civilians, asked why should it be acceptable to
deploy bombing to "terrorize" soldiers but not the munitions workers or
dockyard workers who supplied them?[113] When the British government
announced that it would not ratify the Hague Rules on Air Warfare, other
participants in the negotiation abandoned the project.

The ambivalence remained. In 1924, J.M. Spaight, a legal analyst for
Britain's air ministry, published *Air Power and War Rights*. He denounced
the idea that aerial bombardment could be unleashed to "spread death
and desolation" without limit, which he described as "a doctrine which
can only be described as medieval in its hideous simplicity." But he
acknowledged that bombardment might prove to have a crucial "psychological effect" which could demoralize the enemy and undermine
the will to resist. Governments probably would not be "satisfied with
the limitations which the humanitarians and idealists would impose" on
air power. His solution was to abandon rules limiting lawful targets to
"military objectives" but retain a continuing concern to safeguard human
life. He advocated a "compromise" in international law:

> If you will agree to attack only that kind of non-combatant property which can
> be destroyed without loss of life (I do not speak now of military objectives or
> combatants), I am prepared to admit that such a method of warfare would
> be a reasonable development of the accepted principles of international law.
> In brief, I will give you *property* to destroy if you will give me *life* to save.[114]

Spaight thought this compromise might be achieved by bombing factories at night, when they were unoccupied. Others were less
optimistic, but still envisioned a future in which air power would be
deployed when states saw it as effective.[115] Critics noted that limiting
bombing of civilian centers would simply encourage enemies to place
military installations and weapons production facilities in civilian

areas.[116] In 1938, the academic International Law Association proposed limits on bombing and emphasized protection for civilian life rather than property. It called for the evacuation of women, children, and old men to designated safe zones, which would be exempt from bombing attacks. The proposal took for granted that cities would likely be bombed in the next war.[117]

When war broke out in September of 1939, President Roosevelt urged all sides to refrain from bombing cities.[118] His appeal had no effect. In the first weeks of the war, Germany's Luftwaffe bombed Warsaw. It bombed Rotterdam in the spring of 1940 and English airfields a few months later. But the Germans could plausibly claim that their air attacks had been in aid of ground offensives or focused on military objectives in the spirit of the 1923 Hague Rules. Both Britain and Germany hesitated to attack cities, in what has been described as "deterrence before Hiroshima."[119]

When German bombs fell on London, Britain retaliated with a raid on Berlin. The Germans may have struck civilian neighborhoods by accident, but Britain took the episode as justification to commit to a far more aggressive air war. The RAF continued raids on German cities even when German air attacks on Britain halted in the spring of 1941. The RAF tried at first to hit "military objectives" in night raids. "Business before pleasure," Churchill archly explained to a member of Parliament who complained about excessive restraint.[120]

By the fall of 1941, careful studies, based on aerial photographs, demonstrated that only 15 percent of bombs fell within a five-mile radius of the intended target.[121] Rather than abandon the bombing, the RAF widened the targets. By the summer of 1943, the RAF sent a thousand bombers at a time to attack Hamburg and Cologne in the hope that generalized destruction in the vicinity of important "military objectives," such as factories, rail yards, etc., might do some actual damage or at least make it hard for workers to return to their jobs. When American bombers joined the RAF, they promised to strike "strategic" targets, but their practice was to record almost any attack on a city as a strike on its "marshaling yards" (rail centers), whether bombs destroyed the actual rail center or just the surrounding neighborhoods.[122] Allied leaders were not fussy about proper targets. At the 1943 Casablanca Conference, Roosevelt and Churchill agreed on a "combined bomber offensive" which would, among other things, aim at "undermining the morale of the German people to a point where their capacity for armed resistance is fatally weakened."[123] Was this license to terrorize civilians, after all? Perhaps not in the minds of those directing Allied "strategic" bombing.

The British were already well aware that bombing could do vast damage without imposing a vast death toll. After the Battle of Britain, authorities found that over 1,000,000 homes had been destroyed but only 43,000 people lost their lives.[124] As Churchill noted in his memoirs, far more tonnage was dropped on Germany but the Germans had much more time to prepare shelters and air-raid responses for civilian defense.[125] Britain's air minister told Parliament that the bombing of cities would ensure that workers in German war production would be "de-housed" but not killed.[126]

In later years, many scholars questioned the efficacy of strategic bombing. They have argued that, since it was not clearly effective, it must be regarded as morally questionable or simply immoral.[127] Several important considerations weigh against such confident conclusions. The first is that the effort was extremely costly both in resources and in the lives of Allied aircrews. Aircrew fatalities accounted for nearly one quarter of British combat losses in World War II.[128] It was not a strategy that could have been sustained without expectations that it would contribute to victory. The second is that, whatever else it achieved, the bombing of German cities diverted sizable Nazi resources to air defense. Fighter planes retained at bases in Germany allowed Allied forces to achieve air supremacy in North Africa, Italy, France, and the all-important eastern front.[129] Whatever the views of postwar critics, the German government at the time thought it was vitally important to limit the effect of Allied air attacks, which made the Allied air campaign a major front in the war. When reinforced with American air power, the British air offensive sent an important signal to the Soviets that the western Allies would help draw off German strength, even if western troops were far from the main centers of the ground campaigns.[130]

Finally, it is important to acknowledge that the air campaign was less devastating than it might have been. Proposals to bomb small towns and villages with no war industry but some potential to affect overall German morale were rejected.[131] No efforts were made to penetrate bomb shelters to kill civilians. Proposals to drop poison gas or other chemical agents to make bombing more frightful were also rejected.[132] Efforts to knock out particular strategic supplies, such as ball bearings, oil, and fuel, did not prove as effective as hoped, partly because the Allies did not have the intelligence to track all alternative sources of supply and foresee German adaptation. The bombing could still be seen as a means to disrupt the economy. At least as military commanders saw it, it was not simply designed to terrorize civilians by mass slaughter, though it was hoped that urban destruction would make workers less devoted or at least less productive.

At Nuremberg, prosecutors did not even attempt to charge German commanders with war crimes based on bombing of cities.[133] Britain's most prominent international law scholar in that era, Hersch Lauterpacht (soon after appointed to the International Court of Justice), published an article in 1952 defending air bombardment, along with blockade, on the ground that in a modern economy, it was no longer possible to make sharp distinctions between "work which is and work which is not of direct military importance." Besides, he noted, legal commentators in the United States and Britain had always rejected the claims of "continental writers" who "regarded the distinction between combatants and civilians…as the most fundamental principle of the law of war."[134] There still remained, Lauterpacht claimed, an accepted rule that attacks should not aim at the killing of civilians.

The drafters of the U.N. Charter made their own judgment. The Charter equips the Security Council with an international bomber force, to be made available by major military powers for "international enforcement action." In the late spring of 1945, as this provision was approved by the diplomats gathered in San Francisco, the power most equipped to provide such force was using B-29 bombers to devastate the cities of Japan. The Charter does not limit the use of bombers to "military objectives," let alone try to define that term. In fact, the Charter authorizes bombing attacks as an alternative to "military" action. The Charter contemplates that bombers will be ready to deploy while the organization of land forces awaits Council negotiations with member states on a case-by-case basis. In the circumstances, international enforcement action by Council bombers could not focus on a "military objective" that would provide "concrete and direct military advantage" to a land campaign. A less euphemistic term for what the Charter calls "enforcement action" might be "punitive action."

In the one long war sponsored by the Security Council, the conflict in Korea in the early 1950s, the American-led international force reverted to the bombing of cities. General MacArthur's air force chief announced that "military targets" could extend to "every installation, facility and village in North Korea." The policy was implemented with "incendiary raids against urban areas reminiscent of World War II."[135] World War II bombing was treated as a perfectly adequate precedent for air strikes against North Korea. It was also treated as quite a respectable military precedent in U.S. military manuals and legal commentaries, as late as the 1970s.[136]

Conclusion: War in Context—Technological and Moral

Not everything done in past wars, even in wars of the twentieth century, should be taken as moral guidance. Even the participants had some qualms. At his last meeting with President Truman in 1952, Churchill wondered whether the war leaders would be called to account, in the afterlife, for agreeing to drop atomic weapons on Japan.[137] He did not, however, express public doubts about the bombing of German and Japanese cities.[138] But even J.M. Spaight, who gave unreserved praise to the bombing of Germany during the war, later expressed doubts about the use of atomic weapons on Japan. He worried that toxic radiation, killing long after Japan's surrender, was too much like the use of poison, prohibited in the Hague Convention and in centuries of customary law.[139]

Still, the methods used in previous wars reflect the circumstances. In a long war, impatience leads to more extreme tactics. Extreme tactics are all the more likely when one side can pursue them with more effect. Whatever one might think of the destruction wrought by Union armies in the American Civil War, it was a more inviting policy when Union armies were marching through the South and Confederate armies were in retreat. Southern schemes to launch terror attacks in the North may have been disavowed as too shameful, but surreptitious attempts also proved to be too hard for the isolated Confederacy to pursue.[140]

By contrast, even the more extreme Allied strategies in the world wars built on past practice and the comparative advantages of the Allied powers. The idea of using navies to disrupt enemy maritime trade was standard British and American doctrine long before the First World War. The idea that bomber fleets could be a strategic force on their own, and not merely support for ground forces, prompted the British to create a separate Royal Air Force in 1918. Only two nations invested resources to develop long-range bomber fleets in the 1930s: the world's two great naval powers at the time, Britain and America, which were both thinking about attacking enemies from a distance.[141]

What military capacities are developed and deployed is also a reflection of what nations regard as acceptable. Whether we now think blockades and bombings were carried to excessive lengths, they were not the work of leaders who thought there were no limits at all on warfare. At the 1943 Tehran Conference, when Stalin and Roosevelt talked about the need to execute 50,000 German staff officers after the war, Churchill stormed out of the meeting because "the British Parliament and public will never tolerate mass executions."[142] He already knew Britain would tolerate many times that number of civilian casualties in air raids. He thought bombing was, in moral terms, quite different. So did others. At Nuremberg, German defense attorneys suggested that if German commanders had ordered the killing of civilians, they were not so different, after all, from Allied commanders who directed the bombings of cities. The parallel was indignantly rejected by American judges. Their explanation of the difference was included in a U.S. Air Force manual, decades later.[143]

For centuries, western military thinking has rejected the notion that deliberate killing of unarmed civilians or disarmed combatants is legitimate. The same cannot be said of attacks on civilian infrastructure and property. The idea that civilians should be shielded from direct attack does not mean they must be regarded as mere bystanders. The Lieber Code made the point quite explicit: It is "a requisite of civilized existence that men live in political, continuous societies ... called states or nations, whose constituents bear, enjoy, suffer, advance, and retrograde together in peace and war. The citizen or native of a hostile country is thus an enemy, as one of the constituents of the hostile state or nation, and as such is subjected to the hardships of war."[144]

We may think it is appropriate to have more constraining rules for military operations in the twenty-first century, when technology allows much more precise targeting. Commanders may have good reasons to impose rules of engagement that are even more constraining than the general rules. But we should hesitate to conclude that advocates for humanitarian constraint in our era have better principles than the greatest western war leaders of earlier times.

CHAPTER 4

How the Law of War Was Hijacked

As the previous chapter recounted, western states have struggled for centuries to limit the violence of war. In earlier times, nations would not have considered the new weapons technologies before us, in themselves, a threat to the existing rules of war. Now, critics worry that robotics, cyber, and space weapons may violate the law of armed conflict or, as it is now often called, International Humanitarian Law.

The new concerns may reflect trends in modern culture: utopianism, suspicion of technology, and Western self-doubt. But what gives traction to critics is that the law of armed conflict has changed. Or at least, treaties crafted in the 1970s make it plausible to say so.

Signed in 1977, Additional Protocol I to the Geneva Conventions (AP I) provided the first new framework for the conduct of war since the Hague Regulations of 1907. It sought to provide new protections for guerrilla fighters and even, by implication, terrorists. AP I also sought to provide new restraints on the nation-states fighting them. The negotiations took place at the end of the Vietnam War, a defeat for the United States that sapped American confidence and damaged American prestige. AP I advanced an effort by Third World nations, which formed a majority of the nations at the AP I conference, to augment their power relative to the advanced societies of the West.

AP I not only extended protections to the irregular and unconventional tactics of Third World combatants. It also rejected the West's agenda. The

United States had hoped to improve protections for prisoners of war after North Vietnam's abuse of captured American airmen. AP I did nothing to advance that concern. Serving as secretariat for the proceedings, the International Committee of the Red Cross (ICRC) had originally proposed less constraining restrictions on air attacks, which were more likely to be conducted by western states. It also offered more definite restrictions on the conduct of wars against domestic rebels (which were more likely to be conducted by poor countries in Africa and Asia) in an accompanying Additional Protocol II. The majority at the Geneva Conferences had different priorities. The Red Cross adapted. Eventually, with varying qualifications, most other countries did too. In practice, however, war in the decades since has rarely conformed to these new rules.

In this chapter, we describe the politics behind the new International Humanitarian Law. Whereas once the nations that fought wars set the rules for hostilities, today the law itself has become an arena for ideological struggle between advanced and developing nations. The chapter also tries to highlight the dubious moral pretentions inspiring this effort, which we believe western nations should resist. Critics might find support from some AP I provisions when they criticize the most promising applications of new weapons. But AP I can't be treated as a clean, clear expression of a solid international consensus or a statement of the best moral rules for war.

The Path to the New Geneva

The prominent role assumed by the ICRC in the drafting of the Additional Protocols would have surprised earlier generations of leaders. The Geneva-based organization started in the nineteenth century as an advocate for medical assistance to wounded soldiers on the battlefield. The Red Cross emblem, a red cross on a white field, simply inverted the colors of the Swiss flag. Like the Swiss government, which encouraged and subtly directed its efforts, the ICRC prided itself on its neutrality.[1] It played some role in monitoring conditions in prisoner-of-war camps during the First World War, a role codified in the Geneva Convention of 1929. But "Geneva law," dealing with such humanitarian concerns, covered different issues than the "Hague Rules," which governed the actual conduct of war. In 1936, the ICRC even declined to assist the League of Nations in investigating poison gas attacks by Mussolini's army in Ethiopia because it feared compromising its neutrality.[2]

The ICRC first tried to expand its role during the Battle of Britain in October 1940. Luftwaffe bombers were pounding British cities, while the RAF responded by attacking targets in Germany. The ICRC approached the British government with an offer to monitor bomb damage in both countries so their air forces could confine themselves to proper military objectives. In British eyes, the ICRC proposal did not logically follow from the monitoring of conditions in POW camps. There was no treaty specifying limits on bombing at the time and no agreement on proper targets. Britain's prime minister dismissed the Red Cross offer out of hand. "Under German influence or fear," Churchill scoffed, the Red Cross would "very likely... report that we had committed the major breaches. Anyhow, we do not want these people thrusting themselves in[;]... bombing of military objectives, increasingly widely interpreted, seems at present our main road home."[3]

Churchill's skepticism proved well founded. During the war, Allied governments pressed the organization to condemn Nazi genocide but officials in Geneva, clinging to neutrality, refused to offer a word about the central humanitarian catastrophe of the war. As historians would later discover, when the ICRC did consider condemnation of Nazi extermination camps, it proposed to link this condemnation with criticism of Allied air attacks on German cities—a parallel which appeared in the writings of Red Cross officials decades later.[4] It did not protest Switzerland's imposition of unique restrictions on Jews seeking safety in that supposedly neutral state.[5]

The ICRC was determinedly neutral. Down to the end, it prided itself on its even-handed detachment in the war between the Nazis and Allied liberators. In the last weeks of the war, a Red Cross agent managed to save thousands of lives by directing an advancing American army patrol to the site of a death camp in Austria. His superiors in Geneva issued a stern rebuke for violating Red Cross neutrality. His repudiation by the Red Cross prevented this hero from returning to his prewar career in the Swiss banking industry.[6] After the German surrender, the Red Cross tried to help refugees from Nazi brutality, but also offered assistance to Nazi war criminals, providing them with false documents to escape Allied military justice.[7]

The Additional Protocols of the 1970s came into existence only after a considerable change in fortunes both for the Red Cross and for the western powers which had paid it so little heed during World War II. In 1949, the victorious Allies convened a Geneva Conference to elaborate humanitarian norms for the conduct of war. Four conventions set out protections for wounded combatants in land war, wounded or shipwrecked combatants at sea, prisoners of war, and civilians under wartime occupation. No convention defined limits on the conduct of military operations. The ICRC appears to have played a marginal role in the negotiations of these conventions, which were concluded after a few weeks of discussion among military and diplomatic representatives of the major Allied states.[8]

As early as 1956, the ICRC published a proposal for tighter restrictions on bombing attacks: Draft Rules for the Limitation of the Dangers Incurred by the Civilian Population in Time of War.[9] Two things are notable about this effort. First, it placed all emphasis on protecting civilian life and limb, rather than asserting some inherent immunity for civilian property. It prohibited "attacks directed against the civilian population, whether with the object of terrorizing it or for any other reason...."[10] It depicted protection for property as entirely a derivative concern: "*In consequence* [of the immediately preceding prohibition against attacks on 'the civilian population'], it is also forbidden to attack dwellings, installations or means of transport, which are *for the exclusive use of, and occupied by, the civilian population.*"[11] It restricted permissible attacks to "military objectives," but defined those to include all facilities "generally acknowledged to be of military importance" unless their destruction under the circumstances "offers *no* military advantage."[12] Second, the 1956 Draft Rules stirred no interest from governments. The Red Cross managed to get the rules endorsed by an international conference, but it was only a conference of Red Cross affiliates.[13] It was not until the late 1960s that wider interest emerged.

A 1968 conference in Tehran was supposed to celebrate the twentieth anniversary of the Universal Declaration of Human Rights. Instead of criticizing the most oppressive regimes, the conference focused attention on the Vietnam War, then at its height, and the recent conflict between Israel and its Arab neighbors. The conference voted for a resolution calling for human rights protection for civilians in wartime. The U.N.

General Assembly followed up with similar resolutions in 1968 and 1970.[14] Among other things, these resolutions called on the U.N. Secretary General to assess the need for new international conventions. Rather than see this sensitive subject taken over by U.N. bodies, western states expressed interest in a new Geneva Conference, under the auspices of the Red Cross.

Why the change? Distance from the Second World War was one factor. There had been some criticism of Allied bombing during the war, but it was isolated in Britain and almost inaudible in the United States. Editorials in *The New York Times* defended the firebombings of Hamburg and Dresden when they occurred. Even the use of atomic bombs against Japan won broad support in American opinion at the time.[15] But twenty years later, these tactics were viewed in a different context. The bombing of Dresden was painted in lurid colors in a 1963 book by David Irving, which suggested that a quarter of a million civilians had been killed in pointless slaughter.[16] Decades later, the author became more open about his Nazi sympathies and was eventually sentenced to a prison term in Austria for denying basic facts about the Holocaust.[17] Other Nazi sympathizers made such a cult of the Dresden attacks that the city itself commissioned a team of historians to establish the actual casualties involved. They found the real figure to be less than a tenth of what Irving had suggested. Historians also clarified that Dresden, which sat in the path of the Russian advance, served as a vital transportation and communication center and had a significant war industry.[18] Nonetheless, Irving's account was popularized in Kurt Vonnegut's best-selling 1969 novel *Slaughterhouse-Five*, which in turn inspired a successful film version. Academic works, including Michael Walzer's 1977 *Just and Unjust Wars*, cited Irving's book to justify the claim that the Allies had engaged in "terror bombing."[19]

Revisionist accounts of World War II experiences might have made little difference if the political context of the 1970s had not been so different. The advent of nuclear-armed intercontinental ballistic missiles in the arsenals of both superpowers raised the specter of annihilation in a future great power war. Intense controversy had developed over the Vietnam War, where more than half a million American soldiers were fighting without decisive result. In contrast to the Korean War, the Vietnam conflict did not enjoy the sanction of the U.N. Security Council. The United

States fought without European allies, almost without any allies at all, other than some small contingents from Australia and Korea. Communist states denounced the war in the most extreme terms. A Soviet report to the U.N. in 1970 shrieked that western "imperialist powers" were conducting "a policy bordering on genocide" in which "whole centres of population, together with their peaceful inhabitants are annihilated and such means of mass destruction as chemical weapons are used."[20] As the war became more unpopular, even some respectable American publications began to denounce U.S. measures in strident tones. When the Nixon administration launched bombing raids on Hanoi at the end of 1972, *The New York Times* denounced the resulting destruction as the worst since Dresden, which by then had become a byword for barbarous overkill.[21] As even foreign scholars subsequently acknowledged, however, the more precise attacks on Hanoi did relatively little damage to residential areas in the city.[22] They persuaded North Vietnam to accept the terms of a peace agreement.[23]

Even so, the Tehran Conference and the subsequent U.N. General Assembly resolutions focused on protection for "civilians" or "civilian populations." They said nothing about property. By 1968, the dominant bloc at the U.N. called itself the "Non-Aligned Movement." They were former European colonies in Africa and Asia (along with most nations in Latin America), now claiming independence from both sides in the Cold War. But these Third World nations focused their complaints against western nations, with the support of communist states. Third World nations were not very concerned about property rights. At the same time that they called for restrictions on warfare, they demanded protections for their right to nationalize foreign property, almost all of which belonged to companies based in Europe or North America. By the early 1970s, General Assembly resolutions demanded a "New International Economic Order," sponsoring transfer of resources from affluent to poor countries, with little regard to questions of property rights.[24]

The first human rights treaties that emerged from the U.N. General Assembly in 1966 had adhered closely to the innocuous generalities of the 1948 Universal Declaration of Human Rights. A treaty defining human rights protections in wartime might prove more mischievous.

In this context, the United States and other western states preferred a new conference in Geneva, under Red Cross auspices. The United States had one concern to which the Red Cross might have seemed particularly relevant. It wanted better protection for POWs, since North Vietnam had abused and tortured American prisoners in defiance of the 1949 Geneva Conventions. Following its usual practice, the Red Cross had declined to make any public criticism of North Vietnam's violation of the rules. It had remained silent about abuse of prisoners by North Korea and China during the Korean War. Somehow, its later complaints about improper treatment of prisoners by American authorities at Guantanamo did become public. The Red Cross was neutral, but in a posture that emphasized its patient openness to enemies of the West.[25] In the 1940s, its reputation suffered from its quiet accommodations to Nazi horrors, after most of the world sided against Germany. By the 1970s, a new configuration of power in the world provided more of a platform for such neutrality. A few years later, an American military lawyer scoffed: "It was clear to Western observers that the ICRC is prepared to abandon its principles of impartiality, neutrality and universality where politically expedient."[26]

The Geneva negotiations did not secure new safeguards for prisoners of war taken from Western armies.[27] The negotiations did generate novelties in other areas.

Novelties of the New Conventions

Up until the 1970s, western nations had dominated conferences on the conduct of war. Now the majority represented non-Western, communist, and Third World states. The results served their priorities.

The Third World was feeling its strength in the 1970s. In 1973, the Organization of Petroleum Exporting Countries (OPEC) had organized an embargo of oil sales to western European countries, ostensibly to protest their support for Israel. A string of NATO countries promptly refused to allow the U.S. to use their airfields to resupply weapons to Israel in the Yom Kippur War.[28] The world price of oil soon tripled, which encouraged Third World nations to imagine they could squeeze wealth from developed countries through similar raw-material cartels. Europeans accepted terrorism as a threat that required accommodation. The massacre of Israeli athletes at the Munich Olympics in 1972 was quickly followed by a German government agreement to accommodate Palestinian concerns, following release of the terrorists.[29]

The Third World's political and economic advance extended to military affairs. American military analysts summed up the prevailing view at the time: "Terrorism is seen as the unique weapon of the poor and fanatic, airpower is seen as the symbolic weapon of the West—the means by which the wealthy and advanced countries can bully the poor and weak countries. Thus, bombing is automatically viewed in the Third World as cruel and heavy-handed."[30] Third World states, driving the agenda at the Geneva Conference in the 1970s, were eager to limit the permissible reach of air attacks. On the other hand, Third World countries were sympathetic to "liberation movements," even when they used tactics viewed by Western countries as terrorism. So the conference also aimed to promote new legal protections for guerrilla fighters. Both the Palestine Liberation Organization (PLO) (fighting Israel) and the African National Congress (ANC) (fighting South Africa) were invited to participate and urge their concerns.[31]

Third World governments wanted new constraints on military interventions by Western states. Since 1945, these interventions had always occurred in developing countries, which viewed them as unacceptable interference in their own internal affairs. Developing countries, however, were not always at peace when left to themselves. Far more civilians died from brutal internal conflicts in developing countries than from outside interventions. In the late 1960s, the Nigerian civil war and the tribal conflict in Burundi killed hundreds of thousands of civilians. Western advocates for humanitarian restraint accordingly urged that international rules should be extended to protect civilians in such conflicts. Third World governments viewed such proposals as a new pretext for outside intervention.

The Red Cross acknowledged the competing concerns by proposing two conventions, one for international and one for non-international conflicts. The Red Cross understood that a successful outcome required concessions to the Third World majority, so it offered notably more detail about restraints in international conflicts. Its proposal for the new convention on international conflicts (what became AP I) had 90 articles, while the counterpart for non-international conflicts (what became AP II) had only 47.[32] Even such accommodations proved insufficient amidst the intense divisions among the delegations at Geneva.

Previous conferences on the law of war, whether at The Hague or Geneva, had completed their work in a few weeks. The Geneva Conference of the mid-1970s dragged on for three years. It took that long to work out what compromises could secure general support, at least among the diplomats involved. After years of haggling over each proposed article in the Protocol on non-international conflicts—the conference tried to discuss parallel provisions in each Protocol in tandem—the delegate from Pakistan announced that it was all too complicated for developing countries. He offered a highly truncated version, reducing 47 articles to 27. It soon became clear that the Third World majority regarded this as a take it or leave it offer. The conference decided to take it.[33]

The conference diluted the restraints on the waging of internal conflict. The 1973 Red Cross proposal on non-international wars had contained a provision with the heading "Basic Rules." It declared that "military operations" must take "constant care" to "spare the civilian population, civilians and civilian objects."[34] The final text of Protocol II drops the phrase "Basic Rules" and also the reference to "civilian objects"— along with "constant care." Instead it simply admonishes against making "the civilian population as such as well as individual civilians...the object of attack." In a new and more permissive formulation, it prohibits "acts or threats of violence *the primary purpose* of which is to spread terror among the civilian population."[35] Similarly, the Red Cross draft prohibited attacks directed at military objectives, when "expected to entail incidental losses among the civilian population and cause the destruction of civilian objects to an extent disproportionate to the direct and substantial military advantage anticipated."[36] That restriction disappeared from the final text of AP II, with no counterpart or replacement.

Meanwhile, the diplomatic conference moved in the other direction when it came to the convention for international conflicts (AP I). The "Basic Rule" on distinction remained. Separate protections for "civilian objects" (already included in the Red Cross proposal) were tightened, along with the proportionality requirement. In the 1973 Red Cross proposal, the prohibition against "disproportionate" harm was framed in relation to attacks causing "losses among the civilian population *and*...destruction of civilian objects...." Arab delegations urged that this provision be amended to prohibit *any* attack causing "destruction to civilian objects" even if not causing any "losses among the civilian population," regardless of whether it achieved "substantial military advantage." Communist countries endorsed that approach. Western delegations (especially the British, U.S., and Canadian delegates) insisted that some accommodation must be made for situations where incidental harm was unavoidable, but yielded proportionate advantage to the attacker.[37]

An Egyptian delegate summed up the Third World attitude as follows: "In dealing especially with the Western countries, anything that could be formulated in the very precise terms of an operational rule was considered as nonsense."[38] Western delegates managed to gain agreement on the AP I formula allowing "incidental harm" if not "excessive." In return for getting the conference to agree on the "proportionality" rule in AP I, western delegations accepted more demanding restrictions on attacks against "civilian objects." The final text of AP I lays down an all-encompassing immunity for "civilian objects," defined simply as those which are not "military objectives," with the latter phrase explained as "objects" whose destruction "offers a definite military advantage."[39]

The final text of AP I then added further qualifications. "In case of doubt" whether an object "normally dedicated to civilian purposes . . . is being used to make an effective contribution to military action, it shall be presumed not to be so used."[40] Even reliable indications that fighters had stockpiled weapons in a school or a private home would not justify an attack on that site, unless the evidence also showed this arsenal would likely "contribute" to making fighters more "effective" in the next engagement—a level of intelligence not easy to come by in the midst of ongoing conflict.

Nor could the attack be justified as reprisal for violating the rules. In another reach beyond the Red Cross draft of 1973, the final text of AP I prohibits any attacks on "civilian objects" by way of "reprisal."[41] By contrast, the 1907 Hague Regulations had named protected sites. It listed "buildings dedicated to religion, art, science, hospitals," but stipulated that their immunity was entirely contingent on their "not being used at the time for military purposes." If one side tried to gain military advantage from these immunities, they were forfeited. Because the Hague Regulations said nothing about reprisals, they remained a ready device to retaliate for violation of the rules.[42]

AP I's new approach would encourage defenders to use civilians or civilian facilities to "shield" their military forces. The Red Cross draft tried to anticipate this danger with a provision admonishing against "attempts to shield military objectives from attacks" through the "presence or movements of the civilian population."[43] The final version of AP I embraces most of this language, but then adds a warning that "violation of these prohibitions shall not release the Parties from their legal obligations" to avoid harm to "civilians" or "civilian objects."[44] A subsequent provision warns that state parties must find and punish those responsible for "grave breaches" of the Convention. Its enumeration of such "grave breaches" includes violation of the rules on "distinction" and "proportionality," but not the supposed rule against using "civilian shields" to deflect attack on military fighters or facilities.[45]

The same Third World bias occurs in the provisions on captured fighters. The Red Cross draft sought to assure prisoner-of-war protection for irregular fighters, but limited such protection to fighters who (a) "remain under a command responsible to a Party to the conflict responsible for its subordinates," (b) "distinguish themselves from the civilian population in military operations," and (c) "conduct their military operations in accordance with the Conventions and the present Protocol."[46] As adopted, AP I admonishes that "all combatants are obliged to comply with the rules of international law applicable to armed conflict" but then immediately swerves to the contrary stipulation that "violations of these rules shall not deprive a combatant of his right to be a combatant or…his right to be a prisoner of war."[47] To qualify for POW protection, and thus exemption from prosecution for taking up arms, it is enough if a "combatant…carries his arms openly…during such time as he is visible to the adversary…preceding the launching of an attack."[48] AP I does not make it necessary, after all, to submit to responsible superiors or even to act in accord with the law of armed conflict. A further provision indicates that combatants who do not conform even to these minimal requirements "shall nevertheless be given protections equivalent in all respects to those accorded to prisoners of war…."[49] Lest there be any doubt about the beneficiaries of these new rules, AP I cautions that the special accommodations to irregular fighters are "not intended to change the generally accepted practice of States with respect to the wearing of the uniform by combatants assigned to the regular uniformed armed units of a Party to the conflict."[50]

AP I imposed a one-sided answer to a problem that had long concerned military commanders. The first Hague Peace Conference in 1899 had struggled over the proper limits on an attacking army that faced civilian volunteers in opposition. Targeting irregular fighters could lead to mistaken attacks on civilians; but the volunteers were bound to provoke such indiscriminate responses if they could not be clearly identified. The Hague Conventions accordingly stipulated that resistance fighters would be ineligible for prisoner-of-war protections unless they operated as a distinct organized force and clearly distinguished themselves from ordinary civilians.[51] AP I decided those requirements were too burdensome. But it did not allow nations that observed the rules to pursue irregular fighters with troops of their own operating out of uniform. That might threaten civilians!

Another reflection of AP I's political bias is the different treatment accorded to fighters with ideological claims, compared with other non-state combatants. AP I introduced a novel provision on "mercenaries." They cannot receive "prisoner of war" protection, even if they fight in uniform and follow the international rules applicable to armed conflict.[52] AP I defines a "mercenary" as a non-national of the nations at war who is "motivated to take part in the hostilities essentially by the desire for private gain." Ideologues, such as jihadi or communist volunteers, are not covered. Rich countries, such as South Africa and Rhodesia, had the luxury of employing mercenaries in the 1970s. AP I did not require that nations treat such mercenaries humanely, let alone "with protections equivalent in all respects to those accorded to prisoners of war."

From all that appears in AP I, mercenaries can be shot even after they surrender. Little over a decade before the Geneva Conferences, victorious Algerian rebels slaughtered tens of thousands of Arab soldiers after their surrender—more than 150,000 by some estimates—because they had fought under French command during the long conflict.[53] Western legal scholars protested that denying protection to mercenaries seemed to distinguish categories of combatants based on their purpose for fighting, in disregard of the modern doctrine that *jus ad bellum* considerations should not distort *jus in bello* rules.[54] But Third World liberation ideologies were ascendant at the Geneva Conference. AP I implicitly endorsed the most brutal tactics of past victors in liberation struggles.

AP I openly sought to constrain western states without imposing serious constraints on Third World forces. In another leap beyond the Red Cross proposals, the opening of AP I announces that it applies to "international armed conflicts" but also to "armed conflicts in which peoples are fighting against colonial domination and alien occupation and against racist regimes in the exercise of their right of self-determination."[55] By this provision, an irregular force not connected to its own state—say the ANC fighting the government of South Africa or the PLO fighting Israel—might claim all the benefits of AP I that apply to international conflicts. But for that to happen, nations such as South Africa and Israel would have had to ratify AP I, which they did not do (South Africa only adhered to AP I in 1995, after the transition to majority rule). Their refusal to ratify rendered this provision mostly a theatrical echo of numerous U.N. General Assembly resolutions denouncing apartheid and Israel (sometimes combining these enemies into "Zionist racism"). Like those resolutions, it had no clear legal significance except to gesture at the favorite hate objects of that era.

But AP I expressed an even deeper element of make believe. If it really intended to protect those irregular forces out of uniform and without clear military command, its suggestion of common rules for all participants in an armed conflict was absurd. A force that refuses to show itself openly and hides among civilians cannot win an open confrontation against an actual army. AP I ostensibly requires these forces to attack the enemy military and prohibits them from targeting civilians. In most situations, however, that would be a futile or self-destructive approach for guerrillas. They choose asymmetric methods precisely because the military forces of established states are larger and better equipped. Guerrilla insurgencies have usually trained their attacks on less protected civilian targets. They use terrorism to extort support from the surrounding civilian population. Such brutal tactics were the stock in trade of the ANC and the PLO even at the time of the Geneva Conference in the mid-1970s, as they had been for guerrillas in Algeria and South Asia in the preceding decades.[56] Such tactics have been characteristic of insurgencies across the Middle East, Africa, and Asia since then.

Even if the drafters of AP I hoped that irregular forces would be more restrained in the future, such fighters could not be expected to comply with the actual provisions of the convention. They would not only have to focus their "attacks" on "military objectives," but do so without imposing much "incidental loss of civilian life" or "injury to civilians" or "damage to civilian objects." In other words, they would have to strike "military objectives" in a precisely targeted, almost antiseptic, way. Attacks that cause civilian "loss" or "injury" or "damage" are only allowed under AP I when not "excessive in relation to concrete and direct military advantage anticipated." How much "concrete and direct military advantage" can be "anticipated" from any particular "attack" by an irregular force, when that force is too weak to risk an open battle?

Guerrillas may destroy or kill, but rarely will they achieve a "military advantage" in the normal sense of undermining the fighting capacity of the opposing military force. Guerilla forces may reasonably hope to prevail in a long struggle, but not by securing "military advantage" in the usual understanding of the term. They can only prevail by undermining their enemy's morale. Indeed, the most likely morale target is not the military forces opposing them but the civilian population supporting the enemy. The real target for irregular forces is, almost of necessity, civilians. They are fighting a political struggle, not a military one.

The significance of AP I is that it gives irregular forces license to fight in ways prohibited to the state opposing them. Instead of different rules for different kinds of wars, AP I created different rules for opposing sides in the same wars.

Legalism and Lawfare

Advocates for the new rules faced a challenge in winning their acceptance. The new rules were obviously biased. And the foundational rule in international law is that treaties can only bind nations that have consented to them. In the past, almost all states quickly ratified treaties that imposed humanitarian limits on war, as with the Geneva Conventions in 1949 and the Hague Conventions in 1899 and 1907.[57] But within the first decade of their completion, few western states ratified the 1977 Additional Protocols, though Jordan, Egypt, Syria, and China had already embraced them.[58]

In the final years of the Cold War, western states began to change their attitudes, a change that accelerated after the collapse of the Soviet empire. Belgium, the Netherlands, Italy, and Spain ratified in the late 1980s. Australia, Canada, Germany, and Portugal ratified between 1990 and 1992. Britain did not ratify until 1998, France not until 2002. The United States has never ratified. A number of other states with substantial military capacities and worries about terror insurgencies, including India, Israel, Indonesia, and Turkey, have also declined to ratify. Many of the western states ratified with reservations, claiming a somewhat greater range for military operations (such as the right to strike civilian objects in reprisal).[59]

Faced with this resistance, supporters of the new rules sought ways to apply them universally. Advocates have pursued two general strategies to this end. First, they claim that the new rules have assumed the status of customary international law and are therefore binding on all states, regardless of whether they have ratified the Additional Protocols. The ICRC began urging this doctrine in its commentaries on APs I and II, published in 1987.[60] Many provisions in the treaties had been characterized, even at the 1977 Geneva drafting conference, as codifications or clarifications of accepted practice. But agreement on a background principle does not necessarily constitute endorsement for precise formulations or their applications. Claims about customary law have sometimes looked to treaty provisions as indications of widely shared understandings, as the United States has done with respect to some provisions of the U.N. Law of the Sea Convention. But this approach is most plausible for treaty provisions that states regard as non-controversial.

The ICRC was determined to reach beyond consensus on broad principles. In 2005 it published a massive three-volume study, *Customary International Humanitarian Law*. It tries to demonstrate that virtually every provision in both Additional Protocols has now become binding as customary law. It reaches this conclusion by relying on evidence of what states say, rather than what they do. The evidence adduced ranges from the fanciful to the fantastical. The ICRC's study, for example, claims that Great Britain regards bombing of "civilian objects" as contrary to international law because of a speech by Prime Minister Neville Chamberlain in February 1938. The ICRC editors did not think it relevant that Mr. Chamberlain's immediate successor endorsed a very different approach to bombing during an actual war. In the same spirit, the ICRC reports that Syria's Hafez al-Assad and Iraq's Saddam Hussein opposed bombing civilian objects. As proof, it cites their speeches, ignoring their quite contrary actions.[61]

Meanwhile, the ICRC relies on evidence from more curious sources. A host of small countries are included, such as Ireland and Norway, Cameroon and Togo, which are not known for their martial exertions after gaining independence. Even more remarkably, the ICRC reports the declarations of non-governmental advocacy groups, such as Human

Rights Watch and Amnesty International.[62] This *reductio ad absurdum* is, in its own way, logical. If states that do not engage in combat operations can help establish the customary practice, why not organizations that are not even states? This approach rejects the principle that the rules of war are established by mutual agreement of the "contracting states" (as the Hague Conventions and the 1949 Geneva Conventions call the parties). It is as if the relevant law could be directly established by universal humanity, speaking through any entity that appoints itself to speak for mankind at large. In fact, the ICRC itself has campaigned to call the whole body of law (what used to be called "the law of war" or "law of armed conflict") simply "International Humanitarian Law." The Red Cross does not conduct wars and does not even take sides in armed conflicts but the claims of humanity at large transcend the concerns of particular fighting forces.[63] An American legal scholar aptly summed up this non-state-centered approach to the law of armed conflict in the title of his book, *The End of Reciprocity*.[64]

Scholars of international relations speak of this moral posture as "Kantian," because of its moralism and disdain for practical considerations or ultimate consequences.[65] That may be a bit generous. Given its manifold connections to the Swiss government, the ICRC was bound to adopt a neutralist stance during the Second World War, making it indifferent—at least in principle—to the outcome. It failed to make any comment on the most terrible humanitarian challenges of that war, as even a historian commissioned by the ICRC itself has found.[66] The ICRC maintains the same posture in its advocacy for the Additional Protocols. The ICRC's official commentary on AP I insists, for example, that the proportionality rule "does not provide any justification for attacks which cause extensive civilian losses and damages. Incidental losses and damages should never be extensive."[67] By this criterion, Allied war measures in the Second World War must be condemned, even if they saved many more lives by shortening the war.

That outlook could charitably be described as a sign of tunnel vision. The Red Cross was quite well informed about the Holocaust but chose to say nothing lest that compromise its other humanitarian work. Amnesty International, launched in the 1960s to advocate against torture, remained silent while the Khmer Rouge butchered some two million people in Cambodia, lest denunciation of that slaughter distract from AI's more urgent work, criticizing western-backed governments elsewhere.[68] The ICRC was similarly reticent about the horrors perpetrated by the Khmer Rouge.[69] Responsible governments should have disregarded sanctimonious admonitions from such morally unserious quarters.

But advocates for the new rules have not simply relied on moral appeals to get governments to embrace them. They have also relied on international courts to enforce these standards in individual criminal cases. This was, in itself, a novelty of the 1990s. True, the Nuremberg tribunal and its counterpart in Tokyo tried "war criminals" of the Axis powers. But these tribunals were established by occupying authorities in countries that had surrendered to them unconditionally. Courts controlled by the Allies were the only courts operating in Germany and Japan in 1945.

In earlier times, wars had generated protests that one side or the other (or typically, both) were violating norms of proper military conduct. But almost all previous wars were settled by negotiation. A typical provision of the peace was that abuses that may have been committed would be forgotten for the sake of peace. The Treaty of Westphalia, for example, included a provision that committed all sides to forgive three decades of terrible abuse. Lassa Oppenheim's treatise, *International Law* (first published in 1904-05, updated through twelve successive editions), laid down as a general rule that war crimes must be punished during the war or the charges lapse at the advent of peace.[70] This principle was the logical counterpart to the relaxation of war rules in long wars.

When the object is to win, a nation does what it deems necessary to master its enemy; when the object is to make peace, nations forget what needs to be forgotten. War crimes trials did not follow the Korean War, the Vietnam War, or the conflicts in the Middle East in the 1960s and 1970s. Compromise peace agreements did not provide opportunities for war crimes tribunals. As late as 1991, the U.N. Security Council approved an armistice after U.N.-sponsored forces drove Saddam Hussein's army from Kuwait. Iraq was required to pay indemnities to Kuwait for wanton damage, but the Council did not establish a war crimes tribunal to try Saddam or his top henchmen. The priority was making peace.[71]

But in 1993, the U.N. Security Council established an ad hoc tribunal to prosecute abuses committed in the ethnic conflicts of the former Yugoslavia. Rather than send troops to protect ethnic minorities, the

U.N. sent lawyers to The Hague to judge accused criminals who might turn themselves in (most did not). The war crimes tribunal for the former Yugoslavia turned Nuremberg on its head. Instead of judging after conquest, there would be accusations from the sidelines while fighting continued. The U.N. followed this precedent in Rwanda, to the disgust of the successor government, which had defeated the murderous Hutu government (with no help from the U.N.) and was then told it could not be trusted to try the major Hutu leaders.[72]

In 1998, a conference in Rome agreed on rules for an International Criminal Court (ICC), which received enough ratifications to begin operating in 2002.[73] The statute of the ICC defines war crimes as set out in AP I. Among other things, the list extends to attacks on "civilian objects," without reference to the cause or provocation for such action.[74] The list does not include hiding fighters or weapons among civilians to deter attack. The United States did not join the court. Other states that remained aloof from AP I, such as India and Israel, did not ratify either. Even some that ratified AP I, such as Russia, China, Egypt, Jordan, Syria, and Pakistan, declined to join. But the ICC statute still claims broad jurisdiction. It asserts the right not only to indict members of the armed forces of ratifying states, but also the nationals of non-party states for offenses committed on the territory of a ratifying state. Non-ratifying states can even consent to ICC jurisdiction on a temporary basis to enable the court to prosecute enemies in a discrete conflict.[75] Afghanistan's embrace of the court has potentially exposed American troops to ICC prosecution.

Such threats are not easy to waive away. There is no statute of limitations on the offenses. An explicit provision of the court's charter stipulates that it is not bound by pardons or judicial decisions by national courts.[76] Traditional peace treaty provisions, such as those confirming a general amnesty and forgiving wartime abuses, would not bind the court. The ICC risks reopening conflicts that could be on the verge of settlement. How long would an agreement between Israel and the Palestinian Authority last if the ICC prosecuted their leaders in its aftermath? Settling conflicts, however long-running or destructive, is not the main priority of the ICC.

Here again, the new approach reflects a level of moralism at odds with traditional understandings of war. The ICC, like AP I, makes no exception for reprisals, even if they respond to attacks that first violate the laws of war. Under these rules, a belligerent state cannot deter further abuses by imposing special costs on the perpetrators. Instead of reciprocity, the new approach seems to have a different premise: The rules matter more than the results. The new approach places more importance on upholding its unrealistic vision of the laws of war, regardless of how belligerents might calculate their interest at the time. Upholding the rules takes precedence over the actual fate of combatants and civilians in actual conflicts. Given the murderous character of many regimes in the past century, the nature of the winner should make all the difference—but not, in principle, for the ICC. If murderous tyrants prevail in the struggle, the ICC can subsequently bring them to justice too.

Except, of course, it cannot in real life. The ICC cannot prevent crimes against humanity any more than it can deter war crimes by irregular forces. In fifteen years of operation, the court has achieved three convictions. It has no means to enforce arrest warrants, let alone subpoenas for evidence. It relies on the voluntary cooperation of governments, but has no real means of assuring that cooperation. An ICC indictment of the president of Sudan (on the seemingly most severe charge of genocide) was laughed off by the government of Sudan and by every African state which President Bashar decided to visit. The ICC has not indicted anyone from a western state. Perhaps it is relevant that European states pay most of the court's operating budget, which is not funded by the U.N. but by contributions of ICC members.

It might seem as easy to dismiss the threat of the ICC as to ignore ICRC moralizing. But another factor has given momentum to the new law of war: the growth of human rights advocacy networks. Before the 1980s, the Red Cross was almost alone as a humanitarian advocate operating across borders. In the ensuing years, a whole range of new organizations, such as Amnesty International and Human Rights Watch and dozens of regional counterparts or local affiliates, gained prominence. By the time of the Rome Conference in 1998, these organizations played a large role in the negotiations. They even advised governments on which compromises to accept, as European governments were eager for their approval.[77] These groups have gained much attention because western media often presume their charges to be correct and a considerable audience is eager to hear claims against western states. The most readily denounced western states, the United States and Israel, have actually had to engage in serious combat operations in the past two decades, while most European and Latin American states have not.

There is also more of an audience for charges against western states than the dog-bites-man story that terrorists are attacking civilians. At a deeper level, western governments, themselves, generally report the human rights abuses of rogue states, terrorists, or tyrants. If that were the main point, there would be no need for non-governmental organizations to raise money from donors to tell a different story. When his correspondent in Cuba told the popular press baron, William Randolph Hearst, there was no war to cover in 1898, Hearst is supposed to have said: "You supply the pictures, I'll supply the war." Any NGO can say, "You supply the pictures, we'll supply the war crime accusations."

Three examples may suggest the strength of these trends. First, in 2011, the European Court of Human Rights insisted that Britain had failed to investigate incidents in which its troops had used force to defend themselves against terrorist attacks in the first months after the Iraq invasion. The cases had worked their way forward for several years, with British authorities insisting that the European Convention on Human Rights could not apply to military actions outside Europe and certainly not to military action in what was still a war zone. The European Court of Human Rights rejected these claims and was unimpressed that the British attorney general had determined that none of the incidents had involved unlawful force.[78] Dozens of claims proceeded in British courts against individual British soldiers. Even a Conservative government did not have the self-confidence to enact legislation cutting back on the authority of the Strasbourg-based European Court of Human Rights to judge British military actions, nor a law to constrain British courts.[79] A subsequent ruling of the Strasbourg court even held the Dutch government liable for the conduct of a token Dutch force in Iraq.[80]

This experience has had the unintended consequence of jeopardizing civilian lives in war zones. In 2011, France and Britain agreed to take major responsibility for supporting rebels against Muammar Gaddafi in Libya. Gaddafi's defeat took nearly six months. A quicker victory might have saved many lives and caused less disorder. But as Britain's defense minister explained to Parliament, "We would set our assessment of acceptable civilian casualties as close to zero as was possible." A military aide assured Parliament that "we address very carefully the issues of necessity, proportionality and legality…that is done comprehensively throughout the NATO system," with legal advice on proper bombing targets "delivered at all levels by legal advisers and fundamentally back to the [UK] Attorney-General."[81] Concerns over legal liability have induced a caution in European military operations that will allow civil wars to continue longer and death to civilians to rise.

Rules on force have tightened beyond Europe. In 2016, a group of military officers and officials from democratic countries calling themselves the "High Level Military Group" produced a study of recent battles between western armies and irregular forces. According to this report, in the varied examples of American troops in Afghanistan and Iraq, Israelis in Lebanon, the French in Mali, and Colombian national forces fighting Revolutionary Armed Forces of Columbia (FARC) guerrillas, enemy forces regularly used civilians to shield their own operations and then eagerly blamed all civilian casualties on western forces. Western armies became so cautious that they had to "pay a grave tactical price on the battlefield."[82] According to the report, all governments were more restrictive than even AP I requires, suggesting that the impulse is not simply the result of separate legal assessments but a concern about public expectations of military operations in the twenty-first century.

The burden of the new standards falls with particular weight on Israel, one of the few Western countries obliged to use substantial military force in defense of its own population. If the Red Cross is correct in its claim that AP I rules do "not provide any justification for attacks which cause extensive civilian losses and damages,"[83] then hostile forces can claim immunity from attack by positioning their forces in civilian neighborhoods. In South Lebanon, Hezbollah positioned offensive rockets amidst inhabited villages near Israel's northern border. When Hezbollah launched barrages of rockets in 2006, the Israeli response was denounced, not only in Arab countries but in most European capitals. European governments acknowledged that Israel had a right to defend itself from rocket attacks, but its defense efforts in this case were "excessive" and "disproportionate" because they harmed civilians and damaged civilian property.[84] Israel had a right to defend itself, but not if it hurt civilians in the process.

Lesson learned. In 2009, Hamas launched its own barrage of rocket attacks on Israel from Gaza. It also hid rockets in civilian neighborhoods.

Israel took additional precautions to limit harm to civilians. Nevertheless, it received the same level of denunciation. A U.N. Human Rights Council report blamed Israel for failing to take adequate precautions. It argued that warning the residents of buildings of an attack was insufficient, because the residents could not necessarily believe the warning.[85] Under such rules, there may be no effective way to exercise the supposed right of self-defense.

Nor to give that defense enduring effect. Few noticed the absence of supporting rocket fire from South Lebanon. Israel's campaign against Hezbollah in 2006 may well have prompted caution about starting another round.[86] The damage in the Lebanon war seems to have worked as a deterrent. Achieving such an effect is not the sort of "military objective" permitted under AP I. A Red Cross analyst explained that while terrorists might show complete disdain for all rules, Israeli forces could have no excuse for unleashing "excessive" harm. The proper response, he urged, was to talk more about the importance of adhering to international standards.[87] Under this view, the rules need not accommodate an effective right of self-defense for victim states. International discussion will gradually raise everyone's inhibitions about hurting others, so future conflicts will remain peaceful—or so Swiss analysts like to think. Perhaps that view looks better to people who are confident they will remain safely neutral in future conflicts.

For those living outside Switzerland, better technology may help states defend themselves with less harm to civilians. More precise targeting might achieve necessary objectives, while limiting unintended damage. But AP I can be interpreted as a barrier to the development and deployment of new weapons. Article 35 prohibits weapons that cause "superfluous injury or unnecessary suffering" or "may be expected to cause widespread, long-term and severe damage to the natural environment." Article 36 commands that states must "determine" whether "a new weapon, means or method of warfare" would violate these prohibitions, even if only in "some...circumstances." States must "determine" whether such prohibitions apply even when weapons are in the "study" or "development" phases. This open-ended admonition has no counterpart in any previous treaty on the law of war. A literal reading would prohibit almost any new weapon that could be used improperly (hence causing "unnecessary suffering" or environmental "damage" in "some...circumstances").

AP I effectively seeks to retard the development of new weapons. As the next chapters will indicate, U.N. rapporteurs and NGO advocates have accepted AP I's invitation to criticize any new weapons development. AP I strictures can affect military decision-making even before war.

Working Around Restraints

The challenges posed by AP I and the new law of war are not primarily legal. Certainly that is true for the United States. The United States never ratified AP I, so it has no direct effect on American law. Even if it had consented, the United States can always repudiate a treaty either by statute or by presidential act.

The challenge is more a matter of diplomacy and political leadership. The U.S. has acknowledged that some provisions of AP I represent customary law. There is no consensus, however, on what customary law is in this context and what it requires. American views are not always shared by other western states. There is certainly no assurance that the International Criminal Court will agree. Some national courts in Europe threatened to prosecute American officials for supposed offenses committed in Iraq or in earlier wars, cheered on by human rights advocates in the United States.[88] But in 2002, only a few months after the start of American military efforts in Afghanistan, Congress enacted the American Service-Members' Protection Act to authorize the president to take military action against foreign efforts to prosecute American personnel. It is more popularly known as the Hague Invasion Act. Senator Hillary Clinton voted for it, and, despite pleas from human rights advocates, President Obama left it in place.[89]

An international trial of U.S. military personnel remains unlikely. A U.S. president would be unlikely to hand over an indicted soldier or official to a foreign tribunal. U.S. troops would be demoralized and U.S. public opinion outraged. European governments would almost certainly prefer to maintain good relations with the United States than with the International Criminal Court. Europeans have depended on American military force for their own security for more than 70 years. Their security is not much affected by hand-waiving gestures from the ICC. It is Europeans who pay most of the ICC's costs. In the event of a confrontation, the court would lose more than the United States. The prospect that American soldiers or defense officials might be tried by European national courts under claims of universal jurisdiction worried the Bush administration for a time, but threats to reduce U.S. military cooperation persuaded Belgium, Spain, and Germany to drop any investigations.[90]

Still, if it is wrong to exaggerate the strength of international human rights networks or international legal institutions, it is foolish to dismiss them. The Bush administration had perfectly cogent legal arguments for declining to apply the Geneva Convention to terrorists at Guantanamo. But human rights advocates, encouraged by the Red Cross, successfully depicted the U.S. stance as establishing a "legal black hole" and therefore a challenge to fundamental principles of international humanitarian law.[91] The campaign was so successful that President Obama, on his first day in office, promised to close down Guantanamo and spent two full terms cajoling, wheedling, and bribing foreign countries to accept custody of prisoners judged too dangerous to release.

On the other hand, the United States still invokes interpretations of the law of armed conflict which are not widely accepted by other countries, even by our NATO allies. A manual on the law of war for U.S. navy officers, issued in the 1990s, insisted that in times of war, naval forces may try to intercept not only the import of military supplies to an enemy, but also its export of commercial products, since these might be used to fund military efforts.[92] That view is defensible, but not widely shared. Similarly, the same manual pronounced that bombardment could target not only "war-related" infrastructure (used to supply munitions, say) but also "war-sustaining" infrastructure (which could mean almost anything, as critics pointed out).[93] In 2015, the Department of Defense issued a new Manual on the Law of War, applicable to all services. It embraces both of these doctrines.[94]

The new Pentagon war manual is not light reading. For the army, it was the first full-length manual on the subject in 60 years. The 1956 Manual on The Law of Land Warfare was 193 pages long. The 2015 manual is 1,172 pages long, with an online version to accommodate continuing additions. The 2015 manual covers more subjects, because it is intended for use by all services, but it is also vastly more detailed. It is, in effect, a sourcebook for detailed research efforts (the online version includes links to all relevant treaties and U.S. government policy positions).

There is much to admire about the 2015 manual as a monument to scholarship. It even has a section, near the very end, with links to U.S. government documents noting opposition to particular provisions in AP I. The overall presentation depicts the law of war as a continuous body of precepts and practices, so that episodes from past wars are regularly cited to illuminate current standards. The American Civil War and World War II receive considerable attention in the footnotes. When relevant, the text or a footnote will acknowledge a provision in AP I that parallels the claims made by the manual.

It purports to show that the U.S. military is committed to observing international law. It may not be exactly the law set out in AP I, but it is something similar, parallel, and related. Perhaps it is meant to mollify U.S. allies or critics within the United States. Perhaps it is an effort to reassure American military personnel. The least one can say is that it does not highlight U.S. deviations from AP I. And it is not always completely persuasive on why or how much the U.S. might pursue a different approach. It is the usual instinct of lawyers to downplay any novelty in their arguments. Diplomats often have the same instinct to nurture acquiescence by skirting provocation. But lulling the drowsy or disengaged is not the same as securing their agreement or even their patient respect when real-world events awaken their attention. The lawyering in the manual may be helpful for many purposes but it is not the stuff of public diplomacy or political advocacy. If American arguments come down to arcane citations and creative parsing of words, the resulting fog of legal technicalities creates a moral vacuum that is likely to be filled by the posturing of human rights advocates. Or it may be filled by a hardened cynicism that opens the door to tactics of heedless brutality, tactics that won't be defended when they come to light, because they cannot honestly be defended in broad daylight.

There are several things, related to legal advocacy, which the U.S. government might do—or do better—to avoid entanglement in the legalism that reduces the laws of war to the pronouncements of the Red Cross or of Amnesty International. The first thing we might do is emphasize that the ultimate issues are moral, not legal. It is not necessary to disparage legal arguments, but the legal texts themselves used to acknowledge a necessary background of moral guidance. The 1907 Hague Conventions on land warfare acknowledged the point in its preamble. It cautioned that gaps in the treaty did not leave matters to the "arbitrary judgment of military commanders" but instead to "principles" derived from "the usages established among civilized peoples...the laws of humanity...the dictates of public conscience."[95]

The experiences of the past century should make it easier for us to acknowledge such moral groundings. We can surely distinguish between military operations that depart from some details of AP I, as interpreted by some lawyers, on the one hand, and operations that betray utter contempt for humanity. Military tactics that result in large civilian death tolls must carry a very high burden of justification, while tactics that merely result in economic loss need not. The wording of AP I cannot change the moral force of that fundamental distinction.

Secondly, when enemies use civilians as human shields, the enemy must share responsibility for ensuing loss to civilians. Of course, the attacker must also take precautions, where possible. The police do not rush into hostage situations without thinking about how to limit risks to the hostages. But a rule which puts all responsibility on the attacker, as AP I does, is a rule that invites more enemies to rely on human shields. It should not require elaborate lawyering to explain the problem. It only requires the moral confidence to emphasize the perversity of the AP I rules. A related strategy is to emphasize the lawless depravity of our enemies. There is a tendency to shrink from harsh rhetoric against enemies, lest it inflame conflicts still further. President Bush, for example, was widely criticized for using the term "Axis of Evil." But emphasizing enemy brutality need not aim at stirring hatred so much as supplying perspective. Reciprocal restraints and agreed rules cannot work with jihadis who feel exempt from conformity with any rules. Critics of the Bush administration's Guantanamo policies often warned that failing to supply Geneva protections to enemy prisoners would risk the mistreatment of U.S. prisoners. It was completely lost to the consciousness of such critics that no enemy since 1945 has accorded Geneva protections to U.S. prisoners.[96] This is not an argument for committing abuses in our prisons. It is a way to emphasize that we are not fighting in a world where there are reliably agreed rules, reliably enforced by international legal institutions or NGOs.

This is primarily a moral argument. But it is neither completely removed from legal analysis, nor does it discard law for sheer political rhetoric. Traditional legal principles, even in this area, commonly rest on intuitive moral foundations. When treaties were viewed as contracts, it followed logically that default by one party exempted the other from its obligations. That doctrine is harder to apply in multilateral treaties, but it is still acknowledged in the Vienna Convention on the Law of Treaties, a 1970 treaty that tries to codify approaches to treaty interpretation.[97] The Vienna Convention also states that parties may reasonably adjust their interpretations in light of the conduct of other parties. A treaty's meaning, to some extent, depends on its implementation by the participating states.[98] The same is true, even more so, for customary law. Custom starts with what states actually *do*.

The U.S. State Department now issues an annual survey of the human rights performance of all countries in the world. It does not issue a similar survey on abuses of the law of war. Sometimes we condemn Russian bombing. Sometimes we condemn Israeli bombing. But we do not make any systematic effort to publicize the difference between questionable tactics and outrages against humanity. We leave that to Amnesty International, Human Rights Watch, and the ICRC. They prefer to focus their outrage on western states that are most likely to heed their warnings (and not to retaliate on their researchers with terror attacks). If we want to define moral boundaries rather than belabor legalism, the U.S. should do much more to emphasize what we regard as beyond the bounds.

Every now and then, there is a moment when the light of reason breaks through, even in the dark corners of international legal debate. The United States ought to do more to publicize and salute these episodes and ensure that they have more weight in the world's reckonings of what the law is. In 2005, for a notable example, a claims commission at The Hague handed down a judgment in a series of disputes arising from a border war between Eritrea and Ethiopia in the 1990s. The commission ruled that Ethiopia had not violated AP I when it bombed an electric power plant in Eritrea. "The infliction of economic losses from attacks against military objectives is a lawful means of achieving a definite military advantage, and there can be few military advantages more evident than effective pressure to end an armed conflict that, each day, added to the number of both civilian and military casualties on both sides."[99] No single ruling from an ad hoc arbitration panel can definitively establish the law. But the United States could help to fortify its own claims by publicizing such helpful precedents.

For the same reasons, the United States has an interest in publicizing its own actions and the legal analysis behind them. It must rest its views of customary international law on what nations do more than what they say; and what they say about a particular concrete incident, rather than what they say by way of affirming abstract platitudes. If the United States wants to preserve freedom of action in its deployment of military force, it must publicly reject those who want to restrict such force unduly with new and questionable claims about international law.

The converse is also true. If the rules come to be seen as legalistic wheel-spinning, or schemes to hobble western states, there will be less and less support for maintaining those rules. The result is not likely to be a more peaceful world. Jean Pictet, the Red Cross legal analyst for the Geneva Conferences in the 1970s, is supposed to have said: "If we cannot abolish war, we can make it too complicated to fight."[100] But if we make it too hard for liberal states to use force, we invite a world dominated by ruthless authoritarian states or maniacal non-state actors. Or we will find that when western states do resort to force, they will have lost patience for rules of any kind.

CHAPTER 5

The Rise of the Machines

I n the movie *Terminator*, and its many sequels, a self-aware computer
system wages genocide on mankind. In this dystopian future, Skynet
first triggers a global nuclear war and then launches hunter-killers to
prowl for remaining humans. Drones eerily similar to today's Predators
and Reapers launch missiles from the skies. Advanced autonomous tanks
patrol downtown Los Angeles and killer motorcycles cruise California's
highways. Robot soldiers resembling human skeletons launch ground
assaults and assassinate human leaders. Even the seas contain automated
ships and torpedoes. The movies focus on Arnold Schwarzenegger, both
before and after his stay in the California governor's mansion, who plays
a mechanical assassin designed to look human.

Killer robots inhabit the world of science fiction no more. In its
Middle Eastern wars, the United States depends heavily on unmanned
aerial vehicles (UAVs), known colloquially as drones. At low cost a
Predator or Reaper UAV can hover over hostile territory for hours,
conduct surveillance, and fire a guided missile at remote command.
F-35 stealth fighters can stay on station for only a few hours, depend on
ground personnel for live targeting information, and risk the life of the
pilot. Not only can the U.S. Air Force purchase twenty Predators for the
cost of a single F-35, but it can also operate them at a far lower cost per
hour and keep them on station for far longer, without risking the lives of
pilots who may be captured or killed.[1]

Military strategists have judged the drone to represent a revolution in military affairs. UAVs combine real-time intelligence, precision targeting, and robotic endurance to project power over territory denied to ground forces. They target individual members of the enemy with much less destruction and harm to civilians than conventional bombing or artillery attacks. According to some estimates, the U.S. launched 389 drone strikes in Pakistan against terrorist leaders between 2004-15, with only eleven launched before January 2008. From 2006-15, these strikes killed 2,789 members of the Taliban, al-Qaeda, and their allies, and 158 civilians.[2] In World War II or Vietnam, air forces would have dropped thousands of bombs to eliminate key enemy leaders or command and control facilities that now a few drone strikes can destroy.

And this is just the beginning. Military officials have designs for robots in the air, sea, and land on the drawing boards. Civilian technology gives a hint of the future. Google's auto-driving system has gone more than a half a million miles without an accident. Humans in the United States, by contrast, drive about 3 trillion miles a year at the cost of 32,000 accidental deaths.[3] Google's car may still be learning the subtleties of driving and its millions of variables, but it does not suffer from fatigue, distraction, or poor judgment. Militaries need only marry the technology from self-driving cars to the firing systems of drones to deploy robot tanks far more cheaply than an M-1 Abrams. It is no coincidence that the self-driving cars of today had their start in competitions sponsored by the Defense Advanced Research Program Agency, known as DARPA.

Military advances will occur in other realms as well. A small, unmanned vessel can become a seaborne IED in short order. Existing Unmanned Surface Vehicles (USVs) can carry out dangerous missions, such as reconnaissance or minesweeping. Autonomous submarines can sail faster, deeper, and quieter without crew compartments, large propulsion systems, or narrow depth and danger limits. The U.S. Navy has shown that unmanned vessels can deploy more weapons for longer periods and with greater accuracy than their aerial counterparts.[4] Smaller, cheaper vessels can also deploy in swarms to overcome and destroy larger vessels.[5]

Even without these coming advances, existing robots already provide a peek at the battlefield of the future. Satellite imagery, sophisticated electronic surveillance, drones, and precision-guided munitions allow

American intelligence and military forces to strike enemy targets virtually anywhere in the world at any time. Robotic weapons can reach beyond the traditional battlefield to strike deep into enemy territory, with surgical precision, without risking the lives of their operators. Once U.S. intelligence, for example, locates a terrorist leader in a safe house or moving in a car, controllers in Virginia can order a drone in the area to strike in hours, if not minutes. Although the first such strike occurred as recently as 2002, when the CIA killed Abu Ali al-Harithi, and five other al-Qaeda members while in a car in Yemen, drones have assumed a paramount role in the U.S. war against terrorism.[6] U.S. drones today strike enemy targets throughout Afghanistan, Iraq, Pakistan, Syria, Libya, and Yemen. These capabilities allow the United States to match the unconventional organization and tactics of terrorist groups without the extensive harm to civilians that might arise from pre-2002 bombing.

New warfighting technology naturally improves the effectiveness of military force—otherwise, nations would not adopt it. Crossbows made archery more deadly against armored knights; artillery allowed more destructive bombardment from a greater distance; modern rifles gave draftees the ability to kill at low cost with high accuracy. Robotics' falling costs, flexibility, precision, and the reduction in the risk of harm to combatants and noncombatants alike make them an irresistible choice for the generals of today and tomorrow.

This chapter will defend the use of robots in military combat (we will leave their many domestic uses for another day). Prominent government and academic critics argue that robots pose a severe threat to the laws of war, because they encourage the use of force, enable strikes on protected targets, and threaten a loss of human control. Security analyst Lawrence Korb claims, for example, that robots "will make people think, 'Gee, warfare is easy.'"[7] He worries that leaders will hold the impression that they can win a war with just "three men and a satellite phone." Brookings Institution fellow P.W. Singer agrees, "As unmanned systems become more prevalent, we'll become more likely to use force."[8]

We believe that these alarmist critiques mistake the capabilities of robots and the purpose of the laws of war. First, we will argue that contemporary military robots, popularly known as drones or more technically as unmanned aerial vehicles, should pose little difficulty for the laws or ethics of war. Remote operation does not automatically transform a weapon into an unjustified method of warfare. UAVs, for example, do not differ significantly from long-range artillery, aerial bombing, and ballistic missiles. All of these weapons inflict damage from a remote distance. What remains important is whether drones can effectively attack enemy targets while reducing overall harm to combatants and civilians alike. If robots can aim force with better accuracy so that battlefield casualties decline and can make sharper distinctions between combatants and civilians, we should welcome them, not fear them. The humanitarian goals of the rules of warfare should encourage the broader use of unmanned weapons, not seek to end them.

Second, we address the more difficult question of fully autonomous weapons. Critics claim that independent robots pose a more dire threat because they eliminate human decision-making from the "kill chain." We believe these concerns miss the mark. Nations already use such weapons that do not require direct human decision to pull the trigger. Land mines, for example, kill only based on proximity to the explosive, not by any human identification of a specific target. Cruise missiles make decisions based on programmed flight patterns and can limit themselves to specific targets. Autonomous warriors may reduce, rather than increase, errors in the use of force, not just compared to current technologies but also with regard to human soldiers. By taking humans out of the firing decision, independent robots controlled by computer programming or even artificial intelligence could elevate the humanity of combat. Rather than foreclose research and development of these weapons, as many urge, nations should weigh the improvements in accuracy and decline in targeting mistakes against any risk that robots will run amok.

The Rise of the Machines

Robots are spurring an evolution, rather than revolution, in war. While UAVs have received the most popular attention and sparked the most controversy, nations are developing robots to serve as more than just airborne weapons platforms. The U.S. military is developing a series of new technologies ranging from infantry weaponry to ground vehicles, aircraft, and naval vessels, which employ some type of robotics. These new military technologies portend a revolution in the way that modern militaries will fight wars. Unmanned vehicles can perform what the military calls "dull, dirty, or dangerous" work—constant monitoring, disposal of WMD materials, or high-risk military attacks—that can save the time, effort, or the lives of humans.[9]

Robots also bear advantages in their operations beyond just standing in for human beings. UAVs do not grow tired, fatigued, or hungry. While they need refueling and maintenance, they do not need sleep or rest and relaxation. UAVs can hover over an area for hours, long after a human pilot would have returned to base for rest and refueling. Robots do not suffer from emotion, panic, or fear for their lives. They can follow the orders of human commanders half the world away without misinterpretation, misunderstanding, or delay. They obey their programming, though bugs and viruses could lead them to malfunction.

The U.S.'s signature counterterrorism weapon—the unmanned drone, or UAV—charted the way for the development of military robotics. While unmanned air platforms emerged on battlefields as early as the balloon and as recently as reconnaissance aircraft, these earlier systems could not execute real-time commands, operate over great distances, nor carry out effective, lethal operations. Digital command, control, and communications have vested robots with a quantum leap in their military capabilities. They can stream constant reconnaissance of a battlefield, take account of changing environments, and provide an instant strike ability.[10] In the meantime, they remove human pilots from danger. In these deployments, human operators at a significant distance—some reports put them in Virginia and Nevada, among other locations—make the ultimate decision whether to fire missiles.[11]

Early uses of the drone took the form of solo strikes in locations where ground troops or manned aircraft could not easily deploy. The first reported drone strike, for example, took place in 2002 when a CIA-operated Predator launched a Hellfire missile to kill Abu Ali al-Harithi, the planner of the 2000 bombing of the USS *Cole*.[12] While the strike occurred outside the Yemen capital of Sana'a, the operator made the decision to fire from a base in Djibouti while overseen by commanders in Saudi Arabia. U.S. intelligence and military drone strikes have concentrated in areas of Pakistan, Afghanistan, and parts of Africa and the Middle East. American drone strikes have skyrocketed in the years after. While the Bush administration reportedly carried out 11 drone strikes in Pakistan from 2004-07, and 35 in 2008, the Obama administration launched 53 in 2009, 117 in 2010, 64 in 2011, 46 in 2012, 28 in 2013, and 24 in 2014.[13] The effectiveness of these attacks has led the U.S. Air Force to place more orders for drones than manned aircraft for future deployment.[14]

In this role, UAVs have raised legal questions similar to those prompted by targeted killings, or covert assassinations because of their stealthy nature, pinpoint targeting, and distance from traditional battlefields.[15] National militaries, however, will not limit robots to assassination missions. Aerial drones can eventually replace manned aircraft for most missions, including fighting for air supremacy against enemy fighters, launching strategic bombing campaigns, and conducting tactical ground strikes. While at a great remove from the battlefield, operators can effectively deny access to an area to an enemy force. Digital computing and communication, combined with robotics, can produce what we might call enhanced military operations. Unlike the cyber weapons we discuss in the following chapter, enhanced military operations use high-tech sensors, computing resources, and communications to link weapons and troops to multiply combat effectiveness on battlefields, rather than in cyberspace. Unmanned aerial weapons platforms, precision missiles, and joint forces cooperation allow the U.S., for example, to strike targets farther behind the battlefield. Dominating the information "space" allows nations to wield even greater force by coordinating multiple weapons over great distances, in real time, with constant updating of targets, threats, and costs and benefits.[16]

While criticism has fixed on drone strikes far behind any battlefield lines against discrete terrorist targets, attention has yet to focus on the possibilities of networked drones in support of other military units. Defense planners have raised the idea of deploying multiple drones that provide near-constant, ubiquitous air support, especially when integrated with mortars, artillery, helicopters, and manned aircraft. The Persistent Close Air Support program would give ground troops the ability to select a target, and then rely on computer algorithms to make the optimal choice of weapon system, munitions, and flight pattern to destroy the target.[17] A networked system would gather intelligence from ground troops, airborne vehicles, and space platforms to build the situational awareness necessary for such rapid target selection and weapon launch.

Ground troops would essentially point and shoot, without the delays of communication and calculation with weapons systems.

A mundane weapon like a land mine may illustrate the potential of future weapon development. Land mines are just primitive versions of robotic warfare. Mines automatically detonate their explosives when their sensors detect the presence of certain conditions, most commonly a weight compressing the surface above. They perform a valuable military function by denying an area to enemy military forces. They deter an opponent's offensive operations, slow the speed of advance, and inflict casualties on its ground forces. Along disputed and heavily militarized borders, such as those between North and South Korea or India and Pakistan, mines may play an important role in deterring attacks and providing stability in volatile political environments. Newer technologies will reduce the threat of harm to civilians from mines left on battlefields long after the end of a conflict. Even though the United States and several other countries, such as Russia, China, and India, refused to join the Ottawa Convention banning land mines, the U.S. has worked on improving the devices. New mines, for example, will have limited lifespans and remote monitoring.[18] Enhanced by greater communications, sensors, and remote control, newer mines can inflict the same lethal force, but with greater concentration on combatants and less risk to civilians.

Unmanned systems will come to play an even broader role in ground combat. Militaries already rely on computer-controlled radars and munitions for counter-battery weapons, which respond quickly to intercept enemy fire or destroy its source. Current Defense Department programs have developed small, ultra-light ground robots for intelligence and surveillance.[19] Planners envision unmanned vehicles, the size of small cars and trucks, providing logistical support and transport ground troops. Other models will clear minefields and WMD contamination, breach the entrances of buildings, and open up routes in cities for safe passage. Defense contractors are working on control systems that could transform any ground vehicle, including presumably armored tanks, self-propelled guns, and personnel carriers, into unmanned robots.

Unlike ground units, unmanned maritime systems may enjoy some of the advantages of UAVs, so much so that some military observers call them "the drones of the seas." Like the air, the vast spaces of the ocean provide drones with much greater room to maneuver. Like their early airborne counterparts, unmanned naval vessels could serve in a wide variety of missions including surveillance, intelligence, and reconnaissance, both on the high seas and closer to shore. Unmanned vessels could be smaller, because of the lack of crews, and hence stealthier and faster. By being able to take more damage, they would be more "persistent" and could operate in a wider variety of difficult conditions. They are also cheaper and more numerous, which allows navies to use them in situations where the threat to human life is high. Robotic ships could also be large as well as small. Remote controllers could command military convoys across the oceans, with weapons serving in a defensive capacity only. Indeed, Rolls-Royce predicts that within ten years most civilian cargo vessels will become autonomous.[20]

Armed unmanned naval vessels could take many forms. The most immediate and obvious role would be minelaying and sweeping, which poses severe dangers to human sailors but could be more easily automated. Another stage would involve deploying small, remote-controlled armed vessels from littoral combat ships (LCSs) to conduct operations close to shore. LCSs may end up deploying 12-meter-long USVs capable of speeds of up to 65 kilometers per hour and surviving for two days away from the mother ship. The U.S. Navy is also conducting research and development on technology that automates the role of surface warfare vessels. In 2012, for example, the U.S. Navy launched six missiles from an unmanned, remote-controlled weapons platform that also had machine guns to defend itself. The Navy has also tested the X-47B, an aerial drone designed for takeoff and landing on aircraft carriers. Naval observers speculate that the growing automation of the large surface warships of today, including the largest Ford-class aircraft carriers, may lead some day to fully automated destroyers and frigates.[21]

In the decades ahead, robotic warriors should replace humans for more and more combat missions. UAVs only appeared on the scene first because they could operate with more freedom in the skies and with less chance of effective countermeasures. Their early deployment as tactical ground-strike units should expand to include air supremacy and strategic attack missions. As the technology of robots and their supporting information systems advance, drones could also replace manned armored vehicles and artillery on the ground, and surface warships and submarines on the seas. They will have qualitative advantages over their human counterparts, such as farther mobility and longer endurance, faster response, and greater accuracy. These qualities should reduce the harm visited upon attackers, defenders, and civilians. But drones may also suffer from diluted human command and control over the use of force and weakening of a moral barrier to killing in war.

Robotics and the Laws of War

Prominent international officials and lawyers believe these developments in robotic weapons violate the law. The Obama administration's heavy reliance on drone warfare prompted these criticisms. UAVs have afforded the United States the ability to strike terrorist groups far beyond any conventional battlefield without the need to send ground troops or hold territory. "By his third year in office, Obama has approved the killings of twice as many suspected terrorists as had ever been imprisoned at Guantanamo Bay," observed one journalist.[22] Outside groups estimate that American UAV strikes have killed over 3,000 suspected militants in the Middle East and East Africa, and over a thousand civilians nearby.[23]

Criticism of the "drone wars" takes different forms. Some believe that robotic weapons will make war too easy to start and too cheap to stop. In the hopes that law and morality can reduce the amount of conflict, these officials and scholars believe that war should represent a difficult hurdle to cross. Others charge that robotic weapons will spread combat beyond traditional battlefields to civilian locales governed by domestic legal systems, not war. Critics also argue that the accuracy and speed of drones allow nations to target specific individuals for death, in violation of the ban on assassinations.

These criticisms have come primarily from established international organizations, most visibly the United Nations. In May 2010, the United Nations Human Rights Council appointed a special rapporteur to investigate "targeted killings."[24] Philip Alston, the U.N. expert, argued that U.S. drone practice may violate international law because it targeted the leaders of terrorist groups off any recognized battlefield, which he believed tantamount to using force to kill civilians in peacetime. He also criticized the use of drones because "they make it easier to kill without risk to a State's forces." Alston's U.N. report rejected claims that nations could use drones in anticipatory self-defense to preempt terrorists because such a "hypothetical" "threatens to eviscerate the human rights law prohibition against the arbitrary deprivation of life."

Some legal scholars have expanded upon this argument. They argue that the use of drones in Pakistan, for example, violates the laws of war because they do not take place within an international armed conflict. In their view, private groups and individuals, rather than nations, cannot wage war. War concentrates hostilities in a unified place and time, while terrorists launch attacks sporadically, covertly, and without state support. In the view of some scholars, therefore, terrorists do not meet the standard of an "armed attack" under Article 51 of the U.N. Charter, which recognizes a state's right to use force in self-defense. "An armed response to a terrorist attack will almost never meet these parameters for the lawful exercise of self-defense," argues Notre Dame Professor Mary O'Connell.[25]

Under this view, terrorist attacks should only trigger a law enforcement response. Terrorist attacks, because of their sporadic nature, low casualties, and lack of state support, are really crimes, not acts of war. "Terrorist attacks are generally treated as criminal acts because they have all the hallmarks of crimes," O'Connell declares.[26] Using drones to kill terrorists off a conventional battlefield would qualify as extrajudicial killing, or, in domestic law terms, murder. Following this line of thinking, the Swedish foreign minister criticized a U.S. drone strike in Yemen as "a summary execution that violates human rights," a view shared by Amnesty International.[27] Instead of sending drones to kill, these critics argue, nations must use law enforcement personnel to arrest terrorists and try them in court.

These criticisms confuse the legality of an armed conflict—its *jus ad bellum*—with how it is waged—its *jus in bello*. At the outset, we should make clear that precision strikes used to coerce an enemy or pursue terrorists might not even rise to the level of "war." Attacking al-Qaeda leaders or destroying an illicit WMD facility does not rise to the level of hostilities of a full-scale invasion or occupation of another nation. But even if use of precision weapons were to cross the line into war, in its twentieth-century sense, the means a nation chooses in war does not exert a feedback effect on the antecedent question of whether a nation should use force in the first place. Similarly, even if a nation uses force for illegitimate reasons, soldiers who participate in the conflict do not violate *jus in bello*.[28] German soldiers during World War II did not automatically become war criminals simply because they participated in a war of aggression; only those who violated limits on the means of war (such as deliberately killing civilians) violated the laws of war. A nation's decision to use force does not automatically limit its choice of weapons. Once a conflict has begun, the laws of war switch from the lawfulness of force to the narrower, repeated question of whether the choice of weapon in a particular context is reasonable. Whether to use a drone, or a ballistic missile, or a commando team to kill an enemy commander has no bearing on whether the United States legitimately can use force against al-Qaeda.

This mistaken criticism of drones draws on broader criticisms made against the Bush administration that the September 11, 2001 attacks did not trigger a state of war, which would make military detention and trials of terrorists illegal. "The U.S. Constitution contains no wartime or emergency exception to the scope of the President's powers," advised Professors Louis Henkin of Columbia Law School and Harold Koh of Yale Law School. "Indeed the word 'war' appears nowhere in Article II of the Constitution," they argued in urging the U.S. Supreme Court to free José Padilla, a U.S. citizen who was also a suspected al-Qaeda operative, from military detention.[29] No war, no detention. If the U.S. must use the police to arrest terrorists, and try them in civilian courts, the law must also require the government to arrest them rather than to use force. Police cannot use force unless reasonably necessary to prevent a serious imminent harm to the officer or a third party. Under the critics' logic, terrorists off the battlefield do not pose the required imminent threat. No war, no drone strikes.

These arguments, however, do not uniquely apply to drone warfare. Instead, they attack the very concept of a war against terrorist groups. Nations, of course, have long struggled with enemies who have chosen terrorist tactics. National liberation movements fought using irregular, guerrilla tactics and attacks on civilians during the period of post-World War II decolonization. Groups such as Shining Path in Peru and the Moro National Liberation Front in the Philippines continue attacks against government and civilian targets today. In the 1970s and 1980s, radical Marxist groups in Europe—Action Directe in France, the Baader-Meinhof Group in Germany, and the Red Brigades in Italy—sought to overthrow capitalism using terrorist tactics.

Nations should not limit themselves merely to domestic criminal justice approaches to fighting these types of groups. Admittedly, if governments could not use military methods, the current use of drones would violate most western domestic law. In the United States, for example, the Supreme Court has read the Fourth Amendment to bar the use of deadly force unless the officer has "probable cause to believe that the suspect poses a significant threat of death or serious physical injury to the officer or others."[30] Under this standard, police cannot use force against terrorists who are merely organizing their group, conducting training or providing logistical support, or even planning an attack. Instead, they must pose an *imminent* threat of serious harm, which under current understandings depends on the proximity in time of the attack.[31] The September 11th and subsequent terrorist attacks show that such law enforcement standards cannot successfully defeat terrorism, because by the time the attacks become imminent, it is too late.

When terrorist groups launch military attacks, the United States and other nations must respond with force in order to prevent them. They should be entitled to use weapons that reasonably achieve the military goal. Robotic weapons should not bear any special scrutiny beyond those that apply to any other weapons systems. Attacks on terrorists using manned aircraft, guided missiles, or artillery should equally offend U.N. officials and academics. Nor should distance matter. If a Navy SEAL can kill a terrorist leader with a rifle, the U.S. should be able to use drones to kill the same terrorist from a high altitude with a robotic weapon. Robots do not change the legal equation.

While the United States has defended the use of drones, it has not provided a comprehensive explanation for their use. As legal advisor of the U.S. State Department, Harold Koh declared, "It is the considered view of this Administration—and it has certainly been my experience during my time as Legal Adviser—that U.S. targeting practices, including lethal operations conducted with the use of unmanned aerial vehicles, comply with all applicable law, including the laws of war."[32] As dean of Yale Law School, Koh had vociferously criticized the administration of President George W. Bush for its detention, interrogation, and use of force policies against terrorists. Once in the Obama administration, however, he built the legality of drone strikes on the same legal foundations as the Bush administration: that the 9/11 attacks had started a war between al-Qaeda, the Taliban, and the U.S. "As a matter of international law, the United States is in an armed conflict with al-Qaeda, as well as the Taliban and associated forces, in response to the horrific 9/11 attacks, and may use force consistent with its inherent right to self-defense under international law," Koh said.

In the view of the United States, the choice of drones should make no difference for the legality of the use of force. "The rules that govern targeting do not turn on the type of weapon system used," Koh replied. "There is no prohibition under the laws of war on the use of technologically advanced weapons systems in armed conflict—such as pilotless aircraft or so-called smart bombs—so long as they are employed in conformity with applicable laws of war."[33] These laws include the principles of distinction—that nations attack only military objectives and not civilians—and proportionality—military attacks cannot cause damage that is excessive in relation to the military advantage.

Nevertheless, U.N. international law officials have continued to attack drones. Although admitting that drones "are here to stay," Christof Heyns worried that robots would tempt states to "increasingly engag[e] in low-intensity but drawn-out applications of force that know few geographic and temporal boundaries."[34] Their growing availability and falling costs make the weapons a necessary addition to the arsenals of most nations, including the U.S., the UK, France, Russia, China, India, and Israel, among others. States can use drones and other technology, such as cyber weapons, to launch attacks far from conventional battlefields in ways that escape immediate detection or even evade responsibility. The clear line between war and peace will blur as nations use pinpoint strikes and low-level force to coerce each other.

Robots, such critics worry, will encourage states to use force more often, even if less intensely. Because drones risk less harm to an attacking state's forces, they will tempt governments to employ force on a more regular basis. Wider use of force for longer periods of time, Heyns concludes, would "run counter to the notion that war—and the transnational use of force in general—must be of limited duration and scope, and that there should be a time of healing and recovery following conflict." The widespread acceptance and use of drones, Heyns claims, "can do structural damage to the cornerstones of international security and set precedents that undermine the protection of life across the globe in the longer term."[35]

The emergence of robots may create a new dynamic that reduces barriers to the use of force. Modern war deepened conflict but also concentrated it on the battlefield. Robots may have the reverse effect. They may conduct warfare in ways that kill fewer combatants and civilians than the total wars of the last century. They may also expand hostilities beyond a battlefield unified in one place and time to attack enemies thousands of miles from any "front" and weeks before they might launch an attack. In the twenty-first century, robots may spread war farther in reach, but shallower in destructiveness.

Robots are not just like any other weapon, and their use in the twenty-first century will not follow the pathways of the last century's weapons. In the nineteenth and twentieth centuries, the deployment of new weapons technologies exponentially increased death on the battlefield. Industrialization not only made war between mass armies possible, but scientific research eventually developed weapons, such as nuclear bombs, that could kill more people indiscriminately than ever before. After major wars, states naturally sought to limit the most destructive technologies, either through weapon bans or at least through more granular limits on target selection. But by the end of World War II, the Allies engaged in large-scale strategic bombing of entire cities in Germany and Japan in order to destroy their economic capacity to fight as well as their political will to continue fighting. Putting aside the debate over whether "bombing to win" has succeeded, WWII air forces had to use inaccurate dumb gravity bombs to increase their chances of striking an individual target.[36]

Robots make the lethality of force more certain, but less destructive because they are more precise than in these twentieth-century wars. Drones, for example, can gather intelligence that makes a successful attack more likely, and thus reduces the amount of force needed to destroy the target. A Reaper UAV on patrol over Iraq can follow the movements of possible ISIS commanders for weeks, in what intelligence officials call "pattern of life" analysis.[37] Surveillance will allow the U.S. to decide with greater certainty whether the person is more likely to be an ISIS commander, rather than an innocent, and the best time to strike him when he is alone or with other ISIS personnel, rather than near civilians. Greater intelligence increases the probability of killing the ISIS leader while the longer endurance of drones allows the U.S. to strike at the most propitious time and place. Precise munitions lower the likelihood of collateral losses nearby. Destroying the Fuhrer's bunker no longer requires leveling central Berlin. Nations will err if they press for stricter and stricter regulation of new weapons, even as those same weapons reduce death and suffering in combat.

Robots accelerate other important developments in warfare. Technology has allowed for combat at greater and greater distances. Ancient and medieval warriors generally fought within eyesight of each other. An English longbow could disable a target as far away as 275 yards.[38] Twentieth-century rifles can hit targets more than double or triple that distance.[39] Modern artillery gave armies a reach of miles, rather than yards. By WWII, aircraft enabled attacks hundreds of miles away on targets well behind the battlefield—hence the emergence of the "strategic" bombing of political and economic targets. Hiroshima and Nagasaki at the end of World War II introduced a new combination of technology: bombers that could fly across oceans and continents to deliver nuclear weapons capable of destroying entire cities. Missile technology allows nations to project force across continental distances with stunning speed. Missiles, however, suffer from a loss of accuracy and real-time decision-making to engage targets on the fly. A ballistic missile cannot decide to disarm itself if it learns that too many civilians are nearby.

Robots offer the immediacy of a missile strike but with the real-time decision-making of human pilots. Their ability to operate over great distances reduces the chances of casualties for the controllers of the drones. Under the balancing required by the laws of war, the replacement of a human pilot by a remote-controlled computer link should favor the drone as the weapon system of choice. While this calculation may seem cold-hearted because it turns only on the cost to the attacker, while keeping the harm to the target constant, commanders must conduct such balancing under the laws of war. A conclusion in favor of drones shows, however, the perversity of forcing nations to choose the most dangerous and wasteful methods for fighting war.[40]

Drones bear advantages beyond just reducing the potential costs to their users. They also reduce the potential harm to the defenders. This benefit of drones runs counter to the modern trend of military invention. Progress in arms has removed combatants farther and farther from the battlefield: from the distance of a longbow, to a rifle, to artillery, to aerial bombs, to, ultimately, intercontinental ballistic missiles. But as distance has increased, accuracy has decreased. Drones break this link between distance and error. Predators and Reapers allow U.S. Air Force pilots to conduct warfare at an unprecedented remove, once only available to the missile crews in ICBM silos in the Dakotas. Meanwhile, American UAVs offer greater accuracy than missile strikes conducted from the continental United States, even better than the proposed U.S. Prompt Global Strike system, which will use ICBMs and hypersonic cruise missiles to hit any point worldwide in less than an hour.[41] Predators and Reapers should match the superior accuracy of manned ground attack aircraft because they deploy the same armaments, such as the Hellfire or Maverick missile systems. The only difference is the weapons platform. It is possible for drones to even improve on the error rate of fighter-bombers. Drone pilots will suffer less from fatigue and the heat of combat, and they have the greater luxury to loiter over the battlefield to select the best time for an attack. Such high accuracy allows the United States to employ less destructive warheads to effectively eliminate a target.

These advantages help better achieve the ultimate goal of the laws of war to reduce civilian harm. The marriage of constant surveillance and better intelligence with precision munitions should reduce collateral harm to civilians. A missile, for example, once launched, cannot change its flight path based on updated intelligence, nor can a bomber recall a gravity bomb once dropped because civilians suddenly appear near the target. Drones, by contrast, allow changes to targeting and selection of weapons based on real-time updates of information. Because they do not have human pilots in the cockpit, drones can even take greater risks—such as flying at lower altitudes or braving higher degrees of anti-aircraft or antipersonnel fire—to attack their targets in a way that reduces harm to those nearby.[42]

NATO's war in Kosovo provides an example. An intensive air campaign hit not just tactical targets, such as Serbia's armed forces, but also strategic targets such as government ministries and transportation, communications, and energy networks.[43] After 78 days, Milosevic withdrew from Kosovo without the need for NATO ground troops. The attacks represented a success in air-power coercion, with low collateral costs— NATO publicly estimated about 500 civilian deaths.[44] Some international law observers, however, criticized the NATO bombing campaign on the grounds that bombers had deliberately chosen civilian targets, such as Serbian television stations, government ministries, and electrical grids. Others claimed that NATO barred its bombers from flying below 15,000 feet so as to avoid Serbian anti-aircraft defenses, which limited the accuracy of the gravity bombs and increased the risks of harm to nearby civilians.[45]

Such criticisms demand a level of perfection unattainable in war, but which robotic weapons may more closely approach. With UAVs, military planners can better approach the goals of the laws of war of reducing death and destruction. They can accept higher levels of harm to their drones in order to increase the precision of their attacks. During the Kosovo War, NATO kept its aircraft at a high altitude to prevent Serbian forces from killing or capturing pilots, but at the expense of accuracy in hitting targets. An air force armed with UAVs, however, could avoid this problem. It could field drones at lower altitudes to visually confirm the military nature of targets. It could order drones to expose themselves to air defenses at the price of greater certainty in destroying a target. Such efforts would both reduce mistakes in hitting the wrong targets and presumably cut down on collateral damage, as more precise strikes will have less blast damage in civilian areas.

Air war suggests that we should welcome robotics with open arms. Robots offer greater precision in combat, which should reduce destruction to both military soldiers and civilians alike. They should lead to a de-escalation of the intensity of warfare prompted by the technological developments of the twentieth century. We should understand the traditional rules of war to demand that armies choose the least destructive means to achieve a military objective, just as those who argue in favor of precision-guided munitions do today. If this is so, robots will allow nations at war to comply with the grand humanitarian goals of the laws of war far better than a world where drones are banned. Rather than ethically repulsive, robots instead may even be morally required.

Robots and Revolution

Other scholars do not train their criticism on the extensive system of sensors, GPS, and drones currently deployed on the battlefield. Instead, they reserve their fire for the inevitable development of autonomous systems that wage war without direct human decision. As opposed to a weapon system in which automation assists individual human beings conduct warfare, a truly autonomous weapon would acquire targets and make the decision to fire on its own. In 2012, for example, the U.S. Department of Defense defined an autonomous weapons system as one that "once activated, can select and engage targets without further interventions by a human operator."[46]

Under this definition, autonomous weapons systems have already arrived. In the U.S. Navy's Phalanx system, for example, battle computers direct artillery with high rates of fire against attack from multiple missiles.[47] The U.S. Patriot and Israel's Iron Dome systems employ computers and missiles to build a similar shield on the ground.[48] The future promises even more advances. A robotic sentry could automatically fire at certain target profiles, especially along disputed borders (such as the Korean DMZ) or around forward bases during armed conflicts. A drone could seek specific target profiles within specific geographic coordinates and then automatically launch its munitions. Other weapons platforms could employ this combination of sensors, high-speed computing, and precision munitions to similar effect on land and sea.

These developments have prompted fears of a *Terminator* future that justifies a ban on all independent robotic weapons. In 2012, for example, Human Rights Watch and the Harvard International Human Rights Clinic demanded a ban not just on all autonomous weapons, but also their research and development. In their view, such weapons cannot apply the principles of distinction, proportionality, and military necessity. They "would appear to be incapable of abiding by key principles of international humanitarian law."[49] Wendell Wallach, chair of a Yale University committee on technology and ethics, calls on the president of the United States to issue an executive order "declaring that a deliberate attack with legal and nonlethal force by fully autonomous weaponry violates the Law of War."[50] Wallach sets as his goal "terminating the terminator." Both the U.N. special rapporteur and the former head of the ICRC have called for a temporary moratorium on lethal autonomous weapons until the international community can resolve the attending legal and ethical issues.[51]

International and domestic officials question whether international law can even govern such weapons. "What if it is technically impossible to reliably program an autonomous weapon system so as to ensure that it functions in accordance with IHL under battlefield conditions?" asks Jakob Kellenberger, former ICRC president.[52] It will be difficult enough, these critics argue, to devise programs that can methodically apply general principles to specific battlefield situations. It will be even harder to give them the capacity to learn and to apply their rules to new situations. Even supporters of robotic weapons anticipate difficulties in programming them to use force effectively but with restraint. "Restraints on autonomous weapons to ensure ethical engagements are essential," writes a DoD official, "but building autonomous weapons that *fail safely* is the harder task."[53] Some worry that machine learning may produce unpredictable decision-making and outcomes.[54]

Critics make a number of arguments against autonomous weapons, even though their deployment may lie several years, if not decades, in the future. The argument is that they reduce the costs of war so steeply that they will encourage the resort to force. Autonomous weapons reduce the risk to operators to zero. U.S. drone pilots, for example, make firing decisions on foreign targets while sitting at an Air Force base one hour from Las Vegas.[55] If robots produce more precise targeting with lower collateral damage, they will achieve a much higher cost-benefit ratio than conventional manned weapons. These features of drones, however, "also reduce the political costs and risks of going to war," writes Peter Asaro.[56]

Prohibiting such weapons, critics argue, will prevent a slippery slope leading to truly independent robots. Autonomy, critics claim, could lead to unintended consequences, not the least of which is the use of force without human decision. "Autonomous weapon systems also have the potential to cause regional or global instability and insecurity, to fuel arms races, to proliferate to non-state actors, or initiate the escalation of conflicts outside of human political intentions," writes Asaro.[57] A ban will encourage military research to emphasize "human-centred designs capable of enhancing ethical and legal conduct in armed conflicts."[58] It will also prevent broader destabilization of the law of armed conflict, and it will emphasize that killing other humans requires moral consideration by other humans. These critics cite AP I's requirement that a nation must review whether the use of any "new weapon, means or method of warfare" would violate the conventions or the laws of war.[59] Even skeptics of a ban, such as Kenneth Anderson and Matthew Waxman, agree that the U.S. should conduct a thorough review to determine whether autonomous weapons violate the laws of war. Robotics, combined with GPS, sensors, autonomous decision-making, high-speed computing, and precision munitions, represent a new method of warfare that apparently demands special scrutiny.

Arms control advocates no doubt could have made similar claims about new weapons systems at the start of the industrial age. Previous advances gave early adopters large advantages in combat, reduced the ability of opponents to defend themselves, and rendered war less costly and easier to start. Tanks, for example, protect their drivers with armor that makes them virtually invulnerable to small arms fire, while mounting a large cannon and machine guns that can wreak destruction on infantry. At first, airplanes could strike ground targets that had little hope of defense. Aircraft carriers allowed naval forces to project power far beyond a nation's borders, without having to fight through vast fleets of battleships, as the United States learned to its regret at Pearl Harbor on December 7, 1941. Submarines could cripple merchant convoys or attack surface ships without risking a fleet. Ballistic missiles can strike enemies without having to send out any expeditionary forces. While they allow the projection of force over greater distances at less cost, nations do not consider these weapons to violate the laws of war. In fact, as we have seen, efforts to regulate aerial bombing and submarine warfare utterly failed.

Arguments against autonomous weapons really attack progress in military technology and war itself. In some, but certainly not all, international disputes, one nation may hold a wide advantage over its rival. Overwhelming superiority may make it easier for the stronger nation to turn to force. For example, the ability of U.S. and NATO air forces to bomb Serbian targets, without resistance and beyond anti-aircraft missile range, likely made the decision to intervene easier. President Clinton may well have avoided a ground invasion and the prospect of high casualties. There could be other circumstances where a nation may give in to a propensity to wage war because it will be relatively low in cost. One nation may reap an intelligence coup that gives it the benefit of surprise. Another may have far more effective weaponry, tactics, or strategies that give it a profound advantage. Superiority, however, does not equal illegality.

Such mistaken arguments confuse *jus in bello* and *jus ad bellum*. The means of fighting a war do not bear on its justification. A just war need not be fought in an evenhanded fashion; in fact, both sides benefit if the conflict comes to a rapid conclusion with the least loss of life. If we agree with the goal of stopping Serbian ethnic cleansing in Kosovo, we should want NATO to execute the war with the maximum dispatch and effectiveness. A faster war, fought with precision weapons and reduced combat casualties, could end the human rights catastrophe earlier and save more lives. If a nation is defending itself from aggression, we should want it to have the most advanced weapons possible. Superiority itself may not just deter an attack, but it could inflict such high costs in an actual war that the attacker might cease.

U.N. officials and human rights groups could just as well prolong war's death and destruction. Banning advanced weapons systems seeks technological parity among many nations. Nations matched in weaponry and tactics could wage war inconclusively for years, as occurred a century ago in the trench warfare of World War I. Even World War II, which favored offensive weaponry and tactics, lasted for six years and killed millions more than the Great War. Technological discoveries, such as the atomic bomb, shortened the war and saved millions of lives. If today's human rights advocates had persuaded FDR, Truman, and Churchill to preemptively ban nuclear weapons research, the invasion of Japan would have taken an estimated 1 million Allied lives and 8-9 million Japanese.[60] Of course, we would not have wanted Nazi Germany or Imperial Japan to develop the atomic bomb first, but that merely confirms that our approval of superiority in weapons depends on whether we agree with the aims of the war.

The real-world consequences of military technology should lead to a rejection of any categorical ban on new weapons. Autonomous weapons systems may allow nations to wage hostilities with greater lethality, but at lower cost to their own soldiers. A weapon's improved effectiveness should not prompt bans; rather, we should welcome them for reducing the destructiveness of war. Technology that makes war more effective by making targeting more precise, reducing combatant and civilian deaths, and ultimately shortening the conflict, will improve overall global welfare, a result that the rules of war should always promote.

A second main avenue of thought attacks autonomous weapons because they remove human decision from the "kill chain." Dispute continues over whether robotic engineering can even create a fully independent robotic warrior. Mines, automated sentries, and high-speed defense systems, however, already fire on targets without human intervention. Cruise missiles already follow evasive routes once fired; it would not be more difficult to equip them with computer systems to choose among targets once they reach a selected area. UAVs already automate elements of an attack mission, such as takeoff and landing and autopilot; a future computer system could provide preprogrammed responses to certain target profiles in a battlespace. A similar system could adapt to sea warfare, which confronts a combat environment also characterized by three dimensions and large volumes for movement. Less complicated robots could even assist ground troops in difficult urban and insurgent environments by accepting higher damage rates at the front of assaults.

Some argue that the decision to take a human life must be made by another human being. Human Rights Watch has called for a ban on fully autonomous weapons, which "should apply to robotic weapons that can make the choice to use lethal force without human input or supervision."[61] Remotely piloted drones, vessels, or ground vehicles, in which a human operator still pulls the trigger, do not suffer this problem. But autonomous robots will decide to fire on targets based on decision algorithms without human intervention for an individual shot. Nations will especially seek to deploy such systems in battlefield environments where an enemy can cut off contact with remote controllers or autonomy will enhance the stealth and surprise of an attack. In such situations, no individual human may make the ultimate decision to kill. Rather, the choice results from the programming and construction of the weapon by a number of participants, both military and civilian.

The lack of a human being "in the loop" troubles human rights advocates. They argue that robots do not enjoy human consciousness and so lack moral responsibility for their decisions. "Intentionally designing systems that lack responsible and accountable agents is in and of itself unethical, irresponsible, and immoral," argues Asaro.[62] These critics believe that the decision to take a human life must ultimately be made by a human being. Their arguments, however, seem to assume a uniqueness in human decision-making rather than any careful consideration of the moral values at stake. Typically in this vein, O'Connell argues, "What seems unprogrammable is conscience, common sense, intuition, and other human qualities."[63] Without an individual at the trigger, moreover, critics argue that the international legal system will have no one to hold accountable for crimes against the laws of war. Robots will not be deterred by the prospect of *ex post* criminal legal proceedings.

These arguments, however, mistake distance for independence. An autonomous weapon that makes targeting decisions on its own still must receive a command to deploy. It does not seem unreasonable to hold commanders responsible for the foreseeable decisions of their robots.[64] Commanders already bear "command responsibility" for some war crimes committed by their troops. Commanders could bear an even closer responsibility for the actions of autonomous weapons, which would have less individual discretion to make decisions that violate the laws of war. Liability could even extend to the programmers or designers of robotic weapons.[65]

The foundational argument about moral agency is equally weak. It is unclear why morals demand that a human being pull every trigger in war. We have not seen such a principle advocated by the leading moral works on war by moral theorists, such as John Rawls's *Law of Peoples* or Michael Walzer's *Just and Unjust Wars*.[66] If asked, such perspectives might argue that if we want the decision on whether or not to take our lives to be made by other humans, we should adopt the same rule ourselves. Thus, if we do not wish the armies of another nation to use autonomous drones to kill us, we should not use them against others. It is not obvious, however, that our primary interest is in making sure humans make the final decision—making it a but-for cause—of killing in war. We should have a greater interest in making sure that if our lives were taken in combat, that it is done so on legitimate grounds. The laws of war should favor combat methods that reduce harm to civilians and the death and destruction of war itself over any minimum requirement of human participation. If we can program the robot to execute attacks that reduce wartime errors and collateral damage below that of a human fighter, we should choose the robot.

Such criticisms of autonomous weapons also miss weightier reasons for the place of war in the international system. Those who seek a ban on robots for moral reasons narrow the focus to the use of force against a lone target or in a single battle. It is possible that an autonomous weapon might make the wrong moral choice on the battlefield. But it is even more likely that drones might bring war to a more timely conclusion or even help persuade nations never to fight in the first place. We do not argue here that one nation's overwhelming superiority in arms will prevent war from breaking out, though there is some truth to this assumption.

Instead, autonomous weapons could help nations settle their disputes without the resort to force.

Robotic weapons can enhance communication between nations in a dispute, and hence make overall peace more, rather than less, likely. Drones bring into reach a greater range of targets, which permits a wider range of coercion. Nations in a dispute, for example, can use UAVs to temporarily disable infrastructure, both military and civilian, without as great a loss of life or destruction of property. They can also demonstrate varying levels of harm a nation is willing to accept, in between non-coercive, economic measures and those that put soldiers' lives at risk. Banning or limiting autonomous weapons would have the opposite effect. It would narrow the range of targets, which could have the effect of escalating the damage and death of signaling. Reducing the number and types of targets and limiting the means to pursue them could increase the odds of war. The more steps up an escalatory ladder, the more opportunity to jump off before reaching the stage of full armed conflict. On the other hand, limiting the ability of nations to communicate will reduce their ability to reach settlements of their differences.

A broader systemic concern beyond the interests of individual nations is also at stake. Robotic weapons could allow nations to undertake wars that they should fight, but otherwise might not because of the costs. Going to war first can prevent something worse, both for nations and the world. A nation, for example, should have the right to launch a preemptive attack to stop greater aggression that might materialize in the future. Israel's 1981 strike on Iraq's Osirak nuclear reactor and its 2007 bombing of a Syrian nuclear facility prevented a worse future in which the regimes of Saddam Hussein or Bashar al-Assad had successfully acquired the atomic bomb.[67]

Robotic weapons could provide nations with the means to intervene earlier, at lower cost, and with greater precision against looming threats. Such weapons, for example, could allow nations to launch preventive strikes against hardened targets where the odds of high pilot casualties might otherwise deter an operation. Suppose Israel and the United States decided against a strike on Iran's nuclear research facilities because of Tehran's anti-aircraft capabilities and the chances of high civilian casualties. Israeli and American leaders, however, might launch an attack by advanced UAVs because of the zero chance of pilot losses, the higher likelihood of eliminating the facilities, and lower chances of civilian casualties.

Robotic weapons might also provide advantages not just for nations pursuing their individual interests, but also for the world as a whole. States have used force for goals that benefit the world as well as themselves. In the nineteenth century, for example, the British Navy ended the Atlantic slave trade and, later, enforced free navigation and trade on the high seas.[68] The United States used its naval and air superiority in the twentieth century to similar effect. Both countries did not act out of altruism, because their market economies benefitted more from free trade and their militaries could operate more effectively than landlocked rivals. But these expensive policies also increased the welfare of other nations, which could take advantage of globalization to develop their own economies. Robotic weapons will lower the costs for the West to maintain today's free navigation and commerce, which creates the conditions for world economic growth.

Just as public goods theory predicts that the free-riding will discourage nations from undertaking necessary, but expensive, action, so too will similar challenges deter humanitarian intervention. International human rights violations would land low on the list of priorities for military action, as intervening nations would receive almost no material benefit other than an increase in their citizens' psychological well-being. Robotic weapons could reduce the obstacles to humanitarian intervention by lowering the costs of a conflict for the great powers, and thus make it more likely they will use force. Take the Rwandan genocide. Imagine if the United States and its allies could have used drones to inflict costs on Hutu government troops to stop the genocide of the minority Tutsis. Future robotic weaponry would help address the reluctance of western nations to intervene because of the risk of casualties. Lower cost would increase the likelihood that they would intervene in troubled areas, where the worst civilian casualties are now occurring.

Understanding war as an intense form of coercion creates an even more positive role for robotic weapons. As we have argued earlier, nations today are "returning to coercion" as a tool of international politics. Such measures include not just economic embargoes and blockades, but also recent uses of force such as the U.S. threat to bomb Syria for its chemical weapons stockpile or earlier attacks on Saddam Hussein's regime in the

1990s. We believe that recent efforts to purge the international system of punitive responses mistake the traditional principles of the laws of war. The older view acknowledged a much wider range of occasions for the use of force and a wider range of legitimate targets. If there is a place for retaliation, the scope for resorting to force will be enlarged, and it will no longer be obvious that retaliatory measures must actually be limited to attacks on "military objectives." We reject more recent efforts to apply a broad definition of the principle of distinction—the idea that nations at war can only intentionally target each other's military forces—because it may have the perverse consequence of rendering war more likely and more destructive.

For robotic weapons to have this effect, we must return to older understandings of the laws of war. AP I's principle of distinction, for example, forbids combatants from intentionally attacking civilians or civilian assets. Distinction is certainly a moral duty when it comes to civilian lives, but it is less compelling regarding civilian infrastructure or property. But suppose one country could use precision munitions, delivered by drones, to strike civilian infrastructure as a way to pressure another country to accept its demands. In the past, the chance of error of artillery, missiles, and gravity bombs would make it difficult, if not impossible, to hit non-military, yet sensitive, targets without killing nearby civilians. Targeting civilian networks could allow nations to communicate more clearly to each other their capabilities and resolve and, thus, more likely reach a settlement of their dispute. We should prefer an attack on civilian infrastructure instead of an attack on military facilities, if the former required less force and presented less chance of serious death and destruction.

Nations at war already do this. During the 1990s, the United States carried out air attacks on Saddam Hussein's regime for failure to comply with U.N. weapons inspectors. The targets included not only Iraqi military bases, but also buildings in downtown Baghdad, where political, intelligence, and military leaders were located.[69] The aim was clearly coercive. There was no direct connection between destroying Iraqi military assets and enforcing Iraqi obligations to cooperate with inspections.[70] Commentators criticized these exercises as punitive rather than as self-defense.[71] During the Kosovo War, the United States and its NATO allies launched an air war to force Serbia to stop driving ethnic Albanians out of Kosovo and to accept an international peacekeeping force to resolve the dispute. NATO struck targets well beyond military assets in Kosovo or Serbia, including electric power stations, highway bridges, and television broadcasting towers.[72]

Military lawyers have turned somersaults to justify these attacks as meeting the principle of discrimination. At best, their arguments claim that transportation, communications, and power networks served dual purposes to support military and political functions as well as civilian. Under this reasoning, however, almost any civilian resource could qualify as a target, especially because the laws of war demand no minimum military use of a facility to justify an attack. Instead, nations should honestly admit that their militaries are employing force against civilian targets to pressure their enemies. During the Kosovo War, allied commanders fully understood that their strikes sought to coerce Serbia into a political settlement, rather than to destroy discrete military targets. U.S. General Michael Short acknowledged that the ultimate target was civilian morale: "I felt that on the first night, the power should have gone off, and major bridges around Belgrade should have gone into the Danube, and the water should be cut off so that the next morning the leading citizens of Belgrade would have got up and asked, 'Why are we doing this?' and asked [Serb President] Milosevic the same question."[73]

Used in this way, robots could achieve the goals of the laws of war without triggering the negative effects of World War II attacks on farms or industrial plants. Robots, for example, could disable electrical facilities, power plants, or financially sensitive locations to pressure the population to withdraw support from a regime. Or they could destroy nodes, such as airport runways, railroad tracks, or highway intersections, to create traffic logjams primarily for civilian transport. In its ongoing war with ISIS in Iraq and Syria, the United States and its allies have already attacked such targets, such as oil production and central banks, to undermine the terrorist group's financial infrastructure. Israeli strikes against Palestinian terrorist leaders reportedly have destroyed individual apartments or building floors without harming surrounding units.[74] Modern munitions' precision can hit these targets with lower risk to surrounding civilians, but only when combined with the long-range ability of drones and high-quality intelligence. We should prefer such attacks to more direct strikes on military targets, if the latter involve a higher loss of life and greater destruction.

These new capabilities should also change our approach to the other elements of the use of force. As defined by the U.S. Department of Defense, proportionality requires that combatants weigh "the expected loss of life or injury to civilians, and damage to civilian objects incidental to the attack," against "the concrete and direct military advantage expected to be gained."[75] Proportionality recognizes that the laws of war may forbid the intentional targeting of civilians, it does not prohibit civilian losses as a collateral effect of legitimate combat. But the test's focus on military advantage suggests that nations can only use force to reduce an enemy's military capacities. It fails to clarify reasonable standards for force that seek to coerce an enemy's leadership to concede a dispute or give up hostilities, even when it involves less destruction than attacks on the military.

Proportionality's difficulties reflect its failure as a test to regulate robotic weapons. Proportionality requires the measurement and weighing of values that do not lend themselves to comparison. Commentators have observed that proportionality already lacks an objective measure because of the dissimilar variables involved.[76] W. Hays Parks has even argued that proportionality has no content other than to establish that commanders are not intentionally targeting civilians without any military benefit.[77] Under the rule, for example, military commanders must determine the value of a "military advantage," which presumably includes gaining territory, killing enemy soldiers and destroying military assets, and defending their own troops. Military advantage includes not just tactical gains, but also strategic benefits, such as degrading command, control, and communications, transportation, and supporting networks and production. Judgment of advantage would not just encompass the dollar value of enemy resources destroyed, but would involve difficult measurements of tactical and strategic advantages in achieving a war's aim.[78] Against this, commanders are supposed to determine the harm to civilians. This is a difficult task even in the context of domestic regulation; it seems unworkable to ask commanders to set a price for an enemy civilian life and then balance it against military gains.[79]

Commentators admit that no predictable legal rules can provide certainty to proportionality. William Boothby, author of the leading work on the law of military targeting, relies on the idea that most "reasonable military commanders" would agree on most cases. At the same time, he admits that there is no "mathematical formula; there are no hard and fast rules and there is an inevitable element of subjectivity in the judgments associated with the rule."[80] In its 2015 Law of War Manual, the U.S. Defense Department admitted that proportionality "does not necessarily lend itself to empirical analyses" and that instead it calls for "a highly open-ended legal inquiry, and the answer may be subjective and imprecise."[81] Commanders must claim ever more tenuous relationships to military objectives in order to justify attacks whose true purpose is coercion. Strikes on roads and highways become attacks on transportation routes used by the military. Disabling communications nets becomes part of hitting command and control systems. Dams become targets if enemies can use it to flood the approach of friendly troops. Factories that produce dual-use goods become legitimate targets.[82]

Understanding the use of force as coercive would avoid this analytical mess. Attempting to balance military advantages against civilian costs only muddies the waters and places impossible burdens on leaders making decisions under pressure. Instead, proportionality should simply ask whether the costs of an attack significantly outweigh its benefits in bringing a conflict to a more timely, less destructive end. Costs should include all military and civilian losses, while benefits should include not just tactical advantages in territory, lives saved, and strategic gains, but also success in pressuring an enemy's leaders to concede. If an attack does not endanger civilians lives, the analysis should grant a fair amount of flexibility in judging the reasonableness of using force. Permitting attacks that satisfy this analysis should allow nations to achieve their aims at a lower overall cost than strictly following AP I.

The precision offered by robotic weaponry opens up a wider range of legitimate attacks that should make wars less destructive. For example, a swarm of smaller drones, directed by reliable intelligence, could cripple the critical nodes of an enemy's network with small explosives. In the Gulf War, for example, the United States and its allies destroyed airport runways using cluster munitions.[83] While these airports may have primarily hosted civilian traffic, U.S. generals argued that they could also serve military flights. In the Kosovo War, the United States attacked a tractor factory in Serbia because it also engaged in "manufacturing support or parts for tanks and armored personnel carriers as well as for civilian vehicles."[84] In its recent wars in the Middle East, the U.S. and its allies have destroyed roads, bridges, railways, and other transportation hubs. Commanders will struggle to justify such attacks because the facilities involve some military use, or because they are adjacent to legitimate targets. But nations should be able to attack such targets if their destruction coerces an enemy, and hence brings the war closer to an end, at a lower cost—regardless of whether the military advantage outweighs civilian losses. In fact, the superpowers adopted such an approach with the most revolutionary military technology to emerge after World War II: nuclear weapons. During the Cold War, the superpowers aimed thousands of nuclear missiles at each other's major cities. These weapons threatened the destruction not just of military targets, but of most of a rival nation's civilian population.[85] Deterring attack and maintaining a balance of power, however, justified the deployment of such weapons, which by their very nature disregard proportionality.

Precision weapons press proportionality from the other extreme. Drones offer the ability to advance war aims through pinpoint, but minimally destructive, strikes on civilian targets. If commanders can cripple critical enemy networks through precision strikes, they can pressure the enemy's leadership to compromise or concede the dispute. Rather than destroy an airport, drones armed with smaller warheads could disable the radar and communication equipment that control flights. Rather than destroy the tractor factory, precision attacks could disable the power lines or transportation links. If the strikes produce less overall harm to the enemy than more destructive attacks on military targets, they fulfill the overall goal of the laws of war to reduce injury and suffering.

The Persian Gulf War of 1990-91 illustrates the types of targets that come up in an air war that robotic weapons might better attack. In its 1992 report to Congress, the U.S. Defense Department disclosed that one of its primary air campaign objectives was to "isolate and incapacitate the Iraqi regime."[86] In order to achieve that goal, the coalition air force developed three target sets: the first was leadership command facilities; second, electricity production; third, telecommunications, and command, control, and communications nodes.[87] All of these targets involved strikes against civilian sites because of their potential dual-use. Leadership command facilities included "national-level political and military headquarters and command posts," where Saddam Hussein and his aides might be located. The coalition destroyed "virtually the entire Iraqi electric grid" because electricity to military locations could be rerouted through civilian facilities.[88] It also struck "microwave relay towers, telephone exchanges, switching rooms, fiber-optic nodes, and bridges that carried coaxial communications cables" because military communications passed through major switching facilities in Baghdad. Bombing included civilian television and radio facilities because they too could carry military communications and political propaganda.

Attacking these systems no doubt would interfere with military operations. But they also had the effect of pressuring the Hussein regime by escalating their costs during hostilities. Robotic weapons could achieve this effect at even lower human and physical cost. In order to successfully destroy these targets, the U.S. Air Force and its coalition partners have to fly thousands of sorties, drops tons of bombs, and destroy entire buildings and networks. While the coalition attempted to use precision-guided munitions where possible and reduce collateral damage, no doubt civilians at or near these locations were killed. The coalition had to return to these targets repeatedly because the Iraqis could rebuild them.[89] Robotic weapons could provide the ability to incapacitate these civilian facilities with even lower cost. Because of the ability to loiter and fire precise missiles, UAVs could hit critical components that could bring down an electrical or communication grid without permanently destroying the entire network. The less production and transmission facilities hit, the less casualties will result. Western nations might even use robotic weapons to take and hold such facilities—imagine a robotic ground vehicle stationed on top of a critical communications hub—to prevent their repair. Such weapons could achieve military goals with lesser harm, if they could extend their reach to civilian infrastructure.

Less provocative measures could also avoid a rapid escalation of hostilities. For example, the United States currently favors air strikes as a means of placing pressure on another government. It will not, however, risk attacks without first neutralizing enemy anti-aircraft defenses and winning air superiority. Air superiority is also seen as a necessary precondition for successful ground and naval operations.[90] Thus, to engage in successful military force, the United States would first carry out extensive bombing of air defense command and control and munitions as well as ground enemy aircraft—provocative moves that will cause extensive loss of life and damage. Cheaper UAVs, however, provide the opportunity to place pressure on an opponent without risking pilots, and therefore alleviating the need to wipe out a nation's entire air defense system. Unmanned naval and ground weapons could similarly engage in pinpoint attacks that might sacrifice the vehicle, without calling for the suppression of defenses that ground forces would require. Robots' precision with disposability opens up a greater range of uses of force that give nations more space to send signals, negotiate, and ultimately avoid a fuller-blown conflict.

Conclusions

This chapter has described the coming revolution in robotic warfare. The technology that has created aerial drones will produce unmanned versions of many other weapons systems, from tanks to submarines to sentries. Criticism of this advance misses the mark. Rather than an unknown to be feared, new weapons technology will bring a greater precision in the use of force that will reduce casualties and destruction. Allowing the use of robotic weapons against a broader range of targets, such as civilian infrastructure and networks, promises to contain the harm of international disputes and help lead to peaceful settlements. Concerns about autonomous weapons are equally mistaken. Such systems promise to increase the precision and decrease the harms of attack. In a world beset by fresh challenges to international security, reducing the costs and increasing the accuracy of force may reduce the obstacles to action to stop WMD proliferation, terrorist groups, humanitarian disasters, or revanchist powers.

CHAPTER 6

Cyber Weapons

The Wright Brothers achieved heavier than air flight in 1903. A mere eight years later, Italian forces deployed air bombardment against Tripoli—the pilot tossed handheld bombs from the cockpit of his rickety plane. Italian newspapers pronounced the action a decisive contribution to the conquest of Libya.[1] By 1918, a mere fifteen years after the first flight at Kitty Hawk, Britain's new Royal Air Force was planning a major bombing campaign against Germany.[2]

The Internet became accessible to general home use in 1993. That same year, an article appeared warning that future wars would turn on mastery of the cyber domain. Strategists launched the idea of "cyber war" almost simultaneously with the emergence of the Internet.[3] Nearly a quarter-century later, cyber war has yet to happen. No one has died from a cyber attack. No nation has surrendered to a cyber attack. No government has admitted that it launched a cyber attack to force another government to change its policy.[4]

Military services still have much more interest in cyber attacks, of course, than in attack dolphins, seen as an emerging threat not so long ago.[5] The U.S. Defense Department—which denies an interest in attack dolphins[6]—is certainly interested in cyberspace. Beginning in the late 1960s, the Defense Advanced Research Projects Agency (DARPA) provided the critical financial and institutional support for research into networked computers. By 2006, the Air Force established its own cyber command, which became U.S. Cyber Command, linked to the National Security Agency in 2010.

In the meantime, there was a drumbeat of warnings that surprise attacks through computer networks could cripple the United States. CIA Director John Deutch warned Congress in 1996 about the possibility of an "Electronic Pearl Harbor."[7] A 2003 study by a national security analyst, based on extensive consultations with Defense officials, offered an entire chapter entitled "An Electronic Pearl Harbor?"[8] By 2012, CIA Director Leon Panetta, after his nomination to serve as Secretary of Defense, warned the Senate about a "Cyber Pearl Harbor."[9] A few weeks later, two senators used the anniversary of the original December 7 attacks to warn about the same thing, borrowing the title of a famous book on Pearl Harbor for their op-ed: "At Dawn We Sleep."[10]

Some analysts go further. They worry that a terrorist organization, rather than a state, may use the Internet to deliver a catastrophic surprise attack.[11] Some analysts have even offered explicit analogies between today's cyber threat and the threat posed by nuclear missiles during the Cold War.[12] Analysts who emphasize the most alarming possibilities often leap to the most obvious means to head them off: an international agreement by which all powers renounce destructive cyber attacks. In other words, they want arms control.

These warnings are overblown and the prescription is impractical. Even the Obama administration declined to pursue a cyber arms control treaty, while it did acknowledge that U.S. Cyber Command would have vaguely defined "offensive capabilities."[13] Just behind the Cassandras and the utopians, however, are legions of lawyers, insisting that the current law of armed conflict prohibits or constrains the most promising applications of cyber technology to armed conflict. This chapter will examine the nature of cyber weapons and dispel the legal obstacles to their use, before turning to an exploration of the more limited nature of cyber force. We conclude with a description of the appropriate uses of cyber technology against the security threats of today.

Cyber Weapons as WMD: Apocalypse Now, Not

In 2010, Richard Clarke envisioned a cyber attack in these lurid terms:

Within a quarter of an hour, 157 major metropolitan areas have been thrown into knots by a nationwide power blackout hitting during rush hour. Poison gas clouds are wafting toward Wilmington and Houston. Refineries are burning up oil supplies in several cities. Subways have crashed in New York, Oakland, Washington, and Los Angeles. Freight trains have derailed outside major junctions and marshaling yards on four major railroads. Aircraft are literally falling out of the sky as a result of midair collisions across the country. Pipelines carrying natural gas to the Northeast have exploded, leaving millions in the cold. The financial system has also frozen solid because of terabytes of information at data centers being wiped out. Weather, navigation, and communications satellites are spinning out of their orbits into space. And the U.S. military is a series of isolated units, struggling to communicate with each other.[14]

By the time Clarke had published this warning, he had advised a succession of presidents on national security issues. He emerged into the political spotlight when he offered a much-publicized public apology for the government's failure to prevent the 9/11 attacks.[15] As the Obama administration reoriented security policy from terrorist threats, Clark tried to focus public attention on the novel and ostensibly greater threat of cyber attacks.

Other commentators have depicted the potential threat in equally vivid terms. After revelation of the Stuxnet virus directed against the Iranian nuclear program, an MIT researcher warned of a "Stuxnetted future." Just a few years from now, he postulated, a hostile enemy might use porn sites to infect cell phones and order them to overheat and explode, causing mayhem in the subways of major cities. "Hundreds [of passengers] severely burnt and blinded" and "thousands more trampled as panicked commuters struggled to escape the smoke-filled trains," while "above ground . . . along America's East Coast, rush hour trucks and automobiles on freeways, highways and city streets spun out of control as synchronized explosions crippled drivers."[16] Fervid imagination seems to have outrun physical possibility, because electronic signals cannot generate explosions in phones not already packaged with explosive material. Worries about "cyber war" have spread with expressions like "cyber attack" and "cyber weapons."

These metaphors are misleading. Cyber operations are less like battlefield weapons and more like covert operations. In the last years of the Cold War, we might have directed a spy to seek secret data, say, regarding Soviet arms production. If that data were on a Moscow computer, the agent (or some insider he recruited to help) might download it onto discs, so the data could be transferred to the CIA. If the CIA wanted to make it hard for the Soviets to retrieve their own data, the agent might sabotage the Moscow computer to cause it to break down. If the CIA were particularly ingenious, it might try to confuse the Soviets by altering the data on the computers. Cyber attacks allow the United States to carry out the same infiltration, but without physically risking a covert agent inside the Kremlin.

What makes "cyber attacks" seem revolutionary is that they can strike from thousands of miles away. Computers connect to each other in local networks, as within a particular government agency. Networks connect to each other through the Internet. Hackers can infiltrate the communications between computers and networks to steal information or plant new programs that can disrupt the networks or direct computers to operate in new ways. An enemy can instantly attack any computer network linked to the Internet without ever leaving its territory.

The defense against hackers is analogous to the defense against spies. The target network can be programmed to exclude incoming messages that have suspicious electronic markings. Or it can be programmed so that only users with special user passwords can gain access. Computer security services can do periodic inspections to make sure there is nothing lurking in a particular computer or network. Still, as with security controls in the physical world, cyber defenses can be breached. With patience and ingenuity, determined hackers can often disguise their messages or work around security blocks to penetrate the target system.

That does not mean we will face apocalyptic dangers. To begin with, the hacking effects that are easiest to achieve rarely have very severe consequences. By far the most common aim is simply to copy information from targeted computers or computer networks. This is certainly a huge problem. Hackers in the service of foreign governments can penetrate computer networks to obtain government information, commercial trade secrets, and patented technology. Criminal gangs, sometimes with the encouragement of foreign states, seize personal information, such as credit card or bank account numbers, which may be used for criminal purposes. But serious as the problem may be, it is a high-tech version of espionage, which is not, in itself, regarded as comparable to a military "attack."

The next most common aim of hackers is to force a local network to shut down, known as a denial of service (DoS) attack. It can be achieved by overloading the system with incoming messages. The same result can be achieved by infiltrating malicious software into the target system. That can cause considerable inconvenience and, when the target is a private business, serious financial loss. But systems crash all the time, even without outside interference. In most cases, the victim can restore network operation within a few hours or a few days.

Is a temporary denial of service an "attack?" In 2007, in the midst of heightened tensions between Russia and Estonia, hackers shut down major public access websites maintained by the Estonian government. In some cases, the regular site was replaced by a mocking message placed there by the hackers. Still, the Russian-backed hacking did not kill or injure anyone, nor did it cause any physical destruction beyond the damage to the computer networks themselves. When Estonia alerted its NATO allies, they declined to characterize such vandalism as the sort of "attack" that would trigger military assistance under the NATO treaty.[17]

To be sure, worse things can happen. The so-called Shamoon attacks in 2012, which are thought to have been perpetrated by Iran, not only shut down thousands of computers in the offices of Saudi Aramco, but also wiped them clean of all data.[18] In 2014, North Korea apparently inflicted similar damage on Sony Pictures, which had produced a comic picture that satirized dictator Kim Jong-un.[19] It can be very costly and time-consuming to restore normal operations after cyber attacks on this scale. Still, it is not clear such disruptions and property damage should be characterized as "attacks" in the military sense. The attacks did not kill or injure anyone, nor did they cause any physical damage other than the disruption of normal computer operations or the theft of information.

Hacking can achieve even more destructive consequences. Instead of merely shutting down a computer system, hackers might seek to change its code so it operates in dysfunctional ways. Tampering with the computer programs that run complex industrial systems might have destructive consequences. A simulation by American security analysts showed that hackers could take control of a dam in Idaho.[20] The point was demonstrated in the real world with the so-called Stuxnet virus, which reset the spin rate of Iranian centrifuges without discovery by the system's monitoring programs. Ultimately several centrifuges broke apart.[21]

There are good reasons to doubt that even these cyber operations will produce the nightmares drawn by Richard Clarke and other alarmists. The first obstacle is the scale of the technical challenge. A hostile power cannot simply aim a general-purpose cyber weapon at a target system. To take control of a network, the hackers must custom design a special program to penetrate the system. The developers of the cyber weapon must have a detailed understanding of the network, which may take years of snooping inside that system. If the target is disconnected from the Internet, as the Iranian nuclear facility was, the attacker must infiltrate a closed local network. That may prove feasible, but it requires highly specialized and sophisticated intelligence, so that attackers can infiltrate the target system by way of other computers with which it may regularly interact.

The challenge is greater still if the aim is not simply to shut down the target system but to change its operations, as with Stuxnet. The hackers must then figure out how to disguise their program to evade detection by network security teams. The Stuxnet virus is reported to have taken four or five years and billions of dollars to develop. Among other things, the developers built their own model of the Iranian nuclear facility.[22] Stuxnet took over the supervisory control and data acquisition program (SCADA) of the Iranian centrifuges. As engineers have pointed out, "the complexity of SCADA systems is one of the best defenses against attack," because their complexity would prevent all but the most patient, expert, and highly informed hackers from redirecting their operations.[23]

To accomplish a doomsday scenario, an enemy would have to make a huge investment in research and development for each individual target. Enemies are not likely to build models of each mass transit system in the U.S. to work out the right attack program for the controls on that system. Even if they did, they could not expect that all of their efforts would go undetected. If even one such attack were detected or went off ahead of schedule, it would prompt immediate security checks on other transit systems. On the other hand, regular changes in the control systems, which might be updated for any number of reasons, could throw off years of preparation by the hackers. Achieving a simultaneous attack on a series of different targets would be an amazing feat of engineering and deception. Only a handful of states could spare the necessary resources to attempt such a cascade of destruction.

Apart from the technical challenge, there remains the practical question: Why would an adversary want to achieve such mass destruction effects through hacking? If the aim is to generate mass casualties, there are more direct and reliable ways. A hostile state could use ICBMs tipped with nuclear warheads to kill millions. By exploding a nuclear weapon in the atmosphere, an enemy could generate an electromagnetic pulse powerful enough to shut down electrical and communications networks. Aerial bombs and cruise missiles could destroy critical transportation nodes. Terrorists might even introduce poisons to a city water supply or disease agents in the food chain. The more catastrophic the desired effect of the attack, the less point there is to deliver it through computer networks.

Alarmist observers also do not explain why deterrence would not succeed with cyber weapons as it has with WMD. It is the announced policy of the United States government that it stands prepared to respond with "military force" to a cyber attack that causes loss of life or substantial damage to property.[24] The United States need not try to counter each cyber attack with a comparable response in cyber space. A cyber attack could well trigger kinetic retaliation from a wide range of conventional weapons that could cause worse damage to an enemy regime. Whatever one may think about the inherent logic of cyber deterrence, the record of experience suggests that something is at work. Since September 11, 2001 terrorist attacks have killed thousands of Americans, even within the boundaries of the United States. In the same period, there have been no U.S. fatalities attributable to cyber attacks.

But the logic ought to matter. Prominent analysts, looking at the limitations and potentialities of cyber attacks, have doubted that they will prove to be strategic weapons.

Thomas Rid, professor of War Studies at Kings College in London, sums up the case in the title of his 2013 book, *Cyber War Will Not Take Place*.[25] As a "weapon," he argues, hacking operations will be most effective when most specialized and targeted, which means no one attack is likely to have strategic consequences. But, Rid acknowledges, cyber attacks may be quite relevant as ancillary weapons, deployed for espionage, sabotage, or more limited interventions.

Stay Calm about Connectivity

Many commentators worry that, whatever their immediate destructiveness, cyber attacks remain especially dangerous because they are hard to track. The Internet is an immensely complex web of connections. Messages are routed automatically through available channels in this dense network. They may go halfway around the world before they are delivered to a neighboring state or a neighboring country. A sender who wants to disguise the origins can take control of a computer in a distant country and make it appear that this was the source of the hack. It is very difficult to respond when there is doubt about the source of an attack.

Analysts call this the "attribution problem." Even sober officials are concerned that attribution may interfere with the normal incentives behind deterrence. General Michael Hayden, former Director of the National Security Agency, warned in a 2011 essay that, "casually applying concepts from physical space like deterrence, where attribution is assumed, to cyberspace, where attribution is frequently *the* problem, is a recipe for failure."[26] A more recent study, *Cybersecurity and Cyberwar*, asserts that among "dimensions that make the cyber arena so challenging to secure...the most difficult problem is that of attribution."[27] The trouble with cyber intrusions is that they are spectral. We often can't tell where they have come from. We often don't know where they may go next. Cyber attacks may not be inherently more destructive than conventional weapons. But they are harder to identify. For alarmists, the attribution problem makes cyber warfare especially tempting for reckless governments or for terrorists. In Clarke's scenario, the president considers whether to retaliate for the cascade of horrors falling on American cities by ordering cyber command to "turn out the lights in Moscow" or "hit Beijing." But the president is paralyzed because it is not clear whether Russia or China is actually the power responsible for all of those attacks.[28]

There is some ground for this concern. Cyber attacks can be routed through a chain of computers in different countries.[29] Tracing the proximate source of an attack does not always indicate where it was actually planned, directed, or launched. Computers in the chain may be redirected, without the collaboration or even the awareness of their own operators. They can be made to perform certain commands in robotic fashion, working as "botnets." Determining who should finally be blamed for a cyber attack can prove a considerable technical challenge. In the episodes mentioned previously, such as the disruption of Estonian government websites, the Stuxnet disruption of Iran's nuclear program, the disruption of computers at Saudi Aramco, and the vandalism at Sony Pictures, no government officially acknowledged responsibility.[30]

When no attacker claims credit for a cyber attack, its attribution may be disputed. Residual uncertainties, however, need not prove an obstacle to deterrence. As in clandestine operations, non-avowal is not always about confusing the intended target. Israel's spy agency, Mossad, has tracked enemies to foreign capitals and killed them. It rarely acknowledges responsibility. Deniability gives diplomatic cover to host nations, which can claim to be "concerned" without having to strain their own relations with Israel. It may also make the intended targets and their organizations less certain about their safety and freedom to operate. The possibility of obscuring responsibility for lethal attacks has not emboldened governments to use assassination regularly around the world. Past a certain point, other states will insist on tearing off the pretense that they have "no idea" who may be responsible.[31]

As with kinetic attacks using bombs and bullets, attribution in the cyber realm is not an all or nothing enterprise. Analysts can assemble information that can identify the source of an attack with a fair degree of probability. They can compare characteristics of one attack with those of other attacks known to be associated with particular countries. Government agencies can assemble evidence from other sources (regarding the capacities and intentions of foreign powers) to compare with assessments by cyber specialists.[32] A state that is suspected of involvement can be pressed to cooperate with the investigation and much may be learned from how it responds, or how it does not.[33]

Concern over the attribution problem also ignores the purpose of the inquiry. Attribution is not for etiological analysis in a medical sense, let alone for adjudication of criminal guilt. If an attack causes enough damage, an investigation for national security purposes can proceed under the standard of a "preponderance of the evidence" or reasonableness, rather than the criminal justice system's "beyond a reasonable doubt."

Furthermore, the United States can hold nations liable for cyber attacks that originate on their territory. Just as they do with terror networks or militia groups, governments sometimes protect or work through hacker gangs, which commit cyber mischief to extort payments, perpetrate scams, or steal valuable information. The United States and other nations have long maintained the right to use force to stop attacks emanating from foreign countries, and to hold accountable the governments that refuse to stop them. In the wake of the 9/11 attacks, for example, the U.N. Security Council authorized an invasion of Afghanistan, even though the Taliban leadership was not accused of plotting the attacks. In the cybersphere, the United States could reasonably extend this claim to countries whose territory serves as a base for cyber attacks, which the host government will not help to control.[34]

The supposedly severe problem of attribution has not made cyber weapons attractive to the very actors most often desirous of secrecy. Terrorists groups depend on their ability to conceal their attacks and disguise their operations as normal civilian activity. Judging from experience to date, terrorists have not carried out destructive cyber attacks. A study by political scientists tracked "cyber incidents" between 2001 and 2011.[35] Almost all occupied the low end of the spectrum of destructive impact. Whether it was the "Cyber Gaza" group attacking websites in Israel or the "Syrian Electronic Army" (loyal to Assad) attacking websites in the U.S., the damage involved resembled vandalism more than serious injury.[36] And in the twenty interstate conflicts where cyber incidents occurred, traditional terror attacks (involving on-the-ground violence aimed at killing or wounding human beings) were almost 600 times more frequent than these cyber incidents.[37] "Terrorists" rely on "violence that instills a sense of fear and horror," writes a defense analyst. "To that end, terrorist attacks tend to be extremely violent, bloody, and photogenic. They want to hurt or kill their victims in a way that disturbs as many people as possible and is seen by as many people as possible."[38] Cyber attacks do not lend themselves to this strategy. Nor have terrorist groups been able or willing to invest the considerable resources required to execute the most fearful sorts of cyber attacks.[39]

While major states might be capable of concealing a major cyber attack, it is doubtful that they would rely on such tactics. For most purposes, an attacker will want the victim to know who delivered the attack. The point of an attack is to coerce an enemy so it ceases harmful conduct. In Clarke's hypothetical, Russia or China wish to inflict catastrophic harm on the United States, but anonymously. The question is why. For all the talk of a cyber Pearl Harbor, potential attackers will surely recall that the United States responded to the original Pearl Harbor attacks with a full-scale war that brought crushing defeat to the Japanese attackers in less than four years. It is conceivable that a reckless foreign leader would hope that mass casualties would so demoralize the United States that American public opinion would demand a wholesale repudiation of U.S. international commitments. Perhaps that foreign adventurer would hope that by concealing the source of the attack, his own country would escape American retaliation. But he could not, in fact, be sure that the United States would fail to penetrate his country's efforts at concealment. The broader the attack, the harder it would be to conceal.

Even if the United States did not immediately retaliate, it might plan future revenge and refuse to accept denials of responsibility. The risk, however, is not only that subsequent denials will be discounted. A confused America might lash out in the wrong direction. The United States might misunderstand the intended message which might be, for example, a Russian warning about American policy toward Ukraine or Syria. The misunderstanding might lead the United States to lash out against another state, without affecting the policies Russia had meant to protest. A mistaken attribution of a cyber attack might even lead to a destabilizing conflict elsewhere, that could prove counterproductive to Russia's aims. If there are potential benefits in anonymous cyber attacks, there are also great risks. It is hard to see why adversary powers would see the benefits exceeding the risks, especially when the attacks cause enough havoc to provoke the defender.

Some writers, however, dwell on the fear that cyber attacks and retaliation could spark a spiral of uncontrolled escalation that unleashes mass destruction. The underlying thought seems to be that cyber attacks always risk harm to unintended targets because of their unforeseen consequences.[40] The Stuxnet virus, for example, did not just cause Iranian nuclear centrifuges to crash, it also found its way into thousands of computers around the world. Hence, cyber weapons are likely to generate more harm than originally intended.

The concern is exaggerated. The rhetoric used to describe cyber attacks may heighten the sense of the risk, such as when analysts speak of computers as "infected" with a "virus." The biological metaphor is misleading. Humans have similar physical structures, which is not generally true of electronic control programs. A virus that interferes with respiration in one person is likely to restrict lung function for a great many others. But all computer systems do not possess the same "physiology" with slight variations. Systems are custom designed to do different things in different settings. A virus that successfully disrupts or redirects one network will not likely have the same effects against others. Researchers in Europe, analyzing software oddities circulating there, discovered the Stuxnet virus used to "infect" the Iranian nuclear program.[41] But the virus seems to have done no serious harm to anything other than the Iranian nuclear program. Its engineers specifically designed Stuxnet to disrupt specific machines controlled by German computer software. Stuxnet's sharp focus on the Iranian centrifuges rendered it harmless to other computer networks.

It is possible for a "virus" to disable the hardware elements of a network, as happened in the Shamoon attack. The effects of such an attack are costly, especially if they crash electric power supplies or delete important government data. But those well-known costs will encourage governments and corporations to back up valuable data in several places and build redundancies into vital control systems. Such safeguards would mean cyber attacks cause temporary inconvenience, but are not likely to cause widespread, permanent damage. If an attacker wants to turn off the lights everywhere, there are easier ways than cyber-based attacks.

Alarms over shutting down computer networks overlook their resiliency. Computers are immensely complicated and hence inherently temperamental. Designers of computer systems have always known that. At any one time, some computers in commercial networks may be experiencing technical difficulties—as air travelers know from experience trying to acquire boarding passes from "self-help" kiosks.[42] Network designers build their systems to work even when significant portions of the hardware and software go offline. Such resiliency would pose a serious obstacle to the success of a cyber attack. As new risks become known, network engineers will build in more robust defenses.

Finally, even if nations could build cyber weapons that could shut down networks on a large scale, they may never use them. Such a weapon could be equally dangerous for the attacker as for the defender if its effects spread beyond the target system. The more networked an attacker's economy and military, the more exposed it will be to such harms. Even if the attacker could deploy a prophylactic defense for its own computers, it would still need those computers to communicate with external networks in other countries. A world paralyzed by computer problems would prevent the attacking nation from reaping the benefits of the Internet. Unless it were prepared to isolate itself from the world economy for a lengthy period of time, a nation would not likely deploy an all-destructive cyber weapon.

To think of cyber as a weapon of mass destruction is like noticing that a laptop computer is light enough to swing, while also encased in unyielding metal, and then to conclude that a laptop computer is well suited to deploy as a war club. That conclusion is not demonstrably false. But it misses the main point. The most attractive aspect of cyber operations from a tactical standpoint is that they can be customized, allowing attacks to be highly focused and ratcheted up or dialed back, according to circumstances. Their most effective use is when they are used for espionage and covert action goals, rather than strategic strikes. Their military value will come as an aid to other forms of hostilities, such as diplomatic and economic pressure or kinetic attacks. Cyber weapons have far more value as a more precisely tuned means of coercion between nations, rather than as a weapon of mass destruction.

International Rules and Cyber Weapons

Anxieties that "cyber war" may get out of control have encouraged efforts to use law to constrain it. Proposals for new international treaties—a nostrum urged by Richard Clarke, for example—have not gained much support. Nevertheless, prominent scholars and government officials have been quick to argue that existing international law already imposes extensive controls on cyber operations. But, as we will show, they improperly assume that AP I and novel notions of international humanitarian law automatically apply to cyber warfare as they do to ground warfare. The major powers do not agree on any norms to restrain cyber warfare. As we have argued earlier, the history of technology and war suggest that nations will not agree to significant limits until they have gained experience with the weapons and understand their strategic implications.

Some restraints on cyber conflict may seem obvious. Hacking the controls of an air traffic control system could result in thousands of civilian deaths from air crashes. That looks like wanton murder. If such an attack were launched without warning, it could rightly be seen as an act of aggression, justifying fierce retaliation. Even if undertaken during a conflict, attacks that directly threatened the life and limb of large numbers of civilians would surely violate any understanding of applicable laws of armed conflict.

But to go much beyond that would require speculation beyond experience. In the past, nations governed military operations in different domains with different rules. War at sea had different rules from war on land. At sea, it was lawful to raid enemy shipping, even if merchant ships were carrying entirely civilian cargoes for purely commercial purposes. There was a duty to protect the lives of enemy sailors and passengers, so far as possible, but not to safeguard civilian property (nor return it when seized as a prize of war). In the world wars of the twentieth century, blockades tried to prevent all shipping into enemy territory. Even outside the context of war, nations could use their naval forces to attack another state's commercial shipping as a reprisal or to impose a "pacific blockade" of a major port as a sanction.[43]

Efforts to codify the law of war in the twentieth century acknowledged that different rules should continue to govern different realms of combat. The Hague Conventions of 1899 and 1907 expressly regulated war on land, while different rules were crafted (in 1907) for war at sea.[44] The 1949 Geneva Conference produced different conventions for shipwrecked sailors and for wounded combatants on land. Even AP I acknowledges that its rules do not apply to conflict on the sea.[45] Naval combat should have different rules because collateral damage is less likely or extensive on the high seas. Due to the vast spaces of the oceans, few people are traveling on any part of the ocean at any one time. An attack on a particular building might threaten neighboring buildings, including private homes. An attack on one ship does not usually threaten others. It is also easier, at least in principle, for an attacker to distinguish the character of a ship from brief inspection, based on what flag it flies, whether it is armed, and what cargo it could carry. On land, an attacker cannot know as much about all the individuals who might be in harm's way.

The differences in combat environments demand differences in their regulation. A land army usually relies on civilian cooperation or has to fear civilian resistance in ways that ships at sea do not. There are special rules for occupied territory that do not apply to armies in combat on the front lines. In naval war, all the high seas may be potential scenes of combat, but the rules are supposed to assure that neutral shipping can move freely through the same waters.[46]

Cyber does not fit cleanly into the models governing land, sea, or air. One might think it shares characteristics with the high seas, because cyber weapons may roam through international networks before targeting a particular computer network without interfering with other Internet activities. Or one might think it is its own domain, as implied by the U.S. government's decision to establish a cyber command, separate from existing army, navy, and air force commands. The Defense Department's Law of War Manual seems to take the latter approach. It declines to apply rules of land warfare directly or mechanically to the cyber domain. Instead, the DoD recognizes that some cyber operations "may not have a clear kinetic parallel in terms of their capabilities and the effects they create. Such operations may have implications that are quite different from those presented by attacks using traditional weapons and those different implications may well yield different conclusions."[47]

Most legal analysts, however, have gone to considerable lengths to assimilate cyber capabilities to rules that are supposed to apply to land warfare. In particular, they apply rules from AP I as the most extensive compilation of rules in this area. Articles on the law of cyber warfare have taken this view since the mid-1990s and more recent works have borrowed these assumptions.[48] Most notably, this approach appears in specialized, book-length treatises that have appeared in the last few years.

The most prominent such guidebook was composed by a group of experts on law of war issues, meeting in the Estonian capital of Tallinn, under the aegis of NATO's "Cyber Defence Centre of Excellence." Known as the Tallinn Manual, this book is not a treaty, nor even an official guidance document for NATO forces.[49] A first edition appeared in 2013. The second edition, published in 2017, is twice as long, partly from inclusion of some new topics but mostly from the addition of qualifications and refinements in its comments on the 154 "rules" it finds already governing "cyber operations." The Tallinn Manual assumes that AP I rules constitute obligatory standards for the conduct of all military operations, including cyber. "The law of armed conflict applies to cyber operations undertaken in the context of armed conflict," the Manual declares.[50] The Tallinn Manual also takes a restrictive view of *jus ad bellum* under the U.N. Charter. Citing a decision of the International Court of Justice (a decision repudiated by the U.S. at the time), it reads the Charter as prohibiting any resort to "force," even in response to unlawful attacks, so long as the latter do not rise to the level of an "armed attack" in the sense of Art. 51.[51]

Recent treatises by European scholars Heather Harrison Dinniss in 2012 and Marco Roscini in 2014 have also tried to synthesize the extensive literature in this field into definite rules.[52] They embrace much the same views as the Tallinn Manual, which means they assume away the most important questions in a field that has just opened.

First is the question of when a cyber attack is justified. These commentaries take for granted that the U.N. Charter governs cyber attacks. As we explained in chapter 2, the strictest interpretation of the Charter maintains that nations can use force in "self-defense" only "when an armed attack occurs" or when authorized by the Security Council.[53] One of the most prominent commentators on the U.N. Charter, Bruno Simma, argues that the Charter only allows states to use force to resist a cyber attack while it is in progress.[54] Simma acknowledges that this rule might close the window for a response to no more than a few minutes or seconds, which might often be too little time to determine the source. While they do not go to such extremes, other treatises join Simma in trying to articulate similar constraints on cyber attacks. But imposing a broad ban on cyber attacks would seem to imply a correspondingly broad scope for using cyber operations in "self-defense." If a nation violates the ban on the threat or use of force, it might seem to follow that the defender could use cyber weapons in self-defense. These authors, however, seek to prohibit cyber attacks in responding to limited provocations. They claim the U.N. Charter only allows force in responding to an "armed attack" and not what the Charter describes as "threat or use of force." On this theory, an attack could be a violation of the U.N. Charter but still not trigger a right to use force in response.

Such distinctions make intuitive sense in some areas (detaining a foreign merchant ship in port on questionable pretexts might seem to be a use of "force" but not perhaps the sort of thing that would automatically warrant a military response from the ship's home state). The distinctions are harder to apply to cyber intrusions. The Tallinn Manual does acknowledge that the United States rejects this distinction—between prohibited uses of force in general and uses of force so severe as to justify a forcible response.[55] But rather than endorse or defend the American view, it goes to some trouble to adopt the alternative view. The Tallinn Manual notes that a succession of attacks, even if individually below the threshold of force justifying self-defense, might be rightly considered a sufficient attack in the aggregate. But it then qualifies this rule by insisting that the "smaller-scale incidents" must be "related."[56] It gives further bite to this requirement by stipulating an element of "immediacy" for the period when a victim "may reasonably respond in self-defense,"[57] which would seem to preclude the aggregation of well-spaced attacks into a "related" provocation. The Manual further subordinates these fine distinctions to a broader rule that a state may not even threaten cyber retaliation unless "the threatened action is in itself lawful."[58] These legal ambiguities may have the effect of paralyzing a state with a high regard for legal technicalities from using its cyber weapons as a deterrent.

The abstractness of these analyses is occasionally tempered by concrete examples, without at all clarifying the resulting "law." What about an "attack on a major international stock exchange that causes the market to crash"? The experts responsible for the Tallinn Manual could not reach an agreement on how to characterize such an event because some "were not satisfied that mere financial loss constitutes damage for this purpose."[59] With regard to Stuxnet, the group of experts "was divided as to whether the damage sufficed to meet the armed [attack] criterion."[60] The Tallinn Manual does not even attempt to analyze whether the threat posed by the Iranian nuclear program was sufficient to justify the cyber attack. Roscini suggests that the Stuxnet operation involved enough force to be a violation of the U.N. Charter and may have violated the rule against attacking civilian objects.[61] While noting the "decidedly muted" international response, Dinniss is unsure whether the hesitation to condemn Stuxnet reflects a judgment that the worm did not constitute "force" or that it "merely [reflected] satisfaction at the outcome... regardless of its legal nature."[62] Dinniss does not dare to contemplate that international "satisfaction" might indicate that states believed Stuxnet to be legal.

It may be understandable that experts on the law of armed conflict do not want to divert their inquiry into fundamental questions, where they cannot find consensus. But the effort to fit cyber within existing boxes means that basic issues drop from sight. On the question of justification, for example, further questions arise on the application of cyber to humanitarian intervention. The treatises do not dig deeply, when they notice these questions at all. The Tallinn Manual notes, in one paragraph, that its "International Group of experts was divided over" the legality of "cyber operations in support of a humanitarian intervention...."[63] Dr. Roscini notes in passing that the International Criminal Tribunal for the former Yugoslavia (ICTY) approved the NATO bombing of Serbian broadcasting towers because, in Rwanda, state radio had been used to "incite" the population to commit genocide. But Roscini accurately observes that the ICTY's reasoning was not consistent with AP I, because "propaganda or incitement to commit crimes do not amount to 'effective contribution to military action.'"[64] He fails to ask whether AP I should be disregarded in such circumstances or read to allow a reasonable exception to prevent genocide.

These scholars also give short shrift to the fundamental questions on targeting. They do engage in an extensive discussion of requirements under AP I. But they fail to ask whether the same principles of distinction and proportionality apply to cyber weapons. To start with the most obvious difficulty, AP I imposes a stringent definition of military targets permissible to attack. The only objects that qualify are those that "make an effective contribution to military action" so that their "total or partial destruction, capture or neutralization, *in the circumstances ruling at the time*, offers a definite *military* advantage."[65] Our scholars don't admit the difficulty that, in an exchange of cyber attacks, a cyber attack on an enemy's conventional military assets would not at all prevent it from launching new cyber attacks.

Cyber attacks don't rely on a stockpile of cyber weapons conveniently stored in a cyber-weapon arsenal. The defending side might identify the particular computers used to launch an attack, but shutting them down would not prevent the enemy launching new attacks from other computers. The attacking state might not have had the courtesy to label its hacking squads as fully or officially "military" or house them in a government facility. According to AP I, where there is doubt whether a "civilian object" is "being used to make an effective contribution to military action [and so eligible for attack], it shall be presumed not to be so used."[66]

The defending side could try to block all Internet traffic into the attacking state. It is not certain whether this would be technically feasible or reliably effective, given various means to reroute traffic through third parties. But if feasible, it might seem to be prohibited by AP I's rules against disproportionate damage to "civilian objects" and against targeting that is inherently indiscriminate.[67] The Tallinn Manual, for example, stipulates that shutting down a network shared with civilians could be unlawful, "in much the same way that area bombing [of entire cities] is impermissible."[68] It also warns that depriving civilians of Internet access could be considered a form of unlawful "collective punishment," prohibited by AP I and, in narrower circumstances, earlier conventions.[69] Recall that the U.N. Charter empowers the Security Council to impose "complete interruption of . . . rail, sea, postal, telegraphic, radio, or other means of communication" to pressure a state, and it characterizes sanctions as "measures not involving the use of armed force."[70] But now academic or expert guardians of the law of armed conflict see even the deprivation of Internet access as an impermissible brutality.

If a hostile state disregards these restrictions, the obvious answer, in earlier times, would have been retaliation in kind. The Tallinn Manual warns that while earlier conventions prohibited particular kinds of reprisal (against prisoners, medical facilities, etc.), AP I prohibits reprisals against all "civilian objects" and "civilians" generally.[71] Although noting that some parties to AP I filed reservations against this blanket prohibition, the Manual warns that the ICTY has claimed that the prohibition against all forms of reprisal against civilians has now become customary law, binding on all states.[72]

The dispute about the legality of reprisal actions reflects the overall character of these efforts. There is almost no state practice in this area. States have yet to publicly affirm that they have refrained to use cyber weapons out of a sense of legal obligation. Conclusions offered by expert commentators amount to little more than speculation, extrapolation, and disputable judgments about analogies that should apply. At the same time, these same expert commentators consciously ignore the fundamental questions over whether the laws of war should apply to cyber in the same way as to ground, air, or sea operations. Roscini, for example, concludes that AP I "prohibits belligerent reprisals against 'civilian population, individual civilians, civilian objects....'" He mentions the complications only in passing in a footnote.[73] Dinniss does not mention the difficulties of cyber weapons and civilians at all. Anyone who relied on these commentaries would likely think that international law already forbids interference with civilian websites, computer controls, or access to the Internet, regardless of ongoing state practice to the contrary.

If the purpose is to help states avoid violating the law, these scholarly strictures will, almost certainly, spread wider bans than the law requires. That might seem reasonable if the object is to "stay on the safe side" of legal limits. But it is not obvious why it would be safer to refrain from using new technologies when they might actually help us secure a safer world.

Reasonable Applications

In 2007, Israeli jets destroyed a nuclear research facility in Syria without encountering any resistance. It's obvious why Israel attacked. The interesting question is why Syria failed to mount a defense. It is now part of the lore of cyber war that Israel used cyber intrusion to disable the Syrian air defense system in a way that did not alert its military controllers in Damascus.[74] This episode illustrates an important way in which cyber attacks can contribute to the success of a conventional military attack.

This very episode, however, illustrates the reasons that cyber attacks will not replace conventional weapons. Israel's attack succeeded because it only needed to disable Syrian detection systems long enough for one bombing raid. By the time the Syrians figured out what had happened, it was too late. In all likelihood, top officials immediately understood that Israel had already destroyed Syria's nuclear facility. Assad's government did not make any public protest. It may have wanted to deflect attention from its nuclear program. It probably understood that the Israeli strike was a one-time event.

The episode was unusual in a number of ways. Israel attacked as soon as it disabled the Syrian air-defense system. Its cyber attack only needed to remain effective through the duration of one bombing mission. Israel's cyber action opened a window of opportunity but probably did not have an enduring effect on the Syrian air-defense system, nor was it responsible for directly destroying Syria's nuclear plant. It was not preparing the way for a larger or longer military campaign. If Israel planned to disable Syrian military defenses in advance of a larger intervention, it would have needed to launch a much more intensive cyber attack, which might then have been detected and countered.

Israel's successful cyber attack also highlights the temporary effects of the weapons. It is much easier to shut down an enemy's computer system for a short time than to permanently disable it. Usually, technicians can isolate the infiltrated code that causes affected computers to malfunction. The code or program can then be removed and the computers returned to normal operation. Even if the hardware is damaged, computers can be replaced. Engineers on the defending side will be more likely to limit the damage when they have been alerted to hostile designs. An initial attack, even if it achieves a temporary disruption may make it harder to penetrate defenses in the future. The attacker may learn about the target system from an initial probe, but the defending side can also make changes in response, rendering a future attack less effective. Defenders can most easily detect and guard against the infiltration of codes that have already been used in previous attacks. The more novel and elaborate the new weapon, the more the attacker will hesitate to use it, because once it has been used, defenders will be able to prepare for it in the future.

Nations cannot simply stockpile the most effective cyber weapons, and then use them repeatedly in the course of a long conflict. In a major conflict, the single-use nature of cyber weapons may generate pressure to deploy them early, before an enemy can develop defenses. A similar dynamic affected nuclear deterrence. Ground-based ICBMs with multiple warheads were the most vulnerable to a first strike, because their locations were well known, easy to target, and promised the destruction of several enemy nuclear weapons in a single attack. Such weapons could have encouraged a use-it-or-lose-it attitude early in a conflict. But an all-out war with nuclear missiles still risked frightful outcomes that deterred any direct war between the great powers for more than 70 years. Major powers may also restrain themselves in the use of the most destructive cyber weapons for similar reasons.

Major powers might still have good reasons to deploy substantial cyber attacks in lesser conflicts. One obstacle, however, would be a strict approach to the laws of war. Suppose an unfriendly state launches cyber attacks that harm the U.S. banking system. We would certainly recover from such a blow, but only with some delay and cost. Or suppose the provocation were delivered by more conventional means, such as the seizure of U.S. shipping, or the sponsorship of a terror attack on U.S. personnel within the country or abroad. Depending on the circumstances, a precisely targeted cyber attack might provide a tactically superior response than a response with conventional weapons.

If it does sufficient damage, however, commentators would consider the cyber response equivalent to an "armed attack" and therefore bound by the principle of distinction. On this understanding, the U.S. would have to limit its attack to "military objectives." As noted above, AP I defines a "military objective" as one whose destruction or neutralization "in the circumstances ruling at the time offers a definite military advantage."[75] Retaliation against a computer operations center in the attacking state might not offer any "definite military advantage," given that computer technicians can readily shift their operations to other computers in other locations. The AP I formula does not fit the circumstances of conflicts pursued by hackers wielding malicious computer codes.

On the other hand, a broader attack on the target state's computer networks might give rise to unique dangers. A defender might misread a limited attack on a military control system as a prelude to a broader assault. The discovery that an opponent had tried to disable computer networks in a military installation might provoke an overreaction. Commanders might assume this discovery revealed the imminence of a full-scale military attack. They might worry that the advantages of striking first would go to the enemy unless they acted preemptively. Or they might believe that an attack on some aspects of a control system might be followed by interference with military communications, making it difficult to command conventional assets in defense. Actual interference with command and control systems might make it difficult to reach every ship, airfield, or missile base. These factors might contribute to a rapid escalation in the level of violence.

There were similar concerns about nuclear weapons during the Cold War. To address them, the United States and the Soviet Union exchanged information about the methods of control over nuclear weapons in order to reduce the risk of stumbling into war accidentally. The two sides engaged in candid discussions about ways to improve command

and control of launch sites. We did not want to undermine the Kremlin's control of its missiles, but instead wanted to assure the U.S.S.R.'s leaders that their control was reliable.[76] The great powers would want to be very cautious about launching a cyber attack on the military computer networks of a hostile state, for fear that it would be seen as a prelude to a broad-based conventional or even nuclear attack.

If we were actually on the brink of large-scale military operations, we might think it worth taking the risks of using the full range of cyber attacks on an enemy's military networks. There would be obvious advantages. Cyber weapons can disrupt command and control systems. They can interfere with intelligence and reconnaissance. They can make it difficult for national commanders to receive an accurate picture of the battlefield and respond accordingly. They can prevent enemy units from coordinating their actions and might disable or degrade the effectiveness of their weapons systems.

If the aim is to retaliate for a hostile attack in a limited way, while limiting the risk of escalation to all-out confrontation, it might be much more prudent to launch cyber attacks on civilian infrastructure. The point is occasionally acknowledged in public. In October 2016, Philip Hammond, then Britain's Chancellor of the Exchequer, urged the development of an offensive cyber capability for exactly this purpose. "If we do not have the ability to respond in cyberspace to an attack which takes down our [electric] power networks, leaving us in darkness, or hits our air traffic control system, grounding our planes, we would be left with the impossible choice of turning the other cheek and ignoring the devastating consequences, or resorting to a military response," he said. "That is why we need to develop a fully functioning and operational cyber counter-attack capability."[77]

Cyber attacks could provide the means of responding to asymmetric attacks, even those that do not fall on computer networks. Opponents that cannot confront the United States directly on a battlefield might adopt unconventional tactics to harm the U.S., such as by guerrilla or terrorist attacks. The United States might hesitate to respond with conventional military attacks for fear of escalating the conflict. But the U.S. may still find it valuable to impose costs on the sponsoring state. A cyber strike might cut electric power in the target state for a few days or shut down its cell-phone network to dramatize the regime's vulnerability. Such action would not, by itself, prevent a hostile state like Iran from continuing to fund and supply terror networks. Here again, some analysts might regard the response as inconsistent with the requirements of AP I's definition of "military objectives." But such attacks might deter future attacks with less risk of escalation than an alternative response with conventional weapons.

Viewed from this perspective, focusing cyber attacks on civilian infrastructure might serve the ultimate aims of humanitarian law. Attacking military assets might be more likely to provoke the target state to retaliate with conventional weapons. By contrast, an attack on civilian infrastructure might reassure a hostile regime that the U.S. does not seek its destruction by eviscerating its capacity to defend itself. We may be more likely to avoid stumbling into all-out war precisely by signaling our willingness to respond to provocations in only limited ways. For this purpose, cyber technology offers many advantages. It can be precisely targeted in space and in time. We can often paralyze the operating component of a network in a way that is reversible, given time. Stuxnet, for example, ceased operating on a definite date.[78] A cyber attack can be annoying and distracting, even unsettling, without necessarily inducing the sort of rage or panic that rushes governments into all-out conflict.[79] This does not mean cyber attacks on civilian targets present no risks. But cyber attacks might involve risks that are more contained.

At the least, it is valuable to have a wider range of options in the use of force. As long ago as the late 1990s, the Defense Department gave consideration to using cyber intrusions to prevent Serb dictator Slobodan Milosevic from gaining access to his bank accounts.[80] Apparently, the idea was rejected for fear of provoking foreign attacks on the U.S. banking system or setting a precedent for such attacks in the future. Similar schemes for seizing Saddam Hussein's personal fortune were considered and rejected at the outset of the 2003 Gulf War.[81] But more recently, attacks on banks under ISIS control seem to have been considered acceptable.[82] Seizing a regime leader's personal assets could raise the costs on an authoritarian enemy without directly harming the civilians under its control, in contrast to the usual effects of economic sanctions, which hurt the population but not the leaders.

Cyber weapons may have the additional advantage of operating behind the scenes. An authoritarian regime might be reluctant to retreat in the face of a public challenge from American arms. The same leader might be much more inclined to concede to pressure that was not publicly known. Cyber threats can be delivered to the top commanders or political leaders in an authoritarian regime. Such measures do not have to provoke an actual coup to have useful effects. Merely sowing mutual doubts at the highest levels of a hostile regime may have an inhibiting effect on its actions.

Conversely, public cyber attacks may lead a population to question its leadership. If electricity, cell-phone service, or radio or TV broadcasts fail for a few days, the entire country will become aware that the regime is losing. That lesson can be valuable, even if it does not spark riots or rebellion. Authoritarian regimes tend to be sensitive to anything that threatens their control, which is why they do not allow free debate, let alone free elections. So what might seem merely annoying to a democracy might seem much more threatening to an authoritarian regime. Officials at U.S. Cyber Command have been quite reticent about uttering public threats or even clarifications of what sorts of interventions are now technically feasible. Some senior military commanders have warned that deterrence requires more explicit statements of the threat to retaliate.[83]

But critics worry that by deploying cyber attacks against foreign countries, we will invite reciprocal attacks against the United States. They warn that the United States and its allies have more to lose, because our societies are much more dependent on computer networks. It is far too late, however, to hope for a general abstention from such attacks or even a fragile cyber cease-fire. Foreign states, notably Russia, China, Iran, and North Korea, have already conducted or sponsored malicious hacking against American government agencies and businesses for two decades. General Keith Alexander, former head of the U.S. National Security Agency, called the theft of trade secrets and patents from U.S. corporations the "greatest transfer of wealth in history," estimating costs to U.S. companies from such thefts at $250 billion with another $114 billion in related expenses.[84] Foreign hackers have infiltrated computers in the Department of Defense, the State Department, and many other U.S. government agencies.[85]

A second consideration is that, despite the scale of these disruptions, foreign hackers have not generated fatal results. There seems to be an implicit agreement that hacking that damages property is different from hacking that causes loss of life or limb. Perhaps we have been lucky. Or perhaps when it comes to cyber attacks that generate casualties equivalent to terrorism, the threat to retaliate need not be very explicit. So far, rival states seem to think the rules of the game allow for a good deal of malicious intrusion, so long as it does not involve bloodletting.

A related point is that if we are afraid to embrace cyber attacks as a form of retaliation or pressure, we either resort to more destructive measures, such as bombardment with conventional weapons, or we remain passive. Both of these alternatives pose serious risks. The appeal of cyber weapons is that nations can more precisely control the harms. With many kinds of cyber attack, the results can be temporary and the damage quickly restored. Cyber attacks may be much more appropriate for times when we want to register protest or inflict costs, but are prepared to back off when satisfied. It is also worth recalling that cyber incursions can gain information without doing any harm to the computers or physical network. Even the cautious international experts behind the Tallinn Manual are in agreement that stealing information is not an act of force.[86] In fact, espionage is not in itself contrary to international law, though it is, of course, punished under a nation's domestic law.[87]

Americans no longer need to be reminded of the damage that can result from a cyber attack, though we do need to see it in better perspective. Russian hackers gained access to the email traffic of the Democratic National Committee in 2016 and released it to the general public via Wikileaks.[88] This may have hurt the public image of the Democratic presidential candidate Hillary Clinton. There is cosmic irony in the fact that the candidate herself had been negligent in protecting U.S. secrets as Secretary of State, by transmitting classified information on an unsecured private server.[89] But the DNC emails did not include any notable bombshells about the personal conduct of the candidate. If they hurt Clinton's image, it was by confirming her staff as people who were dismissive or condescending toward ordinary voters and unscrupulous about the contest for the Democratic nomination. In fact, the leaked emails did not offer any important information not already available from ordinary leaks to the press.

In a contest between efforts to guard secrets and schemes to uncover and reveal secrets, the United States has important advantages over authoritarian rivals. People in free societies may prize their privacy but the outlines of their lives are hard to conceal. In the United States, a great deal of personal data, including records of arrests, civil litigation, and debt problems, can be gleaned from specialized websites. In authoritarian countries, information about leaders is closely guarded, often along with access to foreign news. Cyber interventions might accomplish much by uncovering information about the private lives of leaders in authoritarian countries.

In October 2012, for example, *The New York Times* published a story about the private fortunes and high living of relatives of Chinese premier Wen Jiabao. It provoked protest from the Chinese government and efforts to suppress dissemination of the articles within China. The following June, *Bloomberg News* followed up with stories on the private wealth of other Chinese leaders, including the new Communist party chief, Xi Jinping. The Chinese government apparently hacked a series of American news outlets in retaliation.[90] To keep such stories from reaching ordinary Chinese, the government in Beijing imposes elaborate controls on access to outside Internet sites. But in various ways, technical specialists in the West might help dissidents in authoritarian countries to receive and share such sensitive reports.

Such efforts might be applied even to terror networks. In the 1950s, Britain's anti-insurgency campaign against Communist terror networks in Malaya publicized accounts of Communist leaders frolicking with their girlfriends, which seems to have generated much resentment amidst the austerity of life in the ranks.[91] Cyber surveillance increases the capacity to gather such discrediting information. Modern technology also multiplies channels for disseminating such information. The British in Malaya had to rely on dropping paper leaflets into the jungle, often using comic-style graphics for the illiterate. During the Cold War, American-sponsored programs like Radio Free Europe and Radio Martí (aimed at Cuba) supported dissidents and unsettled regime supporters. Cyber infiltration offers many more opportunities to find and share politically subversive information.

Overheated alarms about reciprocal attack might inhibit western leaders from using cyber tools that are particularly effective against terrorist groups and insurgencies. Terrorist groups such as al-Qaeda and ISIS rely upon the Internet to organize their agents in the West and to encourage homegrown terrorists to attack. They use social media to communicate with members, attract new followers, and publicize their alleged victories. Information warfare can extend to interfering with terror websites, planting embarrassing information, making it dangerous to lurk, and making it clear that the webmasters are vulnerable. U.S. agents also might allow such sites to appear undisturbed in order to monitor activities of unwary sympathizers.[92] The appeal of cyber intrusions is that they are not all or nothing: There may be value in interfering with some sites, even while leaving others undisturbed.

On projects that deal with the dissemination of information, the private sector may have much to contribute. Every day the American private sector generates a new "app" that allows people to do something—call a car service, arrange a private apartment rental, or summon delivery of a food order—which they couldn't previously do so well or do at all. Much of the time, consumers could not have appreciated the benefit of the new technology before it was demonstrated to them. What's true when it comes to improving life is also true for techniques of harassment, retaliation, and distraction. Cyber technology has many more applications than we now recognize. Surely, we should be experimenting to discover options, even if we choose not to deploy them. And we should find ways to engage the inventive genius of the private sector, which, in contrast to many other fields of defense, does not require vast subsidies to maintain itself.

Conclusions

Cyber technology has roused more alarm and panic than other new weapons. Government officials and scholars warn of an "Electronic Pearl Harbor" in language usually associated with weapons of mass destruction. Nations certainly are extending their rivalries to cyberspace. China has stolen the U.S. government personnel database, Russia has launched denial of service attacks against Ukraine and the Baltic states, and the United States likely used a computer virus to delay the Iranian nuclear program. Claims that Russia interfered with the 2016 U.S. presidential elections continue to beset American politics. Undoubtedly, hostile nations have launched further cyber attacks that have not yet come to light.

But the emergence of a new field for great power rivalry does not mean that an apocalypse is on the way. Commentators have widely exaggerated the capabilities of cyber weapons. Stealing information or interfering with computer networks, while a serious problem, amounts to high-tech espionage more than military attack. Cyber operations can launch highly focused attacks that are most effective for espionage and covert action, rather than strategic strikes. Cyber weapons have far more value as an aid to other forms of hostilities, such as diplomatic and economic pressure, and ultimately as a more precisely tuned means of coercion. Efforts to ban or heavily regulate cyber weapons cannot yet succeed because nations still have little experience with their effects. Claims that the laws of war already place severe limits on cyber attacks may amount to wishful thinking. In the meanwhile, such claims may have the counterproductive effect of discouraging reasonable uses of cyber weapons to replace more destructive and less reversible methods of attack. It makes little sense to refrain from using new technologies when they might actually help secure a safer world.

CHAPTER 7

Coercion in Space

Control of space underlies the United States' predominant position in world affairs. Communications satellites provide the high-speed data transfer that stitches the U.S. Armed Forces together, from generals issuing commands to pilots controlling drones. Other satellites monitor rival nations for missile launches, strategic deployments, or troop movements. America's nuclear deterrent itself uses space: land- or sea-based ballistic missiles leave and then reenter the atmosphere, giving them a global reach that is difficult to defend against.

Since the end of the Cold War, space-based military systems have come to exert a more direct terrestrial impact. The global positioning system (GPS) allows U.S. aircraft, naval vessels, and ground units to locate their whereabouts and to direct their fire with precision. The stunning speed of the initial invasion of Iraq in 2003, like the earlier triumph of the Persian Gulf War in 1991, demonstrates the lethal success of military operations that integrate satellite communications and information gathering. The drone campaign against terrorist leaders in the Middle East and Pakistan depends on satellites to locate targets, conduct real-time surveillance, and then control the fire systems of the drones.

The future holds even more advances in store. Building on precision-guided munitions, the U.S. Defense Department is developing a "prompt global strike" system that will use GPS satellites to guide hypersonic missiles, armed with conventional warheads, to targets anywhere in the world within an hour.[1] More exotic versions envision bombardments from orbital platforms using rods, which would generate their explosive force purely from the kinetic energy created by their high terminal velocity upon reentering the atmosphere. American planners speculate that such systems could replace the need for tactical nuclear weapons because of their combination of precision, speed, and destructive potential.

Space-based weapons will not only appear in offensive operations. In 2002, the Bush administration formally terminated the Anti-Ballistic Missile Treaty with Russia, which had prohibited the development of space-based anti-missile systems. Washington soon developed a National Missile Defense system that seeks to intercept ballistic missiles in mid-flight using sophisticated satellite detectors, ground-based radar, and interceptors launched from land. In the past year, the U.S. Department of Defense accounted for an estimated 69 percent of global defense-related expenditures on its space security programs.[2]

Civilian networks similarly depend on space. GPS has transformed the transportation industry. Navigation products allow for quicker driving for individual cars, more efficient cargo transport by trucks, rail, and ships, and fuel-saving routes for airplanes. Autonomous cars, ride-sharing, and delivery services similarly rely on GPS. Other satellites predict the weather, while yet others transmit communications and data. Private industry has also begun to exploit the commercial potential of space. The space economy is now estimated to be a $330 billion global commercial enterprise, $251 billion of which is contributed by private commercial actors, with the rest of the revenue being generated by government spending.[3] The U.S. Defense Department relies on commercial satellites for about 40 percent of its communication needs.[4] The idea of sending civilians into space is even beginning to take flight. Elon Musk's SpaceX has developed rockets to transport cargo to the International Space Station, while Virgin Galactic is already selling seats for space tourism.

While space-based systems enhance military operations and civilian networks, they also expose vulnerabilities. Anti-satellite missiles could shut down a nation's communications networks. Directed beam or radiation weapons could cripple a GPS system, paralyzing transportation networks. Enemy destruction of a nation's reconnaissance satellites would blind its strategic monitoring and degrade its operational and tactical abilities. Space especially invites asymmetric warfare because anti-satellite attacks could even the technological odds against western powers that have developed information-enhanced operations.

The potential for space warfare has led to calls to ban the "militarization" of space. Such efforts began as early as the Outer Space Treaty of 1967, which declares its purpose "to promote international co-operation in the peaceful exploration and use of outer space."[5] The Treaty forbids the stationing of nuclear weapons (and other WMD) in orbit and bans military installations or operations on the moon and other celestial bodies.[6] The Treaty also forbids any nation from claiming sovereignty over the moon and planets or even the space above their territory (unlike airspace, for example). Ever since, some have argued that space must be an arms-free zone, and any use of space for military purposes, even non-aggressive ones, violates international law.[7] The United Nations General Assembly has repeatedly passed resolutions "to prevent an arms race in outer space."[8] Some scholars argue that the U.N. Charter's ban on the use of force, except for self-defense or Security Council authorization, must also apply to outer space.[9] They hope that international agreements and cooperation can head off the U.S. and other great powers from their quests for military supremacy in space. "The United States has by choice and by overconfidence bordering on folly embarked upon a course that relies primarily on technology, including space weapons, to protects its space assets, rather than diplomacy and cooperation, which had been the cornerstones of U.S. policy until the Reagan administration."[10]

In this chapter, we argue against adopting any broad prohibition on the use of force in space. At the level of legal doctrine, the great powers have already carefully crafted treaties to limit a nuclear arms race in outer space. But at the same time they have left open significant routes for other military uses of space. Current law, for example, does not prohibit the passage of weapons through space, such as ballistic missiles, the stationing of reconnaissance satellites, or the basing of conventional weapons in orbit. We believe that states can use force in these ways to achieve the same goals set out in the cyber and robotics chapters: for self-defense, to pursue terrorist groups, to stop international crises, and to resolve disputes between states. Combat in space raises the same questions as other technologies, due to the integration of civilian and military networks in space, but also realizes the same benefits: greater precision in attack, a reduction in battle casualties, and clearer negotiations between states to settle their controversies. Nations can coordinate to place certain areas of space off limits to occupation, rendering them akin to the legal status of Antarctica. But it would deny reality to expect the great powers to ignore the military and technological advantages made possible by space.

Weapons in Space

The global positioning system illustrates the importance of space. GPS uses two dozen satellites in geosynchronous orbit to send out a signal that allows receivers to pinpoint their locations. Ride-sharing services, for example, use GPS to allow drivers and passengers to coordinate rides. Logistics and transportation companies, such as FedEx or UPS, use GPS to improve the speed and reliability of package delivery. Apple, Google, and Microsoft offer mapping technology that allows individual smartphone users to navigate routes efficiently and provide detailed information on locations, such as shopping, restaurants, and entertainment. Airliners rely on GPS to reach their destinations quickly and safely, while trucking and railroad companies use it to keep track of their fleets. The value of such enterprises is astonishing: Just one ride-sharing company, Uber, operates in about 300 cities worldwide and in only five years reached an estimated value of more than $50 billion.[11]

Satellites also provide communications services that are equally as important as location. A system of satellites transmits voice and data across the globe instantly. While once limited to voice communications, satellites can now upload and download Internet data and video content at broadband speeds. In 2015, AT&T paid $49 billion for satellite television provider DirecTV, which beams television shows and movies directly from space to users on the ground.[12] In 2016, the entire industry of satellite television services generated $98 billion in revenue.[13] Communications satellites also allow automated teller machines to process withdrawals, cash registers to verify credit cards, and financial institutions to execute transactions quickly and reliably.

These capabilities have military roles too. Strategists divide military space missions into four areas. First is space support, which refers to the launching of missiles and satellites and the management of satellites in orbit. The second is force enhancement, which seeks to improve the effectiveness of terrestrial military operations. These missions include the use of space for passive surveillance and support of terrestrial operations, both military and civilian. Indeed, the very first satellites performed a critical surveillance role in the strategic competition between the United States and the Soviet Union.[14] Spy satellites replaced dangerous aerial reconnaissance flights, such as the U-2 flight shot down over the Soviet Union in 1960, in providing intelligence on rival nuclear missile arsenals. Later space-based systems provided the superpowers with instant early warnings of ballistic missile launches. Both of these programs, scholars believed, helped bolster strategic stability between the superpowers and even aided the progress in nuclear arms reduction talks.[15] Satellites thus created "national technical means" of verification, the capability to detect compliance with arms control treaties without the need to intrude on territorial sovereignty.[16] They also reduced the chances of human miscalculation by increasing the information available to decisionmakers about the intentions of other nations. While space technologies have given the superpowers the means to launch nuclear weapons against any location on the planet, they have also provided the means for nations to trust each other enough to reduce their stockpiles of those same weapons.

At the level of the second mission, force enhancement, the U.S.'s development of space-based technologies has boosted conventional military abilities to the point where strategists describe it as a "revolution in military affairs."[17] GPS technology makes possible exact deployment of units, the synchronization of combat maneuvers, clearer identification of friend and foe, and precision-guided force. Sensors in space, combined with dense communications networks, allow swift, pinpoint targeting of crucial enemy units, effectively multiplying U.S. military force. Displayed in the two wars with Iraq, as well as the 1999 Kosovo air war and the continuing conflicts in Afghanistan and the Middle East, the U.S. uses satellite information to find the enemy, even to the level of individual leaders, deploys on-station air or ground forces to the area, and fires precision-guided munitions to destroy targets with lower levels of destruction than in the past. Supporters of this revolution in military affairs, which include former Defense Secretary Donald Rumsfeld, hope that the integration of intelligence, communication, and joint services action on land, sea, and air, all made possible by space-based systems, will allow the military to fight more effectively with less resources—in other words, to boost the productivity of the American soldier. Such gains will allow the U.S. armed forces to organize themselves more flexibly to handle the twenty-first century threats of terrorism, rogue nations, asymmetric warfare, and regional challengers.[18]

Satellites do not just accelerate U.S. tactical operations, but also provide an intelligence advantage by intercepting rivals' electronic emissions to learn their plans or to interfere with their operations. A constellation of satellites provides the network of command, control, communications, information, and reconnaissance necessary for enhanced military operations to succeed. Satellites make possible the transmission of real-time video and data from the battlefield to improve targeting and conduct a campaign across continents, as required by the struggle against al-Qaeda, ISIS, and other radical Islamic terrorist groups.

Examples from the last major conventional wars illustrate the manner in which satellite reconnaissance and communications enhance conventional military operations. In the Iraq war of 2003, the United States used GPS to create a system called "Blue Force Tracker" which provided the exact locations of U.S. and enemy units. Even in the midst of a sandstorm from March 25-28, 2003, American bombers used the system to identify and destroy multiple Iraqi targets without harming friendly forces.[19] During the course of the Iraq invasion, the United States launched thousands of GPS-guided joint direct attack munitions (JDAMs) with an accuracy of as much as five meters.[20] The integration of information, communication, and precision force no doubt led to the incredibly low rate of U.S. casualties in the conflict compared to the rapid destruction of the main Iraqi battle force.

Rather than supporting ground operations, the third and fourth space missions focus on space itself. Space control, the third mission, refers to the ability to freely use space to one's benefit while denying it to opponents. In 2006, for example, the head of the U.S. Air Force Space Command testified before Congress that his "top priority is to ensure Space Superiority," which "is akin to Air Superiority."[21] As early as 2001, a special national commission on space warned that the U.S. had become so dependent on satellites in orbit that it could be vulnerable to a "Space Pearl Harbor."[22] For example, an attack on U.S. satellite systems via an electromagnetic pulse explosion that fries their electronics or an attack on the ground-space communication link could blind the U.S. military and prevent it from sending critical orders to tactical units. Space control thus begins with defense: hardening command, control, communications, and reconnaissance facilities to prevent enemy interference. It includes shielding satellite components, giving them the ability to maneuver to avoid collisions, disguising their location with decoys or stealth technologies, and arming satellites or their escorts to destroy attackers.[23]

Use of such forms of active defense can blend space control into the fourth mission: space force. Space force envisions weapons systems based in orbit that can strike targets on the ground, in the air, or even in space.[24] Observers argue that the United States and other countries are developing weapons to use force in space, despite a practice of keeping space demilitarized. They can point to a number of publicly announced policies to support this claim. "Our nation may find it necessary to disrupt, degrade, deny or destroy enemy space capabilities in future conflicts," U.S. Space Command declared in the wake of the September 11, 2001 terrorist attacks, for example.[25] In an important respect, space control and force application demand a far greater exercise of power than air or naval superiority. In times of war, the United States may seek to control certain strategic areas, such as the air over Iraq or the seas next to Taiwan. But it takes time to deploy assets to those areas and any degree of control that is achieved is retained only for the duration of the conflict. In times of peace, the United States does not station the density of air and naval units in those areas necessary for complete force superiority. In space, however, dominance requires a broad geographic scope and long-term duration—a constellation of space weapons, for example, would circle the globe for years.[26]

It is in this realm that new weapons technologies are emerging, and the same questions are arising as those surrounding cyber and robotics. Some argue that the United States and other spacefaring nations should treat space as they would any other area for great power competition. "The reality of confrontation in space politics pervades the reality of the ideal of true cooperation and political unity in space, which has never been genuine, and in the near term seems unlikely," writes Everett Dolman in *Astropolitik*.[27] Because of the pattern of history and strategy, he argues, "policymakers should be prepared to deal with a competitive, state-dominated future in space." The United States certainly has taken such concerns to heart. In the decade ending in 2008, for example, the

United States increased its space budget from $33.7 billion to $43 billion in constant dollars.[28] All of the increase in spending went to Defense Department space programs, which increased by 50 percent.

These weapons systems, some deployed, many in research and development, take several forms. Already in operation today, the U.S. national missile defense system relies upon satellites to track ballistic missile launches and help guide ground-launched kill vehicles.[29] Ballistic missiles travel in three phases: boost (when the missile launches), mid-course (when the missile separates from the booster rocket and coasts through space), and the terminal (when the warhead reenters the atmosphere). Today, satellites provide early warning, tracking, and guidance for interceptor missiles located in Alaska and California to strike missiles in the mid-course phase. Other systems, such as the Terminal High Altitude Area Defense system, the Navy's Aegis cruiser, and the Army's Patriot use that same data to attack missiles in the most difficult terminal phase, which has been compared to hitting a bullet with another bullet. U.S. Northern Command brought this layered defense system online in 2006 in response to North Korea's testing of ballistic missiles, even though its accuracy remained doubtful.[30]

This use of satellites, however, does not vary much in kind, though it does in sophistication, from the passive reconnaissance performed by satellites during the Cold War. The U.S. Defense Department currently has programs aimed at using space weapons to target ballistic missiles in their launch phase, when they are easiest to destroy. Space-based lasers remain the only viable method to destroy ballistic missiles in their initial boost phase.[31] Research begun under the Reagan administration's Star Wars program promises a significant advance to the U.S. national missile defense system. It envisions space-based platforms that can both detect and destroy ballistic missiles in their boost phase, when they are most vulnerable. Satellites offer far greater range than anti-missile ground, naval, or air units, and the ability to act earlier in the territory of other countries.

Technology that can bring down a ballistic missile in midflight could just as easily be used to destroy objects in space, the goal of the fourth space mission, force application. It could also be adapted by adversaries to challenge U.S. space hegemony. Specifically, American reliance on space-based intelligence and communication for its conventional military advantages has made its satellites a target of potential rivals. Chinese strategists discuss countering U.S. superiority in conventional and nuclear weapons with "soft kill" attacks on American satellites, which would aim to blind American forces and prevent them from communicating.[32] While China has steadily advanced its manned space program, it has also developed the technologies necessary for anti-satellite (ASAT) weapons. In 2007, for example, China tested a ground-launched missile to destroy its own Fengyun 1C weather satellite in low-Earth orbit, in the same region inhabited by commercial satellites.[33] "For countries that can never win a war with the United States by using the methods of tanks and planes, attacking an American space system may be an irresistible and most tempting choice," Chinese analyst Wang Hucheng has written, in a much-noticed comment.[34]

Though the 2007 ASAT test sparked international controversy, China had only followed the footsteps of the superpowers. The United States had carried out a primitive ASAT weapon test as early as 1959 by launching an interceptor from an aircraft toward a U.S. satellite. The following year, the U.S. developed the SAINT system, which used ground rockets to launch interceptors into orbit, where they could maneuver near Soviet satellites and then explode.[35] During the Eisenhower, Kennedy, and Johnson administrations, U.S. development of anti-ballistic missile systems usually fostered application of those technologies to an anti-satellite role. The Soviet Union followed with ASAT weapons of similar design.[36] The superpowers dropped these programs with the signing of the Anti-Ballistic Missile Treaty of 1972, which prohibited interference with satellite reconnaissance necessary to observe nuclear weapon deployments, but they restarted them in the 1990s. As its rivals began to mimic American development of force enhancement and space-control abilities, the U.S. naturally sought ASAT weapons to restore its advantage and to deter attacks. After the 2007 Chinese test, the U.S. used an anti-missile weapon launched from the Navy cruiser USS *Lake Erie* to destroy a malfunctioning satellite.[37]

Anti-satellite weapons may become even more common due to the vulnerability of satellites and the spread of ballistic missile technology. Exploding a nuclear warhead in orbit could easily destroy a satellite without the need for precise targeting. ABM systems themselves possess the latent ability to destroy satellites. It is easier for kinetic weapons to hit satellites, which generally fly predictable, easily detected orbits, than ballistic missiles. Ground-based or airborne lasers can interfere with or even destroy the sensors on a satellite. American planners have also begun research into micro- and nano-satellites, which can also serve as ASAT weapons. These tiny objects can be more easily and efficiently launched into space than their large, complicated counterparts. They could then insert themselves into the same orbits as their targets and collide with them, or, on the defensive, could surround vital U.S. satellites to guard them.[38] Even the debris from an explosion or collision could pose a threat of collision with sophisticated satellites, a concern that arose after the 2007 Chinese test created a cloud of 35,000 particles speeding along at 16,000 miles per hour.[39] As rogue nations such as North Korea and Iran acquire ballistic missile technology, they also are developing the capability to destroy satellites.

Space-based weapons offer the ability not only to use force in the heavens, but also to use force from the heavens. Space may eventually provide an effective means of power projection that does not depend on deploying air, ground, or naval units in foreign territories or in vulnerable waters. The most ambitious, but still conceptual, proposal is "Hypervelocity Rod Bundles," which would use satellites to drop tungsten rods about 20 feet long and one foot in diameter.[40] When dropped, the rod would accelerate to a speed of 36,000 feet per second and hit its target with the impact of penetrating nuclear weapons, thanks simply to the kinetic energy. Similar technology would arm a cruise vehicle, either in high orbit or in space, that could fire a variety of cylinders—popularly dubbed "Rods from God."[41] After the Chinese ASAT test, Senator Jon Kyl and the Pentagon recommended a Space-Based Test Bed program, which would develop a space-based missile defense system to complement the existing ground-based system. Such a system could easily turn to shooting down other satellites, or countering ASAT attacks, in addition to ballistic missiles in midflight. More exotic research explores the possibility of basing chemical lasers on satellites that could strike ballistic missiles in the early boost phase or even ground targets. These projects have decades to go before they might come to fruition, but they illustrate the creative possibilities of space force.

These research programs became threatening to other nations in the context of the Bush administration's 2006 National Space Policy.[42] While the administration began by committing to "the exploration and use of outer space by all nations for peaceful purposes," it immediately declared that "peaceful purposes allow U.S. defense- and intelligence-related activities in pursuit of national interests."[43] The United States further made clear that it had a right of free passage in space, and that any interference would be a violation of its rights. Because space systems are "vital to its national interest," the U.S. would protect its freedoms in space and "dissuade or deter others from either impeding those rights or developing capabilities intending to do so." The 2006 policy even promised to "take action necessary to protect its space capabilities; respond to interference; and deny, if necessary, adversaries the use of space capabilities hostile to U.S. national interests." Control of space was similar to control of the other global commons: "Freedom of action in space is as important to the United States as air power and sea power."

Observers warn against this "militarization of space." Brookings Institution strategist Michael O'Hanlon, for one, argues that the United States should seek agreement with other nations to ban the basing of weapons in space and to limit the development of ASAT weapons. Professor Joan Johnson-Freese of the Naval War College declaims the Bush administration 2006 policy as "a blanket claim to hegemony in space rather than a reasonable demand that we, like any nation, be allowed to traverse the skies in our own defense."[44] She argues that military leaders exaggerate the threat from space in order to justify more aggressive weaponization of space. But it won't work. "Relying exclusively on [space weapon] technology for security," she writes, "does not provide an asymmetric advantage: it creates a strategically unstable environment."[45]

Critics also question whether the benefits of space weapons are worth the cost of strategic instability. National missile defense, for example, may prove physically incapable of actually preventing any ballistic missiles from striking the United States. Instead of improving U.S. safety, a leaky system might encourage nations to strike before the U.S. can deploy a more secure safety net. American ASAT weapons may push other nations to develop their own ASAT weapons, which would have a greater negative effect on the U.S. because of its heavier reliance on reconnaissance and communications satellites. Space weapons might be especially destabilizing because of the reliance by nuclear powers on satellites to detect ballistic missile launches. The possibility that an enemy might blind U.S.

satellites might encourage decisionmakers to use force earlier than they otherwise might. ASAT weapons themselves might share this "use it or lose it" feature. Because satellites are vulnerable—many remain unarmored, for example, because increasing their weight will increase the cost of their launch—satellite-based weapons are equally vulnerable to attack. Nations might choose to use their space-based weapons before they are destroyed by far cheaper, less sophisticated ASAT systems.

The Laws of War in Space

Faced with the slow march of space technology, the United States has vacillated between pursuit of its self-interest and openness to international regulation.

It should come as little surprise that, as historian Walter McDougall argued in ... the Heavens and the Earth, space programs became another arena for Cold War competition between the superpowers.[16] Large government spending, involving technology that had dual civilian and military users, drove an incredible pace—primitive ballistic missiles at the end of World War II led to a landing on the moon in just 24 years. During much of this period, neither the United States nor the Soviet Union could reach agreement on basic questions on the heavens. Moscow, for example, long took the position that nations enjoyed sovereignty over the space above their territory, just as they did with airspace. During the Eisenhower years, the United States conducted significant research into ASAT, ABM, and space-based weaponry.

In the 1960s, however, the superpowers began to see a place for reciprocal limits on their space activities. Nuclear weapons testing in the upper atmosphere had demonstrated that radiation would quickly spread into outer space and threaten both manned missions and satellites. Such concerns led both nations, and other nuclear powers, to sign the Partial Test Ban Treaty in July 1963, which banned underwater-, air-, and space-based nuclear testing.[47] As space exploration continued, American and Soviet leaders came to conclude that exploiting space for weapons deployment would prove extremely expensive, if possible at all, and would only prompt competing programs from the other side. Space-based weapons might also destabilize the strategic balance, as both superpowers came to rely heavily on national technical means (i.e., satellites) to verify compliance with security treaties and to monitor their nuclear forces status. In the period after the Cuban Missile Crisis and the Test Ban Treaty, the U.S. and the Soviet Union ended their race in space and began to seek cooperative means of restraint.

Arms-control momentum culminated in 1967 in the Outer Space Treaty, signed by the U.S., the U.S.S.R., and the world's other major powers. In addition to outlining procedures for launches, debris, and liability, the treaty contained clear disarmament rules. It declares that outer space, including the moon and other celestial bodies, must be used for "exclusively peaceful purposes."[48] It forbids "the establishment of military bases, installations and fortifications, the testing of any type of weapons and the conduct of military manoeuvres on celestial bodies."[49] Nor can any nation make claims of territorial sovereignty over space.[50] It extended its arms-control goals to near-Earth space by forbidding the placement of weapons of mass destruction in orbit.[51] Arms control in space thus far outpaced cooperation on planet Earth. The Strategic Arms Limitations Talks led to an interim accord in 1972 that expired when the U.S. refused to ratify the second, permanent agreement after the Soviet invasion of Afghanistan. It was not until the Intermediate Nuclear Forces agreement of 1988 that Moscow and Washington would agree to reduce a class of nuclear arms, and not until the START I agreement of 1991, after the fall of the Berlin Wall and the end of the Soviet Union, that the U.S. and Russia committed to broad reductions in their arsenals.

Although it is the most significant form of cooperation in space, the Outer Space Treaty still contains important limits. Most significantly, its stand that outer space must be used for "peaceful purposes" has not successfully banned military operations in space. The United States, for example, has long maintained that "peaceful purposes" does not preclude the use of space for self-defense.[52] Under this reading, nations can use space to conduct passive reconnaissance for aggression or even to host systems designed to counter offensive uses of space. Even as it signed the Outer Space Treaty, Washington was deploying satellites to provide early warning of missile launches and to conduct surveillance of Soviet and Chinese military movements. Some scholars argue that the United States and other spacefaring nations still must obey Article 2(4) of the United Nations Charter, which prohibits nations from use of force to threaten the territorial integrity or political independence of others.[53] Indeed,

Article III of the Outer Space Treaty declares that all space activity must be "in accordance with international law, including the Charter of the United Nations."

But as we have seen on terra firma, the U.N. Charter's ban on war has not ended armed conflict. Instead, the United States and its allies have continued to use force to counter aggression, as in the first Persian Gulf War; aid allies in civil wars, as in Korea and Vietnam; and to stop humanitarian crises, as in Kosovo. They have justified other interventions, most controversially the 2003 Iraq invasion, to stop WMD proliferation or, as in Afghanistan in 2001, to pursue international terrorist groups. Western nations helped overthrow the authoritarian Gaddafi regime in Libya, even though it had posed no threat to its neighbors, and are intervening in the Syrian civil war today. In smaller wars, the U.S. used force in places like Grenada and Panama to end leftist regimes that threatened to destabilize their regions. Western nations arguably have adopted an approach to war that abjures the territorial conquest of the nineteenth and twentieth centuries in favor of a global meliorism that seeks to improve global welfare.[54]

In all of these conflicts, the United States and its allies maintained that they had acted consistently with international law and the U.N. Charter. If this practice reflects the contemporary understanding of the U.N. Charter's prohibition on war, it leaves a wide arena for the use of force in space. At a minimum, it would allow nations to station forces in space for the purposes of self-defense, which Article 51 of the U.N. Charter recognizes as an inherent exception to the ban on war. As we have seen, nations have long deployed satellites to aid their surveillance of rivals' nuclear launches, which a critic might claim violates the treaty ban on the use of space for anything other than "peaceful purposes." At the time of the Outer Space Treaty's signing, nuclear powers used space as the transit path for their ballistic missiles. The use of satellites for terrestrial force enhancement, such as target selection, command and control, and reconnaissance, evidences even less peaceful purposes. Article 51 should further permit active military operations in space that serve a defensive purpose, such as blinding the satellites of a nation launching a clear war of aggression. If guiding missiles to a target does not violate the U.N. Charter because the satellites are defending against an unlawful attack, the law should allow the defending nation to launch those missiles directly from space. This understanding of international law could even permit military operations in space that advance the same goals of these earlier wars.

The Outer Space Treaty could not prohibit a nation's right to use force in self-defense. Indeed, the nations that signed the U.N. Charter did not understand the new global framework to limit the right of self-defense. As Article 51 declares: "Nothing in the present Charter shall impair the inherent right of individual or collective self-defense if an armed attack occurs against a Member of the United Nations." The Outer Space Treaty might not even preclude more recent, welfare-maximizing purposes for war, such as removing destabilizing regimes or ending humanitarian crises, insofar as international law accepts such interventions. It is true that the text of the treaty has a generally peaceful agenda in its opening declaration that "the exploration and use of outer space, including the moon and other celestial bodies, shall be carried out for the benefit and in the interests of all countries," and that outer space is "the province of all mankind."[55] It requires equal access for all countries to outer space and forbids "national appropriation by claim of sovereignty" of space or any of the celestial bodies. Article IV clearly forbids the placement of nuclear weapons or other WMD in orbit, on the moon or planets, or in outer space. Article IV forbids the "establishment of military bases, installations and fortifications, the testing of any type of weapons and the conduct of military manoeuvres on celestial bodies." The Treaty requires spacefaring nations to assist others in distress, to allow them access to their moon or planetary installations, and to "be guided by the principle of co-operation and mutual assistance."

But like the dog that didn't bark in the Sherlock Holmes story, the Treaty is as significant for its silences as for its declarations. First, the agreement does not prohibit weapons from passing through space between two terrestrial destinations. Ballistic missiles do not violate the treaty. The superpowers could not have understood the text any other way, as they had already deployed ground- and sea-launched ICBMs by 1967 and would field thousands more in the years following. Second, aside from the ban on WMD, the treaty does not prohibit any military operations in orbit or outer space. The text's ban on all military use of the moon, planets, and asteroids extends only to those celestial bodies, leaving unregulated the rest of outer space. Third, the treaty makes no distinction between defensive and offensive weapons in orbit or space. Again, its clear ban on WMD in space also makes clear that all other weapons remain unregulated. Fourth, the treaty entirely neglects orbital weapons for use against terrestrial targets, or vice versa. The superpowers, for example, would have to resort to another, separate agreement to forbid space-based ABM defenses. They would not have to obey any restrictions on ASAT weapons.

Most importantly, the treaty's overall structure resists the claim that outer space must remain demilitarized. Some scholars interpret Article I's declaration that activities in space must pursue "peaceful purposes" as a prohibition on most military activities in space.[56] U.N. General Assembly resolutions seek the same goal. In 1988, for example, the General Assembly passed a resolution calling for "general and complete disarmament under effective international control" so that "outer space shall be used exclusively for peaceful purposes" and "not become an arena for an arms race."[57] The resolution passed 154 to 1—the United States was the sole vote against.

But subsequent U.N. resolutions cannot cast a backward gloss on the Outer Space Treaty. If disarmament were truly the treaty's purpose, it would have contained a universal ban on all military activities in space. It does not; it only lists piecemeal prohibitions. The specific provisions on WMD, or on military bases on the moon, or against sovereignty over space, belie any intent to universally ban all military activity. Otherwise, the treaty could have been much shorter and more concise. Scholars compare the 1967 Outer Space Treaty to the 1959 Antarctic Treaty, which sought to demilitarize the continent. But Article I of the Antarctic Treaty contains a broader prohibition: "Antarctica shall be used for peaceful purposes only. There shall be prohibited, inter alia, any measures of a military nature, such as the establishment of military bases and fortifications, the carrying out of military maneuvers, as well as the testing of any type of weapons."[58] The Antarctica Treaty does not limit its reach only to specific parts of the continent, or prohibit only specific types of weapons, as does the Outer Space Treaty.

From a broader viewpoint, the Outer Space Treaty does not attempt to rewrite the U.N. Charter's framework for the use of force. A treaty certainly could go beyond the U.N. Charter's prohibition on aggression, excepting the right to self-defense, by ordering a complete demilitarization of space. The Treaty, however, does anything but that. Article III of the Treaty specifically states that spacefaring nations shall follow "international law, including the Charter of the United Nations, in the interest of maintaining international peace and security and promoting international cooperation and understanding." By specifically incorporating the Charter, the treaty acknowledges the international law framework that has permitted—although always subject to controversial and conflicting interpretations—the use of force many times since the end of World War II. Indeed, it would make little sense to infer that the United States in particular would understand the Outer Space Treaty's language here to bar military activity in space at a time when it was interpreting the same language—the U.N. Charter's protection of a right to self-defense—to justify the Vietnam War.[59]

The Outer Space Treaty marked the high point in legal cooperation in space. In the years since détente, the United States has gradually moved away from arms limits toward the open pursuit of the national interest in space. With his Strategic Defense Initiative, President Ronald Reagan launched a program to develop space-based weapons against ICBMs. When critics charged that SDI would violate the ABM Treaty, the Reagan administration argued that research and development would not run afoul of the agreement. Left virtually unmentioned was the Outer Space Treaty.[60] In the 1990s, the Clinton administration continued missile defense research, though at a lesser pace. With the end of the Cold War, the U.S. and Russia cooperated on various space science and manned missions, but the U.S. also resisted broad legal regulation of space. In its 1996 National Space Policy, for example, the Clinton administration continued U.S. support for "passage through and operations in space without interference" and the "fundamental right" to "acquire data from space."[61] While these traditional U.S. policy goals recognized the equal right of all nations to free navigation of space and to engage in commercial activity in orbit, they also rejected treaty-based limits on U.S. military activities in space.

U.S. realism in space reached its apogee in the Bush administration. The stage was set even before the 9/11 attacks with the report of a special congressional commission on space issued in January 2001.[62] Chaired by soon-to-become Secretary of Defense Donald Rumsfeld, the commission warned of a "Space Pearl Harbor" because of the vulnerabilities of U.S. satellites performing vital reconnaissance, communications, and early warning missions. It observed that mankind had fought in air, water,

and on land and that conflict in space was "a virtual certainty." The commission called for the U.S. to field superior space capabilities that could
"negate the hostile use of space against United States interests" by using
"power projection in, from and through space." It found that treaties and
law did not prohibit a wide variety of military space operations. "There is
no blanket prohibition in international law on placing or using weapons
in space, applying force from space to earth or conducting military operations in and through space." After the 9/11 terrorist attacks, followed by
the Afghanistan and Iraq wars, the United States embarked on a massive
defense buildup that provided generously for research and development
of space weapons.[63]

The signal moment in the U.S. movement away from the cooperative
approach of the Outer Space Treaty came soon after the 9/11 attacks. In
early 2002, the Bush administration announced the United States' withdrawal from the ABM treaty, which had blocked full deployment of a
system integrating ground-based interceptors with a space-based sensor
network. Congress cooperated by increasing funding for national missile
defense by 62 percent, from $4.8 billion in 2001 to $7.8 billion in 2002.[64]
As we have discussed, missile defense systems enjoy the capabilities necessary to destroy satellites as well. In 2006, the Bush administration made
even more clear its hostility to legal limits on U.S. space activities in its
revised National Space Policy: "The United States will oppose the development of a new legal regime or other restrictions that seek to prohibit
or limit U.S. access to space."[65] The 2006 Policy also specifically rejected
arms control proposals for space. "Proposed arms control agreements or
restrictions must not impair the rights of the United States to conduct
research, development, testing, and operations or other activities in space
for U.S. national interests." In February 2008, the United States gave life
to these words when the USS *Lake Erie* used a sea-based missile defense
system to destroy a malfunctioning intelligence satellite in orbit.

While the Obama administration took office determined to step away
from its predecessor's foreign policies, it did not advance an understanding of space at odds with traditional American practice. At first glance,
the Obama White House's 2010 National Space Policy appeared to reject
realism in favor of international cooperation. Its first principle declared:
"It is the shared interest of all nations to act responsibly in space to help
prevent mishaps, misperceptions, and mistrust."[66] While also making

clear that "the United States considers the sustainability, stability, and free access to, and use of, space vital to its national interests," the 2010 Policy also declared that, "space operations should be conducted in ways that emphasize openness and transparency to improve public awareness of the activities of government, and enable others to share in the benefits provided by the use of space." The White House ordered agencies to "identify areas for potential cooperation," "develop transparency and confidence-building measures," and preserve "the space environment and the responsible use of space." Unlike the Bush administration's quest for freedom of operation in space, the Obama policy adopted an apparently positive attitude toward new international regimes. "The United States will consider proposals and concepts for arms control measures if they are equitable, effectively verifiable, and enhance the national security of the United States and its allies."[67]

However, the Obama administration's actions did not match its rhetoric. Despite this more cooperative language, the Obama Space Policy continued important elements of his predecessor's approach to space security. It declared that "peaceful purposes" in the Outer Space Treaty and international law "allows for space to be used for national and homeland security activities."[68] While rejecting any claim to sovereignty in space, the United States continued to demand "the rights of passage through, and conduct of operations in, space without interference." Finally, the Obama administration continued to reserve the right to use force to defend American interests in space. "The United States will employ a variety of measures to help assure the use of space for all responsible parties, and, consistent with the inherent right of self-defense, deter others from interference and attack." It further reserved the right to use force to "defend our space systems and contribute to the defense of allied space systems, and, if deterrence fails, defeat efforts to attack them." During the Obama years, the United States did not subject its military operations in space to any new legal constraints, nor did it enter into any new international agreements involving space—unlike its efforts with Iran, which culminated in the Iran nuclear deal, or climate change, which resulted in the Paris accords.

There were certain circumstances that prevented the Obama administration from carrying out any revolutionary change in the U.S. attitude toward space. For one, other nations began to offer more competition.

China continued its development of anti-satellite weapons and announced an ambitious spaceflight program, which included plans to land unmanned and manned missions on the moon. By 2010, China had matched the U.S. in number of space launches—though both remained behind the traditional leader, Russia—which included the deployment of a Chinese GPS system and expanded military reconnaissance satellites.[69] A traditional rival of China, India also made its first military forays into space with the launch of a satellite and plans for anti-satellite weapons. Also worried by the rise of China, Japan in 2008 enacted a new Basic Law authorizing military use of space, which included an early warning system for missile launches and military reconnaissance satellites. Even rogue nations joined the spacefaring club during the Obama years. In 2009, Iran demonstrated a working knowledge of ballistic missiles by placing a primitive communications satellite into orbit. After several failed attempts, North Korea succeeded in placing a satellite in orbit in February 2016 in violation of U.N. Security Council Resolutions.[70]

Legal efforts to rein in growing competition in orbit have failed to achieve liftoff. In 2008, Russia and China proposed a treaty to prevent the placement of weapons in outer space. Their draft declared that states would not "place in orbit around the Earth any objects carrying any kinds of weapons" and that they would not "resort to the threat or use of force against outer space objects."[71] In seeking to change international law with a treaty on these points, both nations implicitly agreed that existing rules permit orbiting space weapons. In response to U.S. criticism, Beijing and Moscow further acknowledged that existing international law did not prohibit ASAT weapons based on ground, sea, or air. They also conceded that international law did not ban ground-based laser weapons or jamming systems aimed at space targets. Their treaty would only establish a new prohibition on space-based weapons, such as a missile defense network or a global strike capability.[72]

European nations, meanwhile, attempted to gather support for their own set of rules to govern space. In 2008, the European Union issued a draft "Code of Conduct for Outer Space Activities" that sought to guarantee "freedom for all states, in accordance with international law and obligations, to access, to explore, and to use outer space for peaceful purposes without harmful interference."[73] It urged members to refrain from the damage or destruction of any space objects, except when justified by threat to human life or health, to reduce space debris, or by the U.N. Charter or self-defense. The Code of Conduct, however, made clear that it was not legally binding. It instead focused its efforts on voluntary transparency measures, such as sharing data on launches and space activity. Even with these light obligations, the United States and other major spacefaring powers refused to join the Code. Nonetheless, the European Code of Conduct is revealing in the same manner as the Russo-China draft treaty—these proposals would be unnecessary if international law already banned the objects of their texts. Without any binding treaties, except the minimal obligations of the Outer Space Treaty, international law permits a wide variety of military activities in space.

The Future of Space Conflict

In this part, we ask how the United States should use space weapons. As we described in part I, technology has advanced to the stage where space satellites provide the informational backbone for real-time, precision warfare. Technology has also brought the world closer to space-based weapons that can destroy satellites, ballistic missiles, and ground targets. In part II, we argued that existing international law places minimal limits on space weaponry, other than the Outer Space Treaty's WMD prohibition and its declaration of the moon and planets as off limits. Otherwise, spacefaring nations have resisted any new restrictions on their space activities.

We shall make the case that the United States should use space weapons in the same manner as robotic and cyber weapons. Nations are already using space-based systems to reduce the chances of war and both combatant and civilian casualties. Satellites perform the critical function of reconnaissance, particularly by verifying WMD arsenals and the movements of conventional forces. Their communications abilities support the location of targets for precision-guided weapons, which reduce harm to combatants and civilians during war. As we have seen, space already serves as an arena for great power competition. Nations should use space weapons in limited circumstances as a strategic mechanism to coerce other nations, which will lead to more peaceful resolutions of crises. But there is an important caveat: because of the importance of satellites to strategic early-detection systems, we believe that nations should carefully limit their deployment of ASAT weapons. We also believe that nations should carefully manage global strike weapons to prevent their first-strike capabilities from destabilizing the strategic balance of power.

Pure realists would object to any restraint on military activities in outer space. They could point out, correctly, that every environment—land, air, water, and now space—has become an arena for combat. Satellites have already supercharged terrestrial combat operations by providing information, transmitting data, and coordinating ground, air, and sea units. The lightning-fast invasions of Iraq in 1991 and 2003 have shown the possibilities for leveraging space-based networks into tangible victories on the earth. But this success has also made the United States dependent on space-enhanced precision warfare, and so more vulnerable to attack. As military space analyst and DoD official Steven Lambakis wrote in 2007, "The proliferation of space technologies offers foreign governments and non-state entities unparalleled opportunities to enhance diplomatic and military influence over the U.S. and strike with strategic effect."[74] "We will be challenged in space," Lambakis observed in 2001, "simply because it makes military sense to do so."[75] Some strategists have gone farther to argue not just in favor of protecting U.S. space assets, but also embarking on space supremacy. Because great power competition has already spread to space, the United States should capitalize on its early lead to control the ultimate high ground. According to Everett Dolman, the U.S. should withdraw from the Outer Space Treaty, deploy weapons in space, and establish a liberal, pro-Democratic, pro-market hegemony in the heavens. "Who controls low-Earth orbit controls near-Earth space. Who controls near-Earth space dominates Terra. Who dominates Terra determines the destiny of humankind."[76] By deploying a system of ASAT weapons first, the United States can dictate how other nations use space.

Another camp of observers worries that these "space hegemonists" will trigger an arms race that will ultimately waste resources and degrade the commercial benefits of space.[77] Deploying missile defenses or anti-satellite weapons, they argue, will only encourage competitors to do the same. Not only do these systems consume enormous sums, due to the costs of lifting these weapons into space, but also they are relatively easy to defeat. Embarking on a military buildup will only result in a stalemate or expose vulnerable U.S. space systems to effective attack. Even if nations were to use such weapons, their costs go well beyond the military—space debris could collide with civilian satellites, while electromagnetic pulses from nuclear explosions would destroy their electronics. Fear of losing space systems might even encourage nations to attack on earth first or to make critical errors of judgment.

These analysts, who probably represent the majority of scholars in the field, argue in favor of international cooperation. They believe that nations must agree to new arms control agreements that prohibit space-based weapons and new treaties that share the commercial benefits of free space navigation. Naval War College Professor Joan Johnson-Freese, for example, puts her faith in the U.N.'s bodies on disarmament and the peaceful uses of space to develop new norms and ultimately new agreements to stop an arms race.[78] James Moltz of the Naval Postgraduate School proposes that nations can learn to overcome the prisoners' dilemma of arms competition through mutual trust and learning.[79] They point to the Outer Space Treaty to support their claim that nations have adopted a cooperative attitude toward space in the past and thus could feasibly enter into agreements prohibiting the military from the moon and planets and banning whole classes of space weaponry. They also claim that even in the absence of formal treaties, the U.S. and U.S.S.R. diverted their Cold War competition away from the militarization of space and toward civilian and scientific exploration.

Space presents difficult intellectual challenges because of its unique characteristics as a global commons. Analogizing space to other environments has important consequences for regulation. Some, for example, have compared space to the discovery of the New World in 1492, opened by voyages of discovery and subject to claims of sovereignty. But while it has territory, in the form of the moon, planets, and asteroids, nations currently do not have the technology and resources to establish a continuous presence on these bodies. Space also shares some of the characteristics of airspace. Air and spacecraft fly above territory for both security and trade. As is the practice with aircraft, nations could require spacecraft to obtain permission to enter their space and launch missiles at satellites that enter without authorization. But space is far vaster than air. It currently seems impossible to exclude other nations from specific parts of the skies, unlike the way in which the United States can prevent the aircraft of other nations from entering its airspace. While the Soviet Union, at first, sought to apply the rules of airspace to outer space, by the 1960s it accepted that territory did not vest ownership of the space above.[80]

For many decades, the most common analogy for space was the high seas, especially in its combination of commerce and military expansion. If similar to the high seas, space would allow any nation to deploy both military and civilian craft free from interference.[81] Nations could not use force to control space, just as they cannot control the high seas, but they could engage in military patrols and use space resources for their own benefit. Popular culture exemplified this way of thinking. Star Trek named its ship the USS *Enterprise*, made its commander a Captain, and placed it under the command of a Starfleet.[82] But space does not yet have land for bases, there are no colonies or trade routes, and no fleets that can control territory. "It is very easy to make the obvious Mahan analogy on 'control of the sea' and talk blithely and superficially of 'control of space,'" strategist Herman Kahn observed. "The analogy was never really accurate even for control of the air, and…it seems to be completely misleading for space."[83]

Another relevant comparison is to a different type of global commons: Antarctica. The Antarctic Treaty clearly inspired the Outer Space Treaty. Like space, Antarctica's harsh conditions make permanent outposts difficult. Nevertheless, nations claimed sovereignty over parts of the continent, and in World War II even stationed troops there.[84] They attempted to commercially exploit the continent, but the environment made it unfeasible. In the depths of the Cold War, nations with research stations in Antarctica decided to sign a treaty placing the continent off limits to all military activity, even for self-defense. Moltz compares the Antarctic Treaty's prohibition on national sovereignty and demilitarization as a model for further developments in space law.[85] But he also recognizes, as he must, that space plays a much more central role in military and civilian life than Antarctica. At the time that the treaty entered into force in 1961, the frozen continent played little role in the superpower competition, while space has become a vital means of collecting data on competitors and providing an information conduit for enhanced military operations. Space also provides an environment for widespread commercial activity, from television transmissions to GPS location services.

The differences between Antarctica and outer space explain why any comprehensive arms control regime cannot succeed. It is true that nations committed to refrain from stationing WMD in orbit or establishing military bases on the moon and planets. But at the time of the Outer Space Treaty, nations did not enjoy the technical or financial resources to deploy such weapons. Ground-based ballistic missiles can perform the mission of space-based nuclear arms at a fraction of the cost and in much greater numbers. Submarine-launched ballistic missiles could provide the same deterrence with much less vulnerability to attack. In committing to a ban on WMD in orbit, nations did not truly give up any practical military abilities. Nor could nations build military installations on the moon or the planets. A half-century after the signing of the Outer Space Treaty, no nation has succeeded in building a base of any kind on the moon. Nor has any nation even managed to send a manned mission to another planet. Again, the agreement did not demand that the great powers relinquish any military capabilities in existence at the time or foreseeable in the near future.

Meanwhile, nations have developed a host of military capabilities unrestricted by any form of international law. International law does not prohibit nuclear warheads from flying through space on their way to ground targets. The arsenals of the nuclear powers depend on the ability of ICBMs to travel through space. International law does not prohibit weapons fired from the ground, sea, or air at space targets. Both superpowers developed ASAT weapons during the Cold War, and since its end both the United States and China have successfully demonstrated ASAT systems. International law also does not prohibit the basing of conventional weapons or new, exotic weapons such as high-energy beams, in space. The United States already uses space assets to assist ground-based interceptors; the next step could deploy an ABM system wholly in space, where it would act earlier to attack ICBMs soon after launch.

The United States could easily turn these weapons toward the same purposes as robotic and cyber weapons. It should use force as a means of coercion when locked in an interstate dispute. A U.S. ASAT weapon, for example, could destroy a single satellite used by a rival to support conventional ground operations. During the Afghanistan and Iraq wars, the U.S. did not destroy commercial satellites that could have provided opponents with valuable reconnaissance information on troop movements. Instead, it purchased all of the satellite time—effectively buying off the civilian operators to take their satellites out of the market. It would achieve the same effect, of course, by destroying the imaging satellites instead. The U.S. could use weapons to escalate a conflict by destroying surveillance satellites or by temporarily jamming or blinding them with space-based weapons. To take matters further, the U.S. could use ASAT weapons to attack a single node in an opponent's military or government telecommunications network, which would not permanently destroy the whole network, but would degrade the system's reliability.

As with cyber and robotic weapons, the targeting of civilian satellites would enhance the effectiveness of space weapons. Many of these satellites would not deserve noncombatant immunity. The U.S., for example, uses civilian satellite networks to transmit military communications and data. In the 1991 Gulf War, commercial satellites carried about 25 percent of U.S. military communications, a figure that rose to 85 percent in the 2003 invasion of Iraq.[86] Other nations similarly rely on commercial space services, such as communications, weather, and remote sensing, provided by companies located in Canada, France, India, Israel, and Russia.[87] Satellites, even those owned by civilian companies, which carry military or government data and communications qualify as military targets, just as commercial shippers who transport military supplies during war. A nation could also attack the support system behind any military use of satellites by destroying ground control stations or jamming their data flows.

Attacking these targets would not pose difficulties under traditional approaches to the laws of war. Military use of civilian systems renders them liable to attack during armed conflict. A harder question arises over whether nations can use force against satellites and their support systems if they have no military function. At first glance, it may be difficult if not impossible to demarcate certain satellites as purely military or purely civilian. Nations can go onto the commercial market and purchase surveillance or communications bandwidth from civilian providers; their opponents should have the right to disable the capabilities of these systems. During the Iraq war of 2003, for example, Baghdad could have purchased imaging services from corporations based in multiple countries. These providers would have allowed Iraq to substitute civilian products for its own lack of aerial or space reconnaissance of U.S. troop movements. In response, the U.S. could have chosen to disable any satellites capable of providing reconnaissance to the Iraqis or could have jammed the ground control station over the satellites during the period of the war. A less destructive approach could have demanded that the corporations refuse to sell their services to Iraq in return for a payment.

But suppose that the U.S. was fighting an opponent with satellites that perform a primarily civilian function, but one that could be used for military support. China, for example, is deploying its own version of the U.S. GPS system and has weather-prediction satellites. While these satellites provide locational services for a host of civilian uses, such as Google Maps and driving locations, they also could help China locate U.S. carrier battle groups in East Asian waters and direct aircraft or cruise missiles for attack. The potential dual-use of satellites should render them legitimate targets, particularly in a contest between military powers with the capability to conduct information-enhanced operations.

But even if nations possessed only civilian space systems, they should be liable to attack during hostilities if they present a comparatively less destructive means of coercion. Disabling the space-based elements of a communications system could pressure an opponent without causing any human casualties, much in the same way as shutting down its Internet or financial markets. An opponent would suffer economic harm until it is able to launch a replacement or purchase alternative services on the market. A nation could even just temporarily disable certain satellites, which would degrade but not ultimately destroy an opponent's communications. The United States and other nations, for example, could use ground-based lasers to temporarily blind satellites or jam their connections with ground control stations. This would cause loss, but not the breadth of death and destruction of kinetic weapons. Once the conflict passes, nations could take measures to restore the full functioning of their satellite systems. Warfare in space would not have the aim of permanently destroying enemy resources, but of simply denying an enemy access to them for the period of the conflict.

Such uses can send costly signals that can improve the bargaining process between nations. As we argued earlier, nations have a rational interest in reaching a peaceful settlement of their disputes so as to avoid the deadweight loss of war. They should agree to a deal that reflects their relative power positions, as they translate into the expected values of each side in the conflict. In order to communicate to each other their military capabilities and political will, nations need ways to send credible signals. Attacks on space-based systems can provide ways for nations to use limited, coercive force against each other without causing the death and destruction of terrestrial combat. More types of force, at varying levels of harm, provide nations with a greater spectrum of more finely tuned gradations of coercion. Each side should be able to reveal more reliable information about their abilities and intentions, and thus create more room for negotiation.

Using force in this way would draw upon the deeper historical parallels we have addressed earlier in this book. As we have argued, the modern version of international humanitarian law represents a break with more traditional approaches to the rules of warfare. International law scholars, however, commonly argue that nations should obey IHL in their military activities in space.[88] Even though no international agreement expressly addresses space *jus in bello* rules, aside from the Outer Space Treaty's WMD ban, these scholars argue that "undoubtedly customary international law and relevant general principles of law would apply to regulate such armed conflict."[89] They point to the ICJ's application of the principles of proportionality, distinction, and necessity to the question of nuclear weapons as an example, as well as the Outer Space Treaty's demand that all space activities follow international law. International institutions will "assimilate legal principles to fill apparent voids whenever encountered, especially in the context of armed force," because to propose a lawless frontier "goes against the progressive thrust and reasoning underpinning the historic trajectory of IHL."[90]

Such reasoning, however, assumes that modern IHL should apply to space. Manfred Lachs long ago argued that outer space is not a lawless area because once nations begin to interact, even in space, international law applies.[91] Accepting that international law applies to space, however, does not supply the rules that should apply. Nations need not automatically extend humanitarian laws beyond the earth because military operations in space do not threaten civilian life and thus do not conflict with the central goal of the laws of war—protecting innocent civilian life. Combat in space poses little risk of killing human beings because of the near total reliance on remote-controlled spacecraft and robots to carry out operations. Neither military nor civilian astronauts have established any significant presence in orbit. Nations can easily avoid civilian casualties entirely by keeping off limits the only quasi-permanent establishment, the International Space Station, and the few spaceflights manned by astronauts. The absence of human beings makes space an even better arena for the use of force than the earth, as the likelihood of the collateral death of civilians is virtually zero.

Military operations in space would threaten civilians not directly, but through interference with satellite systems that support activity on the ground. An attack that disabled the GPS system, for example, would not directly kill any civilians in space. But it would cause damage on the ground by paralyzing transportation networks, such as the air traffic control system, shipping, or even individual drivers using Google Maps. Attacking communications satellites could inflict costs on a civilian economy by halting financial transactions, impeding voice and data communications, and slowing the speed of the Internet.

We believe that reading the traditional principles of the laws of war to prohibit such attacks would run counter to the goal of resolving international disputes with the lowest costs. In a contest that resorts to force, nations will seek to inflict certain amounts of harm to coerce opponents. Space allows nations to harm each other without directly costing the lives of combatants or civilians. Their use of force will destroy satellites that can be replaced and cause only temporary economic losses. Losing GPS or Internet data will slow, but not permanently destroy, communications and transportation networks. But no one dies, no infrastructure is destroyed, and no lands or waters ruined. In this respect, attacks on space assets produce an effect similar to the international sanctions of the late twentieth century and the naval blockades of the nineteenth century. They increase the economic pain on an opponent, which may consequentially inflict harm on civilians, but they do not directly kill or destroy—they only prevent a nation from taking advantage of trade and commerce. If nations today can impose economic sanctions and enforce embargoes, they should have the right to use force to disable space assets.

We should prefer such an outcome compared to the alternatives. Nations resort to economic sanctions, such as those that apply to North Korea, Russia, and Iran, because they seek means of coercion short of war. Prohibiting economic sanctions would simply encourage nations to adopt more violent means of pressure. Similarly, banning attacks on space assets would only reorient coercive measures toward more direct hostilities. Nations may wish to disable a rival's financial exchange or communications networks to force it to concede in a dispute. If they cannot attack the satellites providing the backbone for these networks, these nations may simply resort to conventional air or missile attacks on energy transmission facilities, communications centers, or data storage sites instead. These attacks will risk the destruction of more lives and infrastructure, but also increase radically the chances of collateral damage on innocent civilians. Space provides the opportunity for more directly focused, surgical attacks that minimize civilian damage. In strategic terms, space provides "celestial lines of communication."[92] Nations can coerce each other by applying force to disrupt those lines of communication, just as they would those on earth, but with dramatically reduced civilian harm.

Critics of space warfare raise environmental harms and unforeseen collateral damage as pitfalls. Early anti-satellite and anti-ballistic missile weapons relied on nuclear explosions that could destroy the electronics of nearby satellites and irradiate parts of space for long periods. Testing in the early 1960s showed that nuclear weapons explosions even on earth generated EMP radiation that severely damaged satellites in low-Earth orbit; presumably then, an explosion in space could indiscriminately disable most satellites in its orbital path.[93] Kinetic ASAT weapons produce a different environmental threat. A successful impact can produce large debris fields that turn thousands of fragments into high-velocity weapons, which can hit other satellites with the force of a 10-ton truck traveling at 118 mph.[94] While some of the debris would soon burn up in the atmosphere, much of it could stay in the same orbit for months, if not years. Military attacks on space assets could degrade the space environment for long periods of time.

Such considerations, however, should not lead to a permanent ban on space weapons. Instead, they militate in favor of developing a wide array of space weapons that do not depend solely on kinetic kills for their effectiveness. One sort of weapon often discussed in the space literature is "soft kill" technology. Rather than destroying targets with direct hits, soft kill weapons disable an opponent's celestial lines of communication by jamming satellite controls.[95] The United States, for example, could use either ground-based lasers to blind satellites, or electromagnetic interference to prevent a satellite from communicating information to ground controllers. It could even hack into an opponent's ground-to-space uplinks to take over a satellite's controls and render it inoperable, temporarily offline, or move it to the wrong orbit.[96] Operating directly in space, the United States could deploy micro-satellites into the same orbit as a target and then disable the target by using jamming or interference, or even by attaching the micro-satellites to its hull and changing its trajectory. By the last decade, the U.S. Air Force had at least three programs to develop micro-satellites for surveillance and possible ASAT missions.[97]

These soft kill weapons could bear advantages beyond using force in a "cleaner" way than kinetic weapons. For example, they could be used as a temporary access denial weapon. Soft kill weapons need only prevent an opponent from using its celestial lines of communications during the course of a dispute. Because they do not destroy their targets, soft kill weapons can restore the availability of space as a resource once a conflict ends. In this respect, such use of force in space would have similar characteristics to the Pacific blockades of the nineteenth century, which temporarily interrupted the targets' normal intercourse with the rest of the world. Once a crisis ended, the naval power could lift its blockade and commerce could resume peacefully. A conflict would end without significant damage to lives or property—the only harm would be the lost economic activity during the period of blockade. Such opportunities allow nations to pressure each other in less harmful ways than just conventional, armed hostilities. Thus, these soft kill options should help produce more clear, effective negotiations between nations that can bring disputes to an end faster, and with less cost, than before.

Under this approach, the United States should develop several types of military space weapons. First, it should develop an anti-ballistic missile capability to prevent smaller nations from threatening nuclear weapons attacks on the continental U.S. Even if rogue powers such as Iran or North Korea have only an imperfect command of nuclear and missile technology, the enormous destruction of even one successful strike—no matter how low the probability—would provide their leaders with a powerful tool of coercion against the developed world. A missile defense system would reduce the probability of success and hence the ability of Pyongyang or Tehran to use their missile assets to counter other U.S. military options.

It is important to observe that the U.S. has an interest in limiting the reach of an ABM system to counter the missile forces of a smaller nation.

Constructing a system that could stop hundreds of targets, which would require an extensive deployment of sensors and perhaps even weapons in orbit, could undermine the strategic balance of power between the U.S. and other nuclear powers, such as Russia and China. If those nations were to believe that a U.S. system undermined the effectiveness of their deterrents, they might construct larger arsenals or attempt to destroy the ABM system.[98] Foreign leaders might even feel it necessary to use certain nuclear assets, especially vulnerable ground-based ICBMs with high numbers of MIRV warheads, to prevent defeat by a U.S. system. To be sure, several of the components of an effective ABM system might be easily scalable from the smaller, anti-rogue-nation system to a more comprehensive defense against the ICBMs of the great powers. Either system would demand sophisticated systems for early warning, tracking radars, targeting sensors, and battle-management computers. If the only difference between the limited and comprehensive system becomes the number of interceptors, an effective ABM system might spark competition from other nuclear powers, particularly those with smaller arsenals like China.[99]

Second, the United States should continue its development of ASAT weapons. China has already joined Russia and the U.S. in demonstrating ASAT capabilities. Washington will not put that genie back in the bottle, even if Russia and China wanted to, because missile defense systems will enjoy a latent ASAT capability. Even if it were possible to verify an anti-ASAT agreement, it would not be in the national interest of the United States or other great powers to sign it. ASAT weapons provide nations with a precise means of using force in a dispute that has little chance of civilian death. It provides a measured form of coercion that can induce nations to settle their disputes before they reach higher levels of destruction. When used against military satellites, ASATs can deprive enemies of the ability to wage information-enhanced combat. When used against civilian satellites, they inflict acute economic pressure on an opponent, similar to sanctions or an embargo. The U.S. should continue development of ground- or air-launched ASAT technology, as those are already feasible, and expand the reach of ground-based weapons that can interfere with communications and control of satellites. But it should also pursue a space-based system that could temporarily disable enemy satellites to provide more options in a crisis.

Strategic considerations, however, warrant an important exception for these weapons. Attacks against satellites that provide early warning of nuclear launches could destabilize the existing balance of deterrence. Under the New START treaty, the United States and Russia agreed to limit their arsenals to 1,550 strategic nuclear warheads and about 700 deployed ICBMs, SLBMs, and nuclear bombers.[100] Both nations rely primarily on satellites to provide early warning of launches; the U.S. Space-Based Infrared System uses four satellites in geosynchronous orbit, two more in elliptical orbits, and up to 24 in low-Earth orbit.[101] If an opponent destroyed part of this system, it could partially blind the U.S. to ICBM launches. Under the pressure of a crisis, commanders might conclude that ASAT use against early warning satellites might be preparing the way for a nuclear strike. Concerns about a strike could encourage leaders to use assets most vulnerable to a first strike—specifically ICBMs with multiple warheads based in ground silos.

The risks of triggering a nuclear exchange far outweigh the coercive value in subjecting these satellites to attack. In this specific area, nations should have a high interest in mutual cooperation to limit ASAT. Nuclear powers need a reliable early warning system to prevent misunderstandings and a mistaken decision to launch their weapons. Nations can rely on self-help to solve part of the problem by hardening the defenses of this class of satellites, to make them more difficult to destroy or jam, and by fielding redundant systems that can absorb the losses from an ASAT attack. But they can also address the problem by agreeing to place strategic warning satellites off limits. A formal treaty would prove difficult to verify, as ASAT weapons capable of striking targets in low-Earth or geosynchronous orbits would have the ability to attack any early warning systems. Instead, nuclear powers would have to rely on deterrence to enforce any such agreement. The U.S. ought to only deploy sufficient ASAT weapons for the targeting of military satellites that provide support for terrestrial operations and for disabling commercial satellites, but not enough to overwhelm the early warning systems of its main competitors.

Russia and China may find it difficult to trust American promises to respect their strategic surveillance satellites. Once the U.S. deploys an ASAT system, extending its capabilities to include early warning satellites may just be a matter of adding more interceptors to the stockpile. As with a comprehensive ABM system, the U.S. military will have already achieved the central challenge of integrating sensors, trackers, and battle-management systems. On the other hand, the superpowers confronted a similar problem in agreeing to limit, and then reduce, their strategic stockpiles. Both the United States and Russia could observe the number of launchers on each side, though some—especially bombers and medium-range missiles—could carry either nuclear or conventional warheads. They also permitted on-site verification to monitor warheads and their disposal. Similarly, an agreement to limit but not prohibit ASATs could rely on national technical means to verify launch sites and radar installations, while relying on on-site visits to confirm interceptor numbers. Ultimately, as with the SALT and START agreements, the U.S., Russia, and China would have to rely upon deterrence to enforce an ASAT agreement. The only way to ensure that nations do not use ASAT weapons against strategic surveillance satellites is if they maintain their capacity to retaliate. Deterrence, therefore, requires that the United States develop the ASAT capabilities that it would want to have for coercion purposes anyway.

Third, these principles suggest that the United States should limit the development of space weaponry designed to strike ground targets. Exotic systems, such as hypersonic rail guns, directed energy beams, or gravity rods, could destabilize the strategic balance of power. These weapons initially appear attractive because of their swift speed, explosive force, precise targeting, and minor fallout. According to some estimates, an orbital platform could hit a ground target 12-15 minutes after launch with the kinetic force of a small nuclear weapon. Basing kinetic weapons in high orbit makes a launch difficult to detect, and their speed and angle of descent makes them almost impossible to defeat with anti-missile or anti-aircraft defenses.[102] The speed and destructiveness of these weapons, however, give national leaders little time to decide whether to respond preemptively. The short warning time may create a strong incentive to use military assets that are vulnerable to a first strike—again, ground-based ICBMs armed with multiple reentry warheads. In a crisis situation, such weapons may create the conditions for a mistake of judgment by national leaders that could have disastrous consequences for both nations.

The United States could propose a narrow international ban on these exotic space-to-ground strike weapons. Competitors would no longer have to fear the prospect of U.S. orbital strike platforms, which would impose costs to build their own offensive and defensive systems. In exchange, the United States could remove a potential threat to strategic stability. In fact, an international agreement would not demand as great a concession from the United States as it would from other nations. The U.S. armed forces have multiple alternatives for global strike missions, such as ICBMs, cruise missiles, stealth bombers, and conventional air-, ground-, and sea-based artillery. Washington does not need space-to-ground attack systems in order to coerce opponents, and it could forestall competition from rivals who might hope to leapfrog U.S. dominance in conventional and nuclear arms with exotic space weapons. A treaty would also prove relatively easy to verify: A nation would need a significant launch capacity to lift all of the weapons into space and the orbital platform needed for basing should be easy to detect.

There is an important criticism of these approaches to space weapons, which applies primarily to the United States. Because the United States has made the greatest investments in space for both military and civilian purposes, it may be uniquely vulnerable to military warfare in the heavens. About half of all satellites are American.[103] Many of them support U.S. military and intelligence operations ranging from verification of strategic weapons to tactical information in battle. The U.S. has become more dependent on high-speed communications, precision munitions, and space-based information than any other nation. Meanwhile, anti-satellite weapons rest in the grasp of any nation that can launch a ballistic missile into orbit. Nations that suffer from a disadvantage in conventional, terrestrial armed forces could quickly narrow the gap by launching an attack on U.S. space systems. Without the information and communications provided by satellites, U.S. military effectiveness will be significantly degraded—all without harming anyone or destroying anything on the ground.

But arms control over the entire class of space-based weapons is extremely unlikely. As we have argued earlier, nations will agree upon limits or prohibitions on weapons and their use when there is a rough symmetry in their capabilities. An agreement must not grant a decisive advantage to any nation that does not exist under the status quo; otherwise, the treaty will create strong incentives to cheat. In the case of space-based weapons, neither the United States nor its rivals can have confidence that an agreement will survive. First, the United States currently enjoys an overwhelming advantage in military activities in space; it would be unlikely to give up its superiority in space-enhanced operations. Second, other nations may see that space weapons, particularly ASATs, provide a quick and relatively inexpensive means to threaten the U.S.'s advantage in conventional military systems. Nor would these nations, such as China or Iran, have any incentive to sign a ban on ASATs since they have few space resources themselves under threat of attack.

Instead of an international agreement, the better course for the United States lies in defensive strategies. Its best response to the growing ASAT capabilities of its rivals is to harden its satellites and build redundancies into its systems. It can also threaten conventional terrestrial attacks on opponent targets in response to interference with its satellites and celestial lines of communication. As other nations build their own space-based networks, they will increasingly fall subject to the reciprocal threat of U.S. ASAT weapons. Deterrence, rather than international law, will provide the protection for the U.S.'s superior civilian and military space assets.

Conclusions

While President Reagan's dream of building an anti-missile shield to protect the entire United States is still far off, space is quickly joining land, sea, and air as an arena for conflict. In a more modest sense, the great powers began to use space for military activity with the launching of the first satellites in the 1950s. Satellites today provide the information, intelligence, and communications that form the backbone for today's up-tempo, integrated, high-tech military operations. In the next decades, we might see the realization of Reagan's hopes with the deployment of capable anti-missile defenses in space. Nations naturally are developing ASAT weapons to undermine the American advantage in space, which provides support for terrestrial operations and a potential battlefield in its own right.

While the great powers have limited military activities in space, most importantly the ban on WMD, they have left important areas free of regulation. International agreements do not prohibit the passage of missiles through space, the stationing of conventional weapons in orbit, or the gathering of intelligence and the transmission of communications from space. States should continue to use force in these ways for self-defense, to defeat terrorist groups and regional aggression, and to resolve their disputes. Combat in space may spark the same fears as other technologies, specifically of lowering the barrier to armed conflict. But it also offers the same benefits of greater precision, less destruction, and lower risk of general war. In the area where space weapons might prove genuinely destabilizing, as a platform for strategic first-strike weapons against earth targets, we believe that the United States and its allies should take the first steps for an arms limitation agreement. But other than that sole area, the great powers should take advantage of the technological progress in space to pursue their age-old security goals.

Conclusion

Our world still faces threats to peace and security. The United States continues to fight the Taliban in Afghanistan more than a decade and a half after the September 11 attacks. While it withdrew its large combat force from Iraq in 2010, U.S. units returned to fight ISIS only four years later. American forces have intervened in Syria in the midst of a civil war that has killed more than 200,000. U.S. bombers are conducting air strikes on ISIS and al-Qaeda terrorists in the Arabian Peninsula and North Africa. Even territorial aggression, in Eastern Europe and the seas of Asia, has reemerged as a threat, while state-sponsored terrorism and the proliferation of weapons of mass destruction remain serious challenges.

While human evils persist, technology continues to advance. New technologies are changing the character of daily life, from the factory floor to personal communications. Robotics, Internet, and space-based communications have increased economic productivity. These same advances are also generating new kinds of weapons, from robotics to computer network attacks, with similar effects. These weapons offer the potential to change the way we conduct armed conflict. Nations will still use force to defend themselves, to counter aggression, to respond to humanitarian crises, and to compete for influence. But robotics, cyber, and space may allow nations to pursue these goals without engaging in full-blown wars involving conventional weapons and the accompanying death and destruction.

Prominent observers regard this as a problem, not a solution. Recall U.N. expert Philip Alston's warning that drone strikes will be abused because "they make it easier to kill without risk to a State's forces."[1] If intervention is too easy, critics argue, states will be tempted to intervene too readily and undermine the existing norms against resorting to force. They further worry that the ease of attack will erode the rules governing permissible targets. For example, they warn that the "potentially nonlethal nature of cyber weapons may cloud the assessment of an attack's legality, leading to more frequent violations of the principle of distinction [between proper military and improper civilian targets]."[2] Those who voice such concerns often advocate greater emphasis on legal constraints. They urge us to negotiate new treaties or to extend interpretations of existing conventions and norms, even though the latter were developed for the technologies and strategic challenges of a half-century ago.

We have argued that such appeals are dangerously misguided. The military technologies discussed in this book—robotics, cyber, space weapons—are either already in our arsenals or in advanced stages of development. It is true—and heartening—that nations have shown considerable restraint in deploying the most terrifying weapons of mass destruction. Nations have not used nuclear weapons since Hiroshima and Nagasaki. In the 1965 Treaty on the Non-Proliferation of Nuclear Weapons, nations agreed to cooperate to limit the spread of these weapons. Poison gas, a prominent feature of battle in World War I, has rarely appeared in subsequent conflicts. The 1998 Chemical Weapons Convention seems to provide reassurance against future use, although Syria's use of sarin and mustard gas against its own citizens is putting the ban to the test. The great powers have never resorted to biological weapons in wars between themselves. Almost all states have agreed to a ban on their development and use, as codified in the 1972 Biological Weapons Convention.

Experience with these weapons, however, does not have much application to the weapons discussed in this book. Nations will have little incentive to obey limits or prohibitions on the use of new weapons when their effects on warfare and international politics are still little understood. In the twentieth century, nations declined to apply old concepts of the laws of war to the innovations of the airplane and submarine. Even if today's latest weapons technologies were not so new, arms control would still fail. Nations have rarely embraced, let alone honored, limits on conventional weapons. Agreement is especially unlikely in today's context because nations would find it difficult, if not impossible, to verify compliance with limits on intangible computer programs or miniaturized air- or ground-based attack vehicles.

The strategic implications of WMD on warfare and international politics, by contrast, are better understood and stockpiles are less difficult to verify. Great powers can use national technical means, such as satellite reconnaissance, to monitor each other's arsenals. Both the Nuclear Non-Proliferation Treaty and the Chemical Weapons Convention provide for international inspection to verify that signatories are not secretly developing these weapons to wield against more trusting adversaries. It is dismaying that the world has not yet agreed to an inspection regime to verify that signatories of the Biological Weapons Convention refrain from development. That failure may reflect the difficulty in distinguishing research in this field from legitimate forms of medical or bioengineering research and development.[3] Verifying limits on development of robotics, cyber, and space weapons is more challenging, because they are applications of activities which have become pervasive in a modern economy. We cannot hope to verify that all computers and computer research are used only for civilian activities and not for military applications, nor can we expect to fare much better in monitoring the use of robotic capacities.

Biological, chemical, and nuclear weapons threaten the very opposite of the precision offered by robotics, cyber, and space weapons. Their broad effects cannot distinguish between combatants and civilians. Even using them only in battlefield environments cannot guarantee that their lingering effects or uncontrollable spread will not harm civilians. Nuclear explosions will render land uninhabitable for decades, while biological weapons can easily spread or mutate beyond the battlefield. Use of these weapons signals an intention to cause mass casualties, and invites a massive retaliation in response. The large-scale casualties threatened by WMD give nations an incentive to abide by arms control agreements because their use could trigger a mutually assured destruction that gives neither side an advantage.

Robotics, cyber, and space weapons, we believe, do not threaten the massive, indiscriminate destruction that supports the special dynamics that govern WMD agreements. Their main appeal is precisely that they can be targeted with precision, so they hit with greater effectiveness and less unintended damage. Indeed, new technologies may help solve the challenges of WMD proliferation by allowing nations to disable nuclear, chemical, or biological weapons facilities with less risk of widespread contamination. New technologies create weapons of less destruction, not mass destruction.

But that does not address the nub of the concern for many critics. They worry that gaining the ability to strike more precisely at lower cost will lower the threshold for war. New technologies may give nations the confidence to resort to force too readily because they trust too much in their capacity to wage easy wars. Or great powers may use force too often because technology allows them to avoid the costs of war and instead concentrate them on the enemy.

We have stressed two responses. First, as we argued in chapter 2, our world is becoming more chaotic. We still need to defend against territorial aggression, to stop the proliferation of WMD, and to contain the worst human rights disasters. The costs of conventional conflicts, particularly casualties from ground combat, will discourage nations from confronting these problems. But if the costs of war decline, while the effectiveness of force improves, nations may turn to force to promote desirable ends. New weapons can make it easier to intervene and to signal our resolve to prevent threats to our security. The challenge of our era is not a world where defenders of international order are too quick to act, but too hesitant. We should welcome technologies that make intervention more precise and more readily feasible.

Second, these new weapons may allow nations to coerce others to stop these greater threats to international order more effectively. The preoccupation with the most restrictive standards of AP I, as we argued in chapters 3 and 4, is quite misguided. The United States is not bound by a treaty it has never ratified, nor by customary law it does not accept. Motivated by utopian fantasy and cynical Third World self-dealing, the nations that adopted AP I did not codify past understandings, but leapt beyond them. It is past the time to rethink this legacy of the 1970s. Among other things, we should reconsider whether it makes sense to hold civilian infrastructure and resources immune from attack, merely because they do not provide direct support to military operations. Attacks of this kind may provide more effective, less lethal, and less destructive means of coercing states that threaten the international order, compared with direct military engagements prescribed by 1970s dogma.

In the past, the law of war has allowed attacks on civilian property, but with recognized limits. For centuries, naval strategy has emphasized attacks on civilian commerce. Other actions—such as the deliberate massacre of civilians—have been considered barbarous. That is, of course, reflected in the general aversion to weapons of mass destruction, since these tend to spread death and physical suffering beyond the battlefield in indiscriminate ways. We think commanders should obey the list of immunities laid down in the Hague Conventions on land warfare—"buildings dedicated to religion, art, science, historic monuments, hospitals"—but with the original condition that it does not apply when such places are "used at the time for military purposes."[4] Recognizing the continuing relevance of these historic limitations does not automatically require that everything not directly contributing to the enemy's military must remain exempt from attack.

To recognize a broader scope for attack would not necessarily imply a dramatic change in actual tactics. Current U.S. military manuals authorize attacks on anything that "sustains" an enemy's "war-fighting capacity."[5] This formula is so vague that, as critics complain, it might extend to almost anything. Such evasive formulations may invite misunderstanding regarding actual U.S. commitments. Academic commentators and NGO advocates have rushed in with confident pronouncements on what international law must be understood to prohibit. The "international experts" behind the Tallinn Manual have spun hundreds of pages of exposition purporting to clarify the rules applicable to cyber conflict without the direct endorsement or commitment of any actual government. The United States will be better off if it does not allow such abstract legal reasoning to limit the way it uses new weapons technologies. We should, of course, try to ensure our militaries use new technology carefully to avoid direct physical injury to human beings other than enemy combatants. But we should not take into account notions of harm that arise from formulas devised in earlier times when weapons inflicted broader, more indiscriminate civilian loss. Today's more focused weapons should cause us to rethink the aim and purpose of attacks.

We should not measure the effectiveness of new weapons on their ability to secure an enemy's total submission. Since 1945, no American war has ended with a formal surrender ceremony, let alone a ceremony on a U.S. warship near the enemy capital. For our world, the more pressing question is whether new weapons can compel rogue actors to stop their worst practices. It makes little sense to insist that attacks must be confined to military objectives if they are not delivered in the context of an all-out war, where neutralizing the enemy's military capacity could deliver total victory. Attacks on military assets and civilian infrastructure can induce bargaining that leads to settlement of a dispute. Attacks with modern weapons might also deter adversaries from harmful conduct even when no negotiated deal is possible. New technologies may not prove decisive against terrorist networks, but they can help disrupt their operations and attack their leadership ranks, as well as pressure state sponsors of terror to curtail their support.

We do not presume to lay down a solution for all disputes. We argue here for expanding the range of options that nations may regard as allowable responses to serious international challenges. Technological change creates new possibilities. Some possibilities carry the potential for new kinds of abuse. Social media allows people to reconnect with distant friends and relatives, to organize political movements, to spur academic research—or to engage in cyberbullying or recruitment for terror networks. The resources made available by the Internet greatly expand the possibilities for academic research—or for plagiarism. But these technologies can also enable the solutions for these same problems. More permissive legal standards could open a Pandora's box of new threats. That is reason to think carefully about how we deploy new weapons and how we use armed force. But we also need to remember that adversaries do not necessarily follow legal restraints just because the U.S. demands that they should. Historically, the threat of retaliation, rather than mere legal argument, has restrained enemies from abusive tactics. What we cannot do is pretend that the new technologies make no difference. We cannot ignore their potential for enhancing security, even as we grapple with the challenges.

Notes

PREFACE

1 Donald J. Trump, Inaugural Address, Jan. 20, 2017, available at https://www. whitehouse.gov/inaugural-address.

2 Transcript: Donald Trump Expounds on His Foreign Policy Views, N.Y. Times, Mar. 26, 2016, available at https://www.nytimes.com/2016/03/27/us/politics/ donald-trump-transcript.html.

3 Ken Dilanian et al., Trump Admin Ups Drone Strikes, Tolerates More Civilian Deaths: U.S. Officials, NBC News, Mar. 14, 2017, available at http://www.nbcnews.com/news/us-news/ trump-admin-ups-drone-strikes-tolerates-more-civilian-deaths-n733336.

4 Gerry Mullany, Trump Warns That "Major, Major Conflict" with North Korea is Possible, N.Y. Times, Apr. 27, 2017, available at https://www.nytimes. com/2017/04/27/world/asia/trump-north-korea-kim-jong-un.html.

5 Katie Hunt, Tillerson Sets Stage for Showdown with Beijing over South China Sea, CNN, Jan. 13, 2017, available at http://edition.cnn.com/2017/01/12/politics/ china-tillerson/.

6 Michael Forsythe, Rex Tillerson's South China Sea Remarks Foreshadow Possible Foreign Policy Crisis, N.Y. Times, Jan. 12, 2017, available at https://www.nytimes.com/2017/01/12/world/asia/rex-tillerson-south-china-sea-us.html.

CHAPTER 1

1 Joseph A. Schumpeter, Capitalism, Socialism, and Democracy (1950).

2 General Douglas MacArthur, Remarks at the Surrender Ceremonies, USS Missouri, Tokyo Bay, Sept. 2, 1945, reprinted in General MacArthur Speeches and Reports 1908-1964 166 (Edward T. Imparato ed. 2000).

3 Edmund Burke, Reflections on the Revolution in France 210 (1790).

4 John Yoo, Point of Attack: Preventive War, International Law, and Global Welfare (2014).

5 Special Rapporteur on Extrajudicial, Summary or Arbitrary Executions, Study on Targeted Killings by Philip Alston, Human Rights Council, 9-11, U.N. Doc. A/HRC/14/24/Add.6 (May 28, 2010), available at http://www2.ohchr.org/english/bodies/hrcouncil/docs/14session/A.HRC.14.24.Add6.pdf.

6 Charles A. Duelfer & Stephen Benedict Dyson, Chronic Misperception and International Conflict: The U.S.-Iraq Experience, 36 Int'l Sec. 73, 73-74 (2011).

7 Ronald Asmus, A Little War That Shook the World: Georgia, Russia, and the Future of the West 166 (2010).

8 Jon R. Lindsay, Stuxnet and the Limits of Cyber Warfare, 22 Security Studies 365, 365-66 (2013).

9 See Under Attack: Federal Cybersecurity and the OPM Data Breach, Before the Sen. Comm. on Homeland Security & Governmental Affairs (2015), 114th Cong. 1st Sess. (statement of Katherine Archuleta, U.S. Director of the Office of Personnel Management); David E. Sanger, Nicole Perlroth, and Michael D. Shear, Attack Gave Chinese Hackers Privileged Access to U.S. Systems, N.Y. Times, Jun. 20, 2015. See generally, China and Cybersecurity: Espionage, Strategy, and Politics in the Digital Domain (Jon R. Lindsay et al. eds. 2015) (discussing China's cyber capabilities).

10 Ash Carter, Secretary of Defense, Rewiring the Pentagon: Charting a New Path on Innovation and Cybersecurity (Apr. 23, 2015), available at http://www.defense.gov/News/Speeches/Speech-View/Article/606666; Michael S. Schmidt & David E. Sanger, Russian Hackers Read Obama's Unclassified Emails, Officials Say, N.Y. Times, Apr. 25, 2015, available at http://www.nytimes.com/2015/04/26/us/russian-hackers-read-obamas-unclassified-emails-officials-say.html. See also Ryan C. Maness & Brandon Valeriano, Russia's Coercive Diplomacy: Energy, Cyber, and Maritime Policy as New Sources of Power 102 (2015).

11 For a popular work, see Max Boot, War Made New: Technology, Warfare, and the Course of History, 1500 to Today 463 (2006); a more specialist work is Michael C. Horowitz, The Diffusion of Military Power: Causes and Consequences for International Politics 121, 214-25 (2010). The classic work on the link between economic innovation and war is William H. McNeill, The Pursuit of Power: Technology, Armed Force, and Society Since A.D. 1000 (1982).

12 Patrick Lin et al., Autonomous Military Robotics: Risk, Ethics, and Design, US Dept. of Navy, Office of Naval Research, at 78 (Dec. 20, 2008), available at http://ethics.calpoly.edu/onr_report.pdf.

13 See Special Rapporteur on Extrajudicial, Summary or Arbitrary Executions, Report of the Special Rapporteur on Extrajudicial, Summary or Arbitrary Executions by Christof Heyns, Human Rights Council, U.N. Doc. A/68/382 5 (Sept. 13, 2013).

14 See, e.g., Kristen Eichensehr, The Cyber-Law of Nations, 103 Geo. L. J. 317, 365-79 (2015); Michael N. Schmitt, The Law of Cyber Warfare: Quo Vadis?, 25 Stan. L. & Pol'y Rev. 269 (2014).

15 Office of the Secretary of Defense, Annual Report to Congress: Military and Security Developments Involving the People's Republic of China 2016, at 64, available at http://www.defense.gov/Portals/1/Documents/pubs/2016%20China%20Military%20Power%20Report.pdf.

16 Department of Defense, Law of War Manual 994 (Jun. 2015), available at http://archive.defense.gov/pubs/Law-of-War-Manual-June-2015.pdf.

17 Id. at 1.

18 See, e.g., The Handbook of International Humanitarian Law (Terry Gill & Dieter Fleck eds. 2008).

19 See John Yoo, Using Force, 71 U. Chi. L. Rev. 729, 758-59 (2004).

20 Additional Protocol I to the Geneva Conventions of 12 Aug. 1949 (Jun. 8, 1977), 1125 UNTS 3, 16 ILM 1391 (1977) (hereinafter "AP I").

21 See Letter of Transmittal from President Ronald Reagan to the U.S. Senate (Jan. 29, 1987), reprinted in Agora: The U.S. Decision Not to Ratify Protocol I to the Geneva Conventions on the Protection of War Victims, 81 Am. J. Int'l L. 910 (1987).

22 Rome Statute of the International Criminal Court, U.N. Doc. A/CONF. 183/9 (Jul. 17, 1998).

23 See, e.g., Michael J. Matheson, Session One: The United States Position on the Relation of Customary International Law to the 1977 Protocols Additional to the 1949 Geneva Conventions, 2 Am. U. J. Int'l L. & Pol'y 419, 422, 428 (1987).

24 See, e.g., L. Lynn Hogue, Identifying Customary International Law of War in Protocol I: A Proposed Restatement, 13 Loy. L.A. Int'l & Comp. L. Rev. 279, 280 (1990); Theodor Meron, The Geneva Conventions as Customary Law, 81 Am. J. Int'l L. 348, 364-65, n.52 (1987).

25 See, e.g., Richard R. Baxter, Multilateral Treaties as Evidence of Customary International Law, 41 Brit. Y.B. Int'l L. 275 (1965-66); Anthony D'Amato, The Concept of Custom in International Law (1971).

26 Nuclear Weapons Advisory Opinion, 1996 ICJ Rep. 226, 258 (Jul. 8, 1996).

27 For criticism, see J. Patrick Kelly, The Twilight of Customary International Law, 40 Va. J. Int'l L. 449 (2000).

28 United States Telecom Association v. FCC, 825 F.3d 674 (D.C. Cir. 2016).

29 Red Lion Broadcasting v. FCC, 395 U.S. 367 (1969) (allowing imposition of right-of-reply rules on television broadcasting); Miami Herald v. Tornillo, 418 U.S. 241 (1974) (disallowing imposition of right-of-reply on newspapers); Kyllo v. United States, 533 U.S. 27 (2001) (thermal imaging devices); United States v. Jones, 132 S.Ct. 945 (2012) (GPS tracking devices).

30 Geoffrey Best, Churchill and War 290 (2006).

31 See, e.g., Heather Harrison Dinniss, Cyber Warfare and the Laws of War (2012); Marco Roscini, Cyber Operations and the Use of Force in International Law (2014); Scott J. Shackelford, Managing Cyber Attacks in International Law, Business, and Relations: In Search of Cyber Peace (2014).

32 See, e.g., Oona A. Hathaway et al., The Law of Cyber-Attack, 100 Cal. L. Rev. 817 (2012); Scott J. Shackelford, From Nuclear War to Net War: Analogizing Attacks in International Law, 27 Berkeley J. Int'l L. 1 (2009).

33 See generally William H. McNeill, The Pursuit of Power: Technology, Armed Force, and Society Since A.D. 1000, at 2-62 (1982).

34 See Neil Morpeth, Thucydides' War: Accounting for the Faces of Conflict 105-07 (2006).

35 McNeill, supra note 33, at 66.

36 Victor Davis Hanson, Carnage and Culture: Landmark Battles in the Rise of Western Power (2002).

37 Alexander Gillespie, A History of the Laws of War: Volume 3: The Customs and Laws of War With Regards to Arms Control 12 (2011).

38 Jeffrey L. Singman, Daily Life in Medieval Europe 124 (1999).

39 While captured knights were usually held for ransom (and well treated in the meantime), captured archers were often mutilated, like particularly despicable criminals.

40 J.F.C. Fuller, Armament and History: A Study of the Influence of Armament on History from the Dawn of Classical Warfare to the Second World War 86 (1945).

41 See Angus Maddison, Contours of the World Economy, 1-2030 AD: Essays in Macro-Economic History 379 (2007).

42 Instructions for the Government of Armies of the United States in the Field, General Orders No. 100, art. 15, Apr. 24, 1863, available at http://avalon.law.yale.edu/19th_century/lieber.asp#sec2.

43 John Fabian Witt, Lincoln's Code: The Laws of War in American History 177 (2012).

44 Quoted in id. at 184.

45 U.S. Library of Congress, Congressional Research Service, The New START Treaty: Central Limits and Key Provisions by Amy F. Woolf, R41219 (Feb. 1, 2017) at 26, available at https://www.fas.org/sgp/crs/nuke/R41219.pdf.

46 Yoo, Point of Attack, supra note 4, at 65-75.

47 U.N. Charter art. 42.

48 Id., art. 51.

49 See, e.g., Thomas M. Franck, Recourse to Force: State Action Against Threats and Armed Attacks (2004); Ian Brownlie, International Law and the Use of Force by States (1963).

50 U.N. Charter art. 39.

51 E.S. Colbert, Retaliation in International Law (1948) (describing many episodes of coercive violence outside the context of declared war).

52 U.N. Charter art. 41.

53 U.N. Charter art. 45.

54 See John Yoo, Force Rules: UN Reform and Intervention, 6 Chi. J. Int'l L. 641 (2006).

55 See, e.g., John Lewis Gaddis, The Long Peace: Inquiries Into the History of the Cold War 219-37 (1989); Kenneth N. Waltz, Nuclear Myths and Political Realities 84 Am. Pol. Sci. Rev. 731, 740 (1990).

56 See, e.g., Roger N. McDermott, Brothers Disunited: Russia's Use of Military Power in Ukraine, in J.L. Black et al. eds., The Return of the Cold War: Ukraine, the West and Russia 77, 80-83 (2016).

57 See Maj. Brian P. Fleming, The Hybrid Threat Concept: Contemporary War, Military Planning and the Advent of Unrestricted Operational Art, U.S. Army Command and Gen. Staff College (May 17, 2011), available at http://indianstrategicknowledgeonline.com/web/2753.pdf.

58 See Scott Jasper & Scott Moreland, The Islamic State is a Hybrid Threat: Why Does That Matter?, Small Wars Journal (2014), available at http://www.smallwarsjournal.com/printpdf/18345.

59 See, e.g., Lassa Oppenheim, International Law: A Treatise, Volume 1 48-53 (2d ed. 1912) (describing "pacific blockade").

60 AP I, supra note 20, art. 52.

61 Id., art. 14.

62 David Cortright & George A. Lopez, The Sanctions Decade: Assessing UN Strategies in the 1990s, at 46-47 (2000) (discussing "humanitarian catastrophe" from sanctions on Iraq).

63 Id. at 73-74 (Serbia).

64 AP I, supra note 20, art. 48.

65 Abraham D. Sofaer, Terrorism, the Law, and the National Defense, 126 Mil. L. Rev. 89, 120 (1989).

66 Id.

67 Thomas C. Schelling, The Strategy of Conflict (1960).

68 Abraham Lincoln, Annual Message to Congress, Dec. 1, 1862, in Collected Works of Abraham Lincoln, Volume 5 518, 537 (Roy P. Basler ed. 1953).

69 6 id. at 28, 29.

CHAPTER 2

1 Zeev Maoz & Azar Gat, War in a Changing World 18 (2001).

2 See Steven Pinker, The Better Angels of Our Nature: Why Violence Has Declined 226-27 (2012).

3 Ben Connable et al., Stretching and Exploiting Thresholds for High-Order War: How Russia, China, and Iran Are Eroding American Influence Using Time-Tested Measures Short of War 17 (2016).

4 See generally Geoffrey Wawro, The Austro-Prussian War: Austria's War with Prussia and Italy in 1866 (1997).

5 Kenneth Mouré & Martin S. Alexander, Crisis and Renewal in France, 1918-1962, at 255 (2002).

6 White House Office of the Press Secretary, Government Assessment of the Syrian Government's Use of Chemical Weapons on August 21, 2013 (Aug. 30, 2013), available at https://www.whitehouse.gov/the-press-office/2013/08/30/government-assessment-syrian-government-s-use-chemical-weapons-august-21.

7 See Convention on the Prohibition of the Development, Production, Stockpiling and Use of Chemical Weapons and on their Destruction, art. 1, Jan. 13, 1993, 1974 U.N.T.S. 317.

8 Security Council Report, UN Documents for Syria, available at http://www.securitycouncilreport.org/un-documents/syria/.

9 Anne Gearan & Ed O'Keefe, Kerry, Hagel Lay Out Military Objectives During Senate Hearing on Syria Strike, Wash. Post, Sept. 4, 2013, at A1.

10 Karl P. Mueller et al., Rand Corp., Airpower Options for Syria: Assessing Objectives and Missions for Aerial Intervention 1-2, 9-10, 12-15 (2013), available at http://www.rand.org/content/dam/rand/pubs/research_reports/RR400/RR446/RAND_RR446.pdf.

11 U.N. Security Council, Security Council Requires Scheduled Destruction of Syria's Chemical Weapons, Unanimously Adopting Resolution 2118 (2013) (Sept. 27, 2013), available at http://www.un.org/press/en/2013/sc11135.doc.htm.

12 Michael R. Gordon, U.S. and Russia Reach Deal to Destroy Syria's Chemical Arms, N.Y. Times, Sep. 14, 2013, available at http://www.nytimes.com/2013/09/15/world/middleeast/syria-talks.html.

13 Anne Barnard, Death Toll From War in Syria Now 470,000, Group Finds, N.Y. Times, Feb. 11, 2016, at A6. See also U.N. Security Council, Alarmed

by Continuing Syria Crisis, Security Council Affirms Its Support for Special Envoy's Approach in Moving Political Solution Forward (Aug. 17, 2015), available at https://www.un.org/press/en/2015/sc12008.doc.htm.

14 U.N. High Commissioner for Refugees, Syria Emergency, available at http://www.unhcr.org/en-us/syria-emergency.html.

15 Hans Christian Bjerg, To Copenhagen a Fleet: The British Pre-emptive Seizure of the Danish-Norwegian Navy, 1807, 7 Int'l J. Naval Hist. (2008), available at http://www.ijnhonline.org/wp-content/uploads/2012/01/Bjerg.pdf.

16 Kinga Tibori Szabó, Anticipatory Action in Self-Defence: Essence and Limits under International Law 97-98 (2011).

17 Maj. Jane Gibson & Maj. Kenneth G. Kemmerly, Intercontinental Ballistic Missiles, in Air Command and Staff College Space Research Electives Seminars, Air University, AU-18 Space Primer 236 (2009), available at http://www.au.af.mil/au/aupress/digital/pdf/book/AU-18.pdf.

18 Id. at 238.

19 Legality of the Threat or Use of Nuclear Weapons in Armed Conflict, Advisory Opinion, 1996 I.C.J. 226, 244 (Jul. 8, 1996).

20 D.W. Bowett, Self-Defense in International Law 187-92 (1958); Myres S. McDougal & Florentino P. Feliciano, Law and Minimum World Public Order: The Legal Regulation of International Coercion 232-41 (1961); Julius Stone, Aggression and World Order: A Critique of United Nations Theories of Aggression 44 (1958); Antonio Cassese, International Law in a Divided World 230-23 (1986); Yoram Dinstein, War, Aggression and Self-Defence 191 (4th ed. 2005); Oscar Schachter, The Right of States to Use Armed Force, 82 Mich. L. Rev. 1620 (1984); Ruth Wedgwood, Responding to Terrorism: The Strikes Against bin Laden, 24 Yale J. Int'l L. 559, 556-65 (1999).

21 Letter from Daniel Webster to Henry Fox, British Minister in Washington (Apr. 24, 1841), in 1 British Documents on Foreign Affairs: Reports and Papers From the Foreign Office Confidential Print (Part I, Series C) 153, 159 (Kenneth Bourne & D. Cameron Watt eds., University Publications of America 1986).

22 See Barbara Tuchman, The Guns of August (2010).

23 John F. Kennedy, Radio and Television Report to the American People on the Soviet Arms Buildup in Cuba (Oct. 22, 1962), reprinted in Public Papers of President Kennedy 1962, at 806-07.

24 See, e.g., Myres S. McDougal, The Soviet-Cuban Quarantine and Self-Defense, 57 Am. J. Int'l L. 597, 598 (1963); Quincy Wright, The Cuban Quarantine, 57 Am. J. Int'l L. 546, 563-64 (1963); Abram Chayes, The Legal Case for U.S. Action in Cuba, 47 Dep't State Bull. 763, 764-65 (1962).

25 See Timothy L.H. McCormack, Self-Defense in International Law: The Israeli Raid on The Iraqi Nuclear Reactor 297-302 (1996).

26 S.C. Res. 487, ¶1, U.N. SCOR, U.N. Doc. S/RES/487 (Jun. 19, 1981).

27 U.N. SCOR 2288th mtg., U.N. Doc. S/PV.2288 80 (Jun. 19, 1981).

28 David E. Sanger, Confront and Conceal: Obama's Secret Wars and Surprising Use of American Power 190 (2012).

29 Id. at 199.

30 Id. at 190-92.

31 Priyanka Boghani, Syria Got Rid of Its Chemical Weapons—But Reports of Attacks Continue, PBS, May 26, 2015, available at http://www.pbs.org/wgbh/frontline/article/syria-got-rid-of-its-chemical-weapons-but-reports-of-attacks-continue/.

32 See White House Office of the Press Secretary, Statement by NSC Spokesperson Ned Price on OPCW-UN Report on Syria (Oct. 22, 2016), available at https://www.whitehouse.gov/the-press-office/2016/10/22/statement-nsc-spokesperson-ned-price-opcw-un-report-syria.

33 Bill Clinton, My Life: The Presidential Years Vol. II 167 (2005).

34 Daniel Ness & Chia-Ling Lin, International Education: An Encyclopedia of Contemporary Issues and Systems 374 (2015); Adam Daniel Rotfeld, International Security in a Time of Change: Threats—Concepts—Institutions 127 (2004).

35 K.J. Holsti, The State, War, and the State of War 21-24 (1996); Nils Petter Gleditsch et al., Armed Conflict 1946-2001: A New Dataset, 39 J. Peace Res. 615, 620 (2002).

36 Human Security Report Project, Human Security Report 2013 (2014), available at http://www.hsrgroup.org/docs/Publications/HSR2013/HSRP_Report_2013_140226_Web.pdf.

37 Id.

38 James D. Fearon & David D. Laitin, Ethnicity, Insurgency, and Civil War, 97 Am. Poli. Sci. Rev. 75 (2003).

39 See John Yoo, Fixing Failed States, 99 Cal. L. Rev. 95 (2011).

40 S.C. Res. 1973, (Mar. 17, 2011).

41 John Yoo, Point of Attack: Preventive War, International Law, and Global Welfare 30 (2014).

42 Allen Buchanan, Reforming the International Law of Humanitarian Intervention, in Humanitarian Intervention: Ethical, Legal, and Political Dilemmas 130 (J.L. Holzgrefe & Robert O. Keohane ed. 2003); Mark R. Amstutz, International Ethics: Concepts, Theories, and Cases in Global Politics 154 (2013); John-Mark Iyi, Humanitarian Intervention and the AU-ECOWAS Intervention Treaties Under International Law: Towards a Theory of Regional Responsibility to Protect 221 (2016).

43 U.N. Charter art. 51.

44 For survey of the debate, see Andrew Roberts, The Storm of War: A New History of the Second World War 245-50 (2011).

45 Agnieszka Jachec-Neale, The Concept of Military Objectives in International Law and Targeting Practice 252 (2015) ("The most problematic objectives in this regard appear to be those that facilitate the commission of war crimes, such as concentration camps or means by which violence against the civilian population is incited.").

46 See Islamic State and the Crisis in Iraq and Syria in Maps, BBC, Jan. 20, 2017, available at http://www.bbc.com/news/world-middle-east-27838034.

47 Sam Perlo-Freeman et al., Stockholm International Peace Research Institute, Trends in World Military Expenditure 2015 (2016), available at https://www.sipri.org/sites/default/files/EMBARGO%20FS1604%20Milex%202015.pdf.

48 For a variety of commentary on the implications of China's rise for the balance of power in Asia, see Aaron L. Friedberg, A Contest for Supremacy: China, America, and the Struggle for Mastery in Asia (2012); Robert D. Kaplan, Asia's Cauldron: The South China Sea and the End of a Stable Pacific (2014); Henry Kissinger, On China (2011); Edward N. Luttwak, The Rise of China vs. The Logic of Strategy (2012).

49 Perlo-Freeman et al., supra note 47.

50 Michael O'Hanlon, The U.S. Defense Spending Context, in The Changing Dynamics of U.S. Defense Spending 11 (Leon V. Sigal ed. 1999).

51 See, e.g., Stephen G. Brooks & William C. Wohlforth, The Rise and Fall of the Great Powers in the Twenty-first Century: China's Rise and the Fate of America's Global Position, 40 Int'l Security 7, 18-19 (2015). On the importance of control of the global commons, see Barry R. Posen, Command of the Commons: The Military Foundation of U.S. Hegemony, 28 Int'l Security 8 (2003).

52 See Bill Hayton, The South China Sea: The Struggle for Power in Asia (2014).

53 See Agnia Grigas, Beyond Crimea: The New Russian Empire (2016).

54 Choe Sang-Hun & Jane Perlez, North Korea Tests a Mightier Nuclear Bomb, Raising Tension, N.Y. Times, Sep. 8, 2016, available at https://www.nytimes.com/2016/09/09/world/asia/north-korea-nuclear-test.html; Choe Sang-Hun, North Korea Launches Rocket Seen as Cover for a Missile Test, N.Y. Times, Feb. 6, 2016, available at https://www.nytimes.com/2016/02/07/world/asia/north-korea-moves-up-rocket-launching-plan.html. In March of 2017 alone, North Korea fired an additional four test missiles. See Jonathan Cheng & Alastair Gale, North Korea Missile Test Stirs ICBM Fears, The Wall Street Journal, Mar. 7, 2017, available at https://www.wsj.com/articles/north-korea-missile-test-stirs-icbm-fears-1488802971.

55 See James Q. Wilson, Thinking About Crime 27, 61-62 (1985).

56 Gabriella Blum, The Crime and Punishment of States, 38 Yale J. Int'l L. 1, 94, 113, 115 (2013); Eric A. Posner & Alan O. Sykes, Optimal War and Jus Ad Bellum, 93 Geo. L.J. 993, 1000-01 (2005).

57 Thomas C. Schelling, The Strategy of Conflict 5 (1960).

58 Robert Powell, War as a Commitment Problem, 60 Int'l Org. 169 (2006); Robert Powell, The Inefficient Use of Power: Costly Conflict with Complete Information, 98 Am. Pol. Sci. Rev. 231 (2004); James D. Fearon, Rationalist Explanations for War, 49 Int'l Org. 379 (1995).

59 See, e.g., Robert D. Cooter & Daniel L. Rubinfeld, An Economic Model of Legal Discovery, 23 J. Legal Stud. 435 (1994); Robert D. Cooter & Daniel L. Rubinfeld, Economic Analysis of Legal Disputes and Their Resolution, 27 J. Econ. Literature 1067 (1989).

60 For uses of the bargaining approach to constitutional and international law questions, see Fearon, supra note 58; Robert Powell, In the Shadow of Power: States and Strategies in International Politics (1999). See also Jide Nzelibe & John Yoo, Rational War and Constitutional Design, 115 Yale L.J. 2512 (2006); Jeremy Rabkin & John Yoo, A Return to Coercion: International Law and New Weapon Technologies, 42 Hofstra L. Rev. 1187 (2014).

61 See Richard L. Russell, Sharpening Strategic Intelligence: Why the CIA Gets It Wrong and What Needs to Be Done to Get It Right (2007). The classic work on intelligence failure is Roberta Wohlstetter, Pearl Harbor: Warning and Decision (1962).

62 Guenter Lewy, America in Vietnam 442-53 (1978).

63 See James D. Fearon, Domestic Political Audiences and the Escalation of International Disputes, 88 Am. Pol. Sci. Rev. 577, 578-79 (1994).

64 See, e.g., Robert Powell, Crisis Stability in the Nuclear Age, 83 Am. Pol. Sci. Rev. 61, 67 (1989).

65 See Interview by PBS Frontline with General Wesley Clark, Former NATO Supreme Allied Commander.

66 Powell, supra note 64, at 171-72.

67 See James D. Morrow, The Laws of War, Common Conjectures, and Legal Systems in International Politics, 31 J. Legal Stud. 41, 44, 54-55 (2002); Eric A. Posner, A Theory of the Laws of War, 70 U. Chi. L. Rev. 297, 302-07 (2003).

68 Charles Cheney Hyde, International Law: Chiefly as Interpreted and Applied by the United States, Volume 3, at 1727-32 (2d ed. 1951).

69 U.N. Charter art. 41.

70 See Schelling, supra note 57, at 207; Powell, supra note 60, at 61, 67.

71 Blum, supra note 56, at 58.

72 See, e.g., Stanimir A. Alexandrov, Self-Defense Against the Use of Force in International Law 77-79 (1996); D.W. Bowett, Self-Defense in International Law 223-25, 273-75 (1958); Ian Brownlie, International Law and the Use of Force by States 274-75 (1963); Thomas M. Franck, Recourse to Force: State Action Against Threats and Armed Attacks 41, 50, 65, 98 (2004); Christine Gray, International Law and the Use of Force 86-88 (2000); Louis Henkin, The Use of Force: Law and U.S. Policy, in Right v. Might: International Law and the Use of Force 38-39 (2d ed. 1991).

73 James A. Green & Francis Grimal, The Threat of Force as an Action in Self-Defense Under International Law, 44 Vand. J. Transnat'l L. 285, 298-302 (2011).

74 Laurie R. Blank, Targeted Strikes: The Consequences of Blurring the Armed Conflict and Self-Defense Justifications, 38 Wm. Mitchell L. Rev. 1655, 1670 (2012).

75 See, e.g., Model Penal Code §3.04 (1985).

76 David Rodin, War and Self-Defense 118 (2002).

77 John Stuart Mill, The Contest in America 31 (1862).

78 S.C. Res. 487, U.N. SCOR, U.N. Doc. S/RES/487 (Jun. 19, 1981). But see U.N. SCOR, 2288th mtg., U.N. Doc. S/PV.2288 80 (Jun. 19, 1981).

79 See John Yoo, The Powers of War and Peace: The Constitution and Foreign Affairs After 9/11, at 169 (2005) (discussing legality of the Kosovo War).

80 U.N. Charter art. 42.

CHAPTER 3

1 Letter to James C. Conkling, Aug. 26, 1863 in Lincoln, Speeches and Writings, 1859-1865, at 497 (Don E. Fehrenbacher ed. 1989). Note that the Emancipation Proclamation was actually implemented by the penetration of Union forces into Confederate territory during operations in which slaves were often enlisted into support services for Union armies, sometimes enlisted as soldiers and often protected from recapture in special encampments.

2 Burrus M. Carnahan, Act of Justice: Lincoln's Emancipation Proclamation and the Law of War 117-33 (2007); John Fabian Witt, Lincoln's Code (2012).

3 Letter to James C. Conkling, supra note 1.

4 Protocol Additional to the Geneva Conventions of 12 August 1949 (AP I), art. 48, Jun. 8, 1977.

5 Id. at art. 51, ¶5(b).

6 Commentary on the Additional Protocols of 8 June 1977 585-87 (Yves Sandoz ed. 1987).

7 Herodotus, The Histories, 9.79, at 702 (Robert B. Strassler trans., Landmark Herodotus 2007).

8 Hugo Grotius, The Law of War and Peace, Book II, xix, §1, at 450 (Francis W. Kelsey trans., Carnegie 1925).

9 Michael Bryant, A World History of War Crimes: From Antiquity to the Present 31-37 (2016).

10 On mutilation of Japanese corpses in World War II, see E.B. Sledge, With the Old Breed: At Peleliu and Okinawa 118-21 (2007) ("like Indian warriors taking scalps").

11 Thucydides, The History of the Peloponnesian War, Book III, §44, §50, at 182, 184 (Richard Crawley trans., Landmark 1996). The most recent study, Mary P. Nichols, Thucydides and the Pursuit of Freedom (2015), notes that Diodotus, who argued for the strategic advantages of displaying clemency in the Athenian debate (as reported by Thucydides), appears nowhere else in classical literature, so may have been an invention of Thucydides to indicate what should have been said. Nichols at 65.

12 Thucydides, The History of the Peloponnesian War, Book V, §89, at 352 ("the strong do what they can"); Book V, §116, at 357 (Athenians "put to death all the grown men").

13 Herodotus, Histories, 8.105 ("ungodly practice"—performed here by an Ionian in the Persian empire on behalf of Persians who subsequently suffers a particularly lurid version of the same fate in retaliation); 6.9, 32 (Persians threaten a Greek city—and then follow through on the threat—to make "the most handsome boys...eunuchs"). No comparable episode is recorded in Thucydides, nor in the Hellenic history of Xenophon.

14 Plutarch, Caesar in Lives of the Noble Grecians and Romans 863 (Clough ed., Modern Library 1992).

15 Barry Strauss, Masters of Command: Alexander, Hannibal, Caesar, and the Genius of Leadership 12 (2012).

16 Robert C. Stacey, The Age of Chivalry in The Laws of War: Constraints on Warfare in the Western World 33 (Michael Howard et al. eds. 1994).

17 Kant, Perpetual Peace: A Philosophical Sketch 116 (1795) in (Ted Humphrey trans., Hackett 1983).

18 Emer de Vattel, The Law of Nations, Book III, Ch. 8, §145, at 282-83 (Charles G. Fenwick trans., Carnegie Institution 1916).

19 Id.

20 Id., III, 8, §201, at 311.

21 Id., III, 8, §151, at 285.

22 Id., III, 9, §167, at 293.

23 Robert Kolb, Origin of the Twin Terms Jus ad Bellum/Jus in Bello, International Review of the Red Cross, Vol. 37, at 553 (1997).

24 Vattel, The Law of Nations, III, viii, §137, at 279.

25 See Barbara Alice Mann, George Washington's War on Native America (2009).

26 David Hackett Fischer, Washington's Crossing 377 (2004).

27 Henry Adams, History of the United States During the Administration of James Madison (1889): Second Administration, Vol. II, Ch. 5 at 1014 (Library of America ed. 1986).

28 Elizabeth Longford, Wellington: The Years of the Sword 337 (1969).

29 Letter of James A. Seldon, Confederate Secretary of War, to Robert Ould, Agent of Exchange, 24 June 1863, reprinted in Lieber's Code and the Law of War 120-30, quoted passage at 128 (Richard S. Hartigan ed. Precedent 1983). Seldon particularly denounced provisions authorizing "destruction of [civilian] property" and allowing Union forces to "bombard" and "to starve" civilians,

but seems most incensed by provisions he took to be instigating "servile war" (that is, rebellion by slaves).

30 Robert R. Mackey, The Uncivil War: Irregular Warfare in the Upper South, 1861-1865 56-60 (2005) (on burning of houses in Arkansas and destruction of property along the Mississippi, seen to be consistent with Lieber Code which allowed execution of irregular fighters—though this penalty was rarely imposed): "Most responsible for the defeat of Confederate irregulars" in Arkansas, according to this study, was the mobilization of "indigenous counter guerrilla units formed of loyal Unionists" who "conducted a brutal and effective counterinsurgency campaign...." See also Richard S. Brownlee, Gray Ghosts of the Confederacy: Guerrilla Warfare in the West, 1861-1865 158-169 (1984) on "banishment" or "confinement" of "disloyal" civilians in Missouri, such as relatives of known guerrillas, along with "social assessments" (enforced payments) imposed on those suspected of being "disloyal" to cover "damage caused by guerrillas."

31 William T. Sherman, Memoirs of General William T. Sherman, at 290 (civilian expulsions), 300 (threats to property). Lieber Code, art. 156: "The commander will throw the burden of the war, as much as lies within his powers, on the disloyal citizens of the revolted portion or province, subjecting them to a stricter police than the non-combatant enemies have to suffer in regular war...he may expel, transfer, imprison, or fine the revolted citizens who refuse to pledge themselves anew as citizens obedient to the law and loyal to the government."

32 Convention (II) With Respect to the Laws and Customs of War on Land, Jul. 29, 1899, reprinted in Laws of Armed Conflicts 60-82 (Dietrich Schindler & Jiri Toman 1988).

33 L. Oppenheim, International Law 190-91 (2d ed. 1912); Percy Bordwell, The Law of War Between Belligerents: A History and Commentary 153 (1908).

34 Bordwell, supra note 33, at 155.

35 Isabel V. Hull, Absolute Destruction: Military Culture and the Practices of War in Imperial Germany 88 (2004); Jeremy Sarkin, Germany's Genocide of the Herero: Kaiser Wilhelm II, His General, His Settlers, His Soldiers (2011); Jurgen Zimmerer & Joachim Zeller, Genocide in German South-West Africa: The Colonial War of 1904-1908 and Its Aftermath (2008).

36 For accounts of these episodes see On the Road to Total War: The American Civil War and the German Wars of Unification, 1861-1871 (Stig Förster & Jorg Nagler eds. 1997).

37 Convention (IV) Respecting the Laws and Customs of War on Land and its Annex: Regulations Concerning the Laws and Customs of War on Land, The Hague, Oct. 18, 1907, 36 Stat. 2277, 1 Bevans 631, entered into force Jan. 26, 1910.

38 Geoffrey Best, Restraints on War by Land before 1945, in Restraints on War: Studies in the Limitation of Armed Conflict 27 (Michael Howard ed. 1979).

39 Substantive prohibitions in the Annex to each convention, known as "Regulations": art. 28, 47 (no pillage), art. 25 (against bombardment of "towns, villages, dwellings, buildings which are undefended").

40 Convention (IV), supra note 37.

41 Hague Regulations, art. 23(a); Declaration (IV, 2) Concerning Asphyxiating Gases, Jul. 29, 1899, reprinted in Laws of Armed Conflict 95 (Schindler & Toman 1988).

42 For account of the initial episode, see Jonathan B. Tucker, War of Nerves: Chemical Warfare from World War I to Al-Qaeda 13-16 (2006).

43 Protocol for the Prohibition of the Use in War of Asphyxiating, Poisonous or Other Gases, Jun. 17, 1925, reprinted in Laws of Armed Conflict 107 (Schindler & Toman 1988) (emphasis added).

44 Rick Atkinson, The Day of Battle: The War in Sicily and Italy, 1943-1944 271-75 (2007), describes widespread injuries in 1943 when a German bomb attack inadvertently released poison gas stockpiled (in secret) by U.S. forces in Italy, to have ready for retaliation.

45 L. Oppenheim, International Law Vol. II, §247, at 305 (2d ed. 1912).

46 Grotius asserts that Roman precedents show the right to kill applies "to all persons who are in the enemy's territory" since "injury may be feared from such persons," even those who do not "actually bear arms." Grotius, The Law of War and Peace, supra note 8, Bk. III, Ch. iv, §6, at 646. But Grotius also urges restraint toward "the innocent," including children, women, farmers, and others presumptively in this category. Id. at Bk. III, Ch. xi, §§8-15, at 733-40.

47 Michael Bryant, A World History of War Crimes, supra note 9 at 41.

48 Hague Regulations, art. 29 stipulates that "soldiers and civilians...entrusted with delivery of despatches [sic]" should not be treated as spies. The one reference to "civilians" is to those providing direct and open assistance to the military.

49 James Kent, Commentaries on American Law 55 (12th ed. 1989) (1826).

50 Henry Wheaton, Elements of International Law 362-63 (8th ed. 1995) (1836).

51 Jean-Jacques Burlamaqui, The Principles of Natural and Politic Law, §30, at 475 (2006) (1751).

52 Nicholas Parrillo, The De-Privatization of American Warfare: How the U.S. Government Used, Regulated, and Ultimately Abandoned Privateering in the Nineteenth Century, 19 Yale J. L. & Human. 1, 1 (2007).

53 Albert Edmond Hogan, Pacific Blockade 151-57 (1908).

54 James Cable, Gunboat Diplomacy 1919-1991 37-42 (3rd ed. 1994).

55 James M. McPherson, War on the Waters: The Union and Confederate Navies, 1861-1865 225 (2012), describing the effectiveness and comprehensiveness of the blockade by war's end, including reduction of cotton exports by some 90 percent.

56 Benjamin R. Curtis, "Executive Power" in Union Pamphlets of the Civil War, 1861-1865 (Frank Freidel ed. 1967): "This penalty [of confiscation of slaves]...is not to be inflicted [exclusively] on those persons who have been guilty of treason....It is not, therefore, as a punishment for guilty persons, that the commander-in-chief decrees the freedom of slaves."

57 Prize Cases, 67 U.S. 635 (1863).

58 For review of French, German, and Italian commentary opposing wartime naval capture of civilian commerce, see Jeremy Rabkin, Anglo-American Dissent from the European Law of War: A History with Contemporary Echoes, 16 San Diego Int'l L. J. 1, 12-16 (2014).

59 John Westlake, "Belligerent Rights at Sea" reprinted in The Collected Papers of John Westlake on Public International Law 614-15 (L. Oppenheim ed. 1914) (1894).

60 Id. at 247 (originally published in Chapters on International Law, 1894).

61 For recent assessments of historians, see John Horne & Alan Kramer, German

Atrocities, 1914: A History of Denial (2001) and Alan Kramer, Dynamic of Destruction: Culture and Mass Killing in the First World War (2007). For accounts at the time, John Hartman Morgan, German Atrocities: An Official Investigation (1916).

62 Letter of W.T. Sherman to Henry Halleck, Dec. 24, 1864, reprinted in William Tecumseh Sherman: Memoirs of W.T. Sherman at 705 (2d ed. Library of America 1990) (1875).

63 Id. at 659.

64 Ulysses S. Grant, Memoirs and Selected Letters: Personal Memoirs of U.S. Grant 646 (Library of America 1990) (1885).

65 Sherman, Memoirs, supra note 62 at 670.

66 Philip Henry Sheridan, Personal Memoirs of P.H. Sheridan, General, United States Army Vol. I 267 (1888).

67 Robert M. Utley, Frontier Regulars: The United States Army and the Indian, 1866-1891 51 (1973): Punitive raids "aimed at finding and destroying Indian villages" though in the "majority of actions, the army shot noncombatants incidentally and accidentally, not purposefully."

68 C.E. Callwell, Small Wars: Their Principles and Practice 40-42 (1990) (1896).

69 Winston S. Churchill, The Story of the Malakand Field Force: An Episode of Frontier War 164-67 (1990) (1898). Among those who congratulated the young author on his insight and honesty was George Curzon, about to become Viceroy of India. Con Coughlin, Churchill's First War: Young Winston and the Fight Against the Taliban 228 (2013). As the author notes, frontier security "remains as problematic for the modern generation of soldiers fighting the Pashtun tribesmen on the Northwest Frontier as it was in the 1890s." Pakistan has preserved the fort where Churchill drafted original dispatches from his punitive expedition and a military guide insists today's Pakistani army has "fond memories of the British empire." Id. at 229, 234-35.

70 Robert Tombs, The Wars Against Paris in On The Road to Total War 546-48 (Stig Förster & Jorg Nagler eds. 1997), describing indiscriminate shelling of Paris in 1870—and advice by U.S. military observer who was present, General Philip Sheridan, that Grant had done the same at Vicksburg.

71 Lawrence James, Churchill and Empire: A Portrait of an Imperialist 165 (2014); James S. Corum & Wray R. Johnson, Airpower in Small Wars: Fighting Insurgents and Terrorists 53 (2003): By the 1920s, "RAF bombing raids largely replaced the traditional army punitive expeditions...."

72 Jaffna L. Cox, A Splendid Training Ground: The Importance to the Royal Air Force of Its Role in Iraq, 1919-1932, 13 J. of Commonwealth and Imperial Hist. 157, 172 (1985) (quoting Colonial Secretary Churchill telegram to Britain's High Commissioner for Mesopotamia, Sir Percy Cox, June 7, 1921: "Air action is a legitimate means of quelling disturbances ... but it should in no circumstances be employed in support of purely administrative measures such as collection of revenue.").

73 Winston Churchill, The World Crisis 1911-1918, Pt. II at 721 (1939).

74 Id., Pt. I, Ch. I 2-3 (1939).

75 David Stevenson, Cataclysm: The First World War as Political Tragedy 201 (2004). By earlier understandings, codified in the 1856 Declaration of Paris, a belligerent could declare a "blockade" of an enemy port, but only if prepared to enforce it with close-in naval patrols. By 1914, mines and shore batteries made

it too dangerous for the Royal Navy to impose formal blockades. Instead, it announced lists of prohibited imports, using its navy to stop ships on the high seas to prevent them from delivering such supplies.

76 Sir Frederick Smith, The Destruction of Merchant Ships Under International Law 49 (1917) (noting—for the benefit of U.S. readers—that John Paul Jones had been careful to assist survivors after his attacks).

77 Id. at 51.

78 Paul G. Halpern, A Naval History of World War I 291 (1994).

79 Address to a Joint Session of Congress on German Violations of International Law, Apr. 19, 1916. Wilson claimed the American position reflected "our sense of duty as the representative of neutrals the world over" as well as to "a just conception of the rights of mankind...."

80 Eric W. Osborne, Britain's Economic Blockade of Germany, 1914-1919 168 (2004), documents scale of reductions—some 80 percent drop in imports for the Netherlands. Allied controls allowed neutrals to import only what they would consume at home.

81 Howard Levie, "Submarine Warfare" in The Law of Naval Warfare 37-38, International Law Studies, Vol. 65 (Richard Grunawalt ed. 1993).

82 For summary of the gradual escalation of control measures, Stevenson, Cataclysm, supra note 75 at 200-03. For much greater detail, A.C. Bell, A History of the Blockade of Germany and of the countries associated with her in the Great War, Austria-Hungary, Bulgaria, and Turkey 1914-1918 221-46 (H.M. Stationery Off. 1937).

83 Earl of Selborne, Debates in British Parliament 1911-1912 on the Declaration of London and the Naval Prize Bill at 631, warning that a foreign power would "make its plans almost exclusively at the beginning of a naval war with a view to creating a shortage in our food supply."

84 C. Paul Vincent, The Politics of Hunger: The Allied Blockade of Germany, 1915-1919 (1985).

85 A.C. Bell, supra note 82 at 674, argues the "great consequence" of blockade measures was "infusing...a blind and contagious anger at authority" among German civilians. Basil H. Liddell Hart, The Ghost of Napoleon 143 (1934): The world war was "decided by an economic means, the blockade, rather than by any decisive victory in battle."

86 Alexander Gillespie, A History of the Law of War, Vol. 2 at 73 ("Civilians") (2011), reports German postwar estimates of 700,000 civilian deaths, from comparison of prewar and wartime death rates. Niall Ferguson, The Pity of War: Explaining World War I 277 (1999), rejects such figures as "fantastic," emphasizing there is "no evidence anyone starved" in Germany due to blockade measures.

87 Ferguson, supra note 86.

88 Memorandum from Secretary of the Committee of Imperial Defence (Dec. 23, 1929), reprinted in Sea Power and the Control of Trade: Belligerent Rights from the Russian War to the Beira Patrol, 1854-1970 407 (Nicholas Tracy ed. 2005).

89 Treaty Relating to the Use of Submarines and Noxious Gases in Warfare, Feb. 6, 1922, reprinted in Laws of Armed Conflict, supra note 32 at art. 1, Sec. 4 at 85.

90 Id., art. 3.

91 Treaty for the Limitation of Naval Armaments, Apr. 22, 1930, reprinted in Laws of Armed Conflict, supra note 32 at 1143; Procés-Verbal Relating to the Rules

of Submarine Warfare Set Forth in Part IV of the Treaty of London of 22 April 1930 reprinted in Laws of Armed Conflict, supra note 32 at 1145.

92 Payson S. Wild, Sanctions and Treaty Enforcement 195 (1934). The study notes that personal criminal liability for violation of treaty provisions was almost unheard of in modern treaties, before the 1922 Washington Treaty. To find a precedent, the author cites a treaty between Byzantine Emperor Justinian and Cosroe of Persia in 511 CE (a treaty restricting merchants to travel on approved trade routes with personal liability for violation).

93 Speech to House of Commons, The Few, Aug. 20, 1940.

94 Joel Ira Holwitt, Execute Against Japan: The U.S. Decision to Conduct Unrestricted Submarine Warfare 121-31, 142 (2009). Holwitt concludes from the documentary record that the Navy did not bother to consult the State Department in developing its policy, presumably because it did not want to hear diplomatic or international law objections. Navy officials also seem to have received verbal approval.

95 Thomas Parrish, The Submarine: A History 331 (2004). For parallel treatment, see Holwitt, supra note 94 at 140-41.

96 Jeremy Black, Naval Power: A History of Warfare and the Sea from 1500 Onwards 183 (Palgrave 2009). Black notes that the scale of Allied shipping in the Second World War was such that, while many more ships were lost to submarine attacks, the total was less as an overall percentage. And readily replaced: The United States built more new cargo ships in the third quarter of 1943 than it had lost since the beginning of the war. Id. at 178.

97 Robert Gannon, Hellions of the Deep: The Development of American Torpedoes in World War II 194-95 (2006).

98 Peter Padfield, War Beneath the Sea: Submarine Conflict During World War II 476 (1995).

99 Telford Taylor, The Anatomy of the Nuremberg Trials 399-410 (1992).

100 San Remo Manual on International Law Applicable to Armed Conflicts at Sea, art. 47 at 1162 (exemptions from attack), art. 60 at 1164 (liability to attack for enemy merchant ships), reprinted in Laws of Armed Conflicts, supra note 32.

101 Id. at art. 67(f) at 1165.

102 Id. at art. 102(a), 103(b), at 1168 (emphasis added).

103 Commander's Handbook on the Law of Naval Operations, Naval Warfare Publication 1-14 M, Jul. 2007, §8.6.2.2.

104 Department of Defense Law of War Manual (2015), §13.7.2, FN 119 (print version, p. 880).

105 Richard M. Price, The Chemical Weapons Taboo 109 (1997), reviewing studies finding lack of interest in gas among military commanders on all sides in Second World War.

106 For a recent survey, John Horne & Alan Kramer, German Atrocities, 1914: A History of Denial (2001).

107 James S. Corum & Wray R. Johnson, Airpower in Small Wars: Fighting Insurgents and Terrorists 34 (2003).

108 Neville Jones, The Beginnings of Strategic Air Power: A History of the British Bomber Force 1923-1939 29-30 (1987) (1923 Trenchard Memo: "The policy of hitting the French nation and making them squeal before we did was a vital one.").

109 Id. at 44-46 (The senior naval commander warned that "arguments almost

similar... were used by the Germans when they decided to adopt a 'sink at sight' policy which was aimed at our resources and the morale of merchant seamen... [but] reacted against Germany in every sphere of the war.").

110 Draft Rules of Air Warfare, The Hague, Feb. 1923, art. 22.

111 Id. at art. 24, ¶2.

112 Id. at art. 24, ¶2.

113 Charles Webster & Noble Frankland, The Strategic Air Offensive Against Germany 1939-1945 Vol. 4 at 71 (on Trenchard's objection that while it was reasonable to prohibit "indiscriminate attacks on the civilian population," it was "an entirely different matter to terrorise munitions workers [men and women] into absenting themselves from work or stevedores into abandoning the loading of a ship with munitions through fear of air attack upon the factory or dock concerned.").

114 J.M. Spaight, Air Power and War Rights 20 (1924). A subsequent book, while cautioning against unrelenting attacks on "military objectives" in "a crowded city," still noted that earlier wars had witnessed naval "bombardment of undefended commercial cities... for the purpose of bringing the war home to the consciousness of the enemy population." He thought aerial bombing could contribute to that strategy in a future war: "A political end—the compulsion of the enemy population as a whole—and not a military end—the overcoming of the armed forces—is sought in each case." J.M. Spaight, Air Power and the Cities 101, 107, 110 (1930). He did not recoil from the implementation of this strategy in the war that followed. J.M. Spaight, Bombing Vindicated (1944).

115 Morton William Royse, Aerial Bombardment and the International Regulation of Warfare 240 (1928): "Nations will employ an effective weapon to its utmost extent checked only by social sanction as manifested in the accepted minimum standards of the time... questionable whether devastation in war as a means of moral pressure falls below the accepted minimum standards today."

116 Paul Whitcomb Williams, Legitimate Targets in Aerial Bombardment, 23 Am. J. Int'l L. 570, 580 (1929).

117 Draft Convention for the Protection of Civilian Populations Against New Engines of War, Sept. 3, 1938, art. 10-21 at 331-36 reprinted in Laws of Armed Conflicts, supra note 32.

118 Appeal of President Franklin D. Roosevelt on Aerial Bombardment of Civilian Populations, Sept. 1, 1939.

119 George H. Quester, Deterrence Before Hiroshima (1966).

120 Harold Nicolson, Diaries and Letters: 1939-1945 121-22 (1967) (diary for Oct. 17, 1940, describing Churchill's bantering with a small group of MPs in the House of Commons smoking lounge).

121 Richard Overy, The Bombers and the Bombed: Allied Air War Over Europe 1940-1945 69-70 (2013).

122 W. Hays Parks, "Precision" and "Area" Bombing: Who did which, and when?, Journal of Strategic Studies, Vol. 18, No. 1, 154 (Mar. 1995) ("'Marshaling yards' was a USAAF euphemism for city areas.").

123 See Winston Churchill, The Second World War, Vol. 5, 519-20 for text of this "Casablanca directive" of Feb. 4, 1943. It did not focus on "civilian morale" as an isolated objective, but mentioned it as one element in a campaign aimed at "the progressive destruction and dislocation of the German military, industrial and economic system."

124 Martin van Creveld, The Age of Airpower 101 (2011).

125 Winston Churchill, The Second World War, Vol. 2, 365: "In this later phase [when the Allies bombed German cities in strength in the last years of the war] the bombs were much more powerful and the raids far more intense. On the other hand, long preparation and German thoroughness had enabled a complete system of bomb-proof shelters to be built, into which all were forced to go by iron routine.... But in London [in 1940-41], although the attack was less overpowering, the security arrangements were far less developed."

126 Overy, The Bombers and the Bombed, supra note 121 at 92.

127 The most general version of the "ineffectual" argument: Robert A. Pape, Bombing to Win: Air Power and Coercion War (1996)—which rebuts claims that bombing might prevail on its own, without proving that it accomplished nothing as an auxiliary tactic. Among many "moral" condemnations: Stephen A. Garrett, Ethics and Airpower in World War II: The British Bombing of German Cities (1993).

128 RAF Bomber Command reported 47,268 combat fatalities among bomber crews, a loss rate of 41 percent, the highest for any British service. Total American losses from bombing missions in Europe were reported at 30,099. Overy, The Bombers and the Bombed, supra note 121 at 229.

129 Id. at 227-28: "The military consequences of the bombing were clearly more important than the economic, psychological or political ones."

130 Christopher C. Harmon, "Are We Beasts?": Churchill and the Moral Question of World War II "Area Bombing" 14 (1991), explaining bombing as partly a "pursuit of allies" in early years, then "insurance against a second Russian withdrawal from an anti-German coalition" (as in 1939).

131 Ronald Schaffer, Wings of Judgment: American Bombing in World War II 72-78 (1985).

132 Martin Gilbert, Winston S. Churchill, Vol. 7: Road to Victory, 1941-1945, at 865 (1986), records Churchill's acceptance of military resistance to use of poison gas against German troops during Normandy stalemate in July 1944. The previous year, Churchill proposed that if the Germans used "gas on the Russians" (though perhaps only against military formations), "we shall retaliate by drenching the German cities with gas on the largest possible scale." PM's Personal Minutes of Feb. 27, 1943. Id. at 352. The generals did not embrace this suggestion.

133 Telford Taylor, The Anatomy of the Nuremberg Trials 325-26 (1992) (noting Allied raids more destructive than earlier German air attacks).

134 Hersch Lauterpacht, The Problem of the Revision of the Law of War, British Yearbook of Int'l L., Vol. 29, 365-67, 364 (1952).

135 Sahr Conway-Lanz, Collateral Damage: American, Non-Combatant Immunity, and Atrocity after World War II 105, 103 (2006).

136 Morton Greenspan, The Modern Law of Land Warfare 335-36 (1959), describing "area bombing" as response to German location of factories in urban centers but "the purpose of that bombing is the destruction of a military objective, all other damage being incidental"; K.J. Raby, Bombardment of Land Targets—Military Necessity and Proportionality 70 (1968) (defending attacks on Hiroshima and Nagasaki as "proportionate"); Department of the Air Force, International Law—The Conduct of Armed Conflict and Air Operations

5-10 (1976) (discussing World War II city bombing as illustrative of legally permissible air operations, including atomic bombings of Japan).

137 Dean Acheson, Present at the Creation: My Years in the State Department 598-99 (1969).

138 The claim that at war's end Churchill deliberately tried to "dishonor" Arthur Harris, commander of Britain's Bomber Command, is a fabrication embraced by moralistic commentators of a later era. Michael Walzer, Just and Unjust Wars: A Moral Argument with Historical Illustrations 323-25 (2006), describing Arthur Harris, director of strategic bombing for RAF, as conducting "terror bombing...a criminal activity...an entirely indefensible activity"—relying on David Irving's account of Dresden bombing (FN 32), which exaggerated resulting casualties by tenfold. Martin Gilbert, Winston S. Churchill, Vol. 8: Never Despair 1945-1965 178 (1988), records Churchill's 1946 letter to Clement Attlee, urging the new government to bestow honors on Harris and Attlee's reply, explaining that the government had struggled to keep the honors list within bounds—without either suggesting that Harris should be disqualified from ceremonial honors.

139 J.M. Spaight, Air Power and War Rights 274-75 (3rd ed. 1947) (Atomic bombs should be seen as contrary to "accepted principles of law" as opposed to "Harris's method of destroying a city piece meal.").

140 Two recent books explore these secret schemes for unleashing poisons, arson, and assassination in the North and both document Confederate incapacity to implement them: Jane Singer, The Confederate Dirty War: Arson, Bombings, Assassination and Plots for Chemical and Germ Attacks on the Union (2005); John C. Fazio, Decapitating the Union: Jefferson Davis, Judah Benjamin and the Plot to Assassinate Lincoln (2015). General Grant refers to Confederate inspired "plans...to burn our cities, to poison the water supplying them, to spread infection by importing clothing from infected regions, to blow up our river and lake steamers—regardless of the destruction of innocent lives." Grant, supra note 64, at 747.

141 Overy, The Bombers and the Bombed, supra note 121.

142 Winston Churchill, The Second World War, Vol. 5 (Closing the Ring, 1951), 374.

143 Department of the Air Force, International Law and the Conduct of Armed Conflict and Air Operations 5-5 (1976), citing United States v. Ohlendorf, Case No. 9, Judgment at 466-67, Apr. 8-9: A bomb "is aimed at railroad yards, houses along the track area hit and many of their occupants are killed. That is entirely different, both in fact and in law, from an armed force marching up to these same railroad trains, entering the houses abutting them, dragging out the men and women and children and shooting them."

144 Lieber Code, art. 20, 21.

CHAPTER 4

1 Caroline Moorehead, Dunant's Dream: War, Switzerland and the History of the Red Cross 309-13 (1998).

2 Id.

3 Martin Gilbert, Winston S. Churchill, Vol. 6: Finest Hour, 1939-1941 832 (1983), n.1, citing "Personal Minute" from Prime Minister to then Foreign Minister Halifax, Oct. 13, 1940.

4   Moorehead, Dunant's Dream, supra note 1 at 420, 454; Jean Pictet, L'Épopée des Peaux-Rouges (Epic of the Red Skins) 20 (1988): "Since the Second World War and the horror of the concentration camps and the indiscriminate bombing, where millions of innocents found a hideous death, one looks at the barbarism of the Indians with different eyes. . . ." (translated from French original by Jeremy Rabkin).

5   Moorehead, Dunant's Dream, supra note 1 at 421.

6   For the fullest account, see Johannes Starmühler, PhD Dissertation, University of Vienna, Louis Haefliger und die Befreiung des Konzentrationslagers Mauthausen ("Louis Haefliger and the Liberation of the Mathausen Concentration Camp," Jan. 2008, available online) 55-66 on International Committee of the Red Cross (ICRC) response. As Starmühler reports, ICRC pressure prevented Haefliger from finding work in Switzerland after the war, so he lived his life in exile—but lived to see streets named for him in Vienna and Tel Aviv, in recognition of his wartime heroism. ICRC President Cornelio Sommaruga offered public recognition to Haefliger a half-century later— but preserved the tradition of neutrality by combining it with criticism of Israeli treatment of Palestinians. Protecting War Victims: Lessons of the Past, Challenges for the Future, Address at Chatham House, London, Sept. 15, 1997 (available online).

7   Gerald Steinacher, Nazis on the Run: How Hitler's Henchmen Fled Justice 70-71, 97, 99 (2011). "The ICRC continued issuing unverified travel documents, long after it became aware of abuses. Thus the ICRC bears a certain amount of moral responsibility." Id. at 99.

8   Two years before the "diplomatic conference" that convened in 1974, the ICRC convened a panel of "experts" to advise on necessary elaborations to the law of armed conflict and distributed documents related to this consultation, along with complete draft texts for AP I and AP II. No documents of this sort were distributed for the 1949 Convention.

9   Reprinted in The Laws of Armed Conflicts 339 44 (Schindler & Toman eds., 4th ed. 2004).

10   Id. at art. 6, ¶1.

11   Id. at art. 6, ¶2 (emphasis added).

12   Id. at art. 7, ¶1 (emphasis added).

13   Protection of Civilian Populations Against the Dangers of Indiscriminate Warfare, Resolution XXVIII, adopted by the XXth International Conference of the Red Cross, Vienna, 1965, reprinted in Laws of Armed Conflicts, supra note 9 at 345.

14   Human Rights in Armed Conflicts, Res. XXIII, adopted by the International Conference on Human Rights, Teheran, May 12, 1968; Respect for Human Rights in Armed Conflicts, Res. 2444 (XXIII) of the UN General Assembly, adopted Dec. 19, 1968; Basic Principles for the Protection of Civilian Populations in Armed Conflicts, Res. 2675 (XXV), UN General Assembly, Dec. 9, 1970, all reprinted in Laws of Armed Conflicts, supra note 9 at 345-46, 347-48, 353-54 respectively.

15   Douglas P. Lackey, The Bombing Campaign: the USAAF in Terror from the Sky: The Bombing of German Cities in World War II 55-57 (Igor Primoratz ed. 2010), concluding from absence of press criticism "the mass killings of German citizens in air attacks were implicitly endorsed by a large majority of the

American people." On support for use of the atomic bomb, Sahr Conway-Lanz, Collateral Damage: American, Non-Combatant Immunity, and Atrocity after World War II (2006).

16 David Irving, The Destruction of Dresden (1964).

17 David Irving Jailed for Holocaust Denial, The Guardian (UK), Feb. 20, 2006, available at https://www.theguardian.com/world/2006/feb/20/austria. thefarright.

18 Dietmar Süss, Death from the Skies: How the British and Germans Survived Bombing in World War II 502 n.202 (2014) (reporting Dresden historical commission estimate of fatalities from Feb. 1945 attack between 18,000-25,000). Recent studies confirm the military value of disrupting transportation, communication, and production facilities in Dresden at a time when the Soviet offensive was still stalled on the edges of Germany's eastern frontiers. Frederick Taylor, Dresden: Tuesday, February 13, 1945 373-74 (2004); Geoffrey Best, Churchill and War 280-84 (2005).

19 Michael Walzer, Just and Unjust Wars: A Moral Argument with Historical Illustrations 261 (3d ed. 2000), describing the bombings of Hamburg and Berlin as pursued "simply for the sake of terror," then dating the Dresden attack to "the spring of 1945 when the war was virtually won" (it took place in February when western armies were still struggling to recover ground lost in Germany's Ardennes offensive) and claiming "something like 100,000 people killed" (a mere five-fold exaggeration)—following which, the citation to David Irving, at n.19. These mistakes might have been understandable when the book first appeared in 1977, but it's notable the author did not think it worthwhile to correct them a quarter-century later.

20 Statement of Byelorussian Soviet Socialist Republic, Mar. 2, 1970, Appendix to Report of the Secretary General, Respect for Human Rights in Armed Conflicts, U.N. Doc A/8052, Sept. 18, 1970 118.

21 Conrad C. Crane, Bombs, Cities, and Civilians: American Airpower Strategy in World War II 153 (1993), noting that North Vietnam reported 1,318 civilian casualties from U.S. bombing in Dec. 1972 (less than one-tenth of the Dresden casualties, even by the most cautious later estimates).

22 W.J. Fenrick, The Law Applicable to Targeting and Proportionality After Operation Allied Force: A View from the Outside, 3 Yearbook of International Humanitarian Law 53 (2000).

23 Mark Moyar, Triumph Forsaken: The Vietnam War 1954-1965 (2006). For defense of campaign as within existing law of war limits, see W. Hays Parks, Linebacker and the Law of War, Air Univ. Rev. (Jan.-Feb. 1983).

24 Declaration for the Establishment of a New International Economic Order, UN G.A. Res. 3201, May 1, 1974. See also The New International Economic Order: The North-South Debate (Jagdish Bhagwati ed. 1977).

25 On prisoners of war in Vietnam, see Moorehead, Dunant's Dream, supra note 1.

26 W. Hays Parks, Air War and the Law of War, 32 A.F. L. Rev. 1, 112 (1990) (commenting on expulsion of South Africa from the International Red Cross for "racism"—which was not seen as disqualifying to National Socialist German). As Parks also notes, the Red Cross was so one-sided in its approach to the Israel-Palestine conflict that it circulated propagandistic civilian

casualty figures handed to it by the PLO. Id at 166. The ICRC resisted Israeli membership in the International Red Cross movement because its local organization, the Red Star of David, did not feature a cross—or a crescent, like the organizations of affiliated Muslim countries.

27 See Protocol Additional to the Geneva Conventions of 12 August 1949 (AP I), art. 5, Jun. 8, 1977—in which successive provisions for a "Protecting Power" to monitor treatment of prisoners of war seem to assert a duty to cooperate with such a power, then offer a fallback in case cooperation is declined, then offer yet another fallback in case of non-compliance with the fallback.

28 See Henry Kissinger, Years of Upheaval 708-18 (1982) (decrying European "stampede of dissociation [from U.S. and Israel]" after "Arab cutback in oil production" at 711).

29 Simon Reeve, One Day in September: The Full Story of the 1972 Munich Olympics Massacre 157-58 (2001) ("Germany made secret agreements with Palestinian and other international terror groups to keep them away from German borders.").

30 James S. Corum and Wray R. Johnson, Airpower in Small Wars: Fighting Insurgents and Terrorists 429 (2003).

31 Geoffrey Best, War and Law Since 1945 (1994).

32 ICRC, Draft Additional Protocols to the Geneva Conventions of 12 August 1949, Oct. 1973, available at http:/www.loc.gov/rr/frd/Military_Law/pdf/RC-Draft-additional-protocols.pdf.

33 Geoffrey Best, War and Law Since 1945 417 (1994). ICRC, Commentary on the Additional Protocols of 8 June 1977 to the Geneva Conventions of 12 August 1949 at 1335 (condemning western acquiescence: The Red Cross Commentary claims, rather wistfully, that this "radical simplification . . . does not reduce the degree of protection which was originally envisaged, for despite its brevity [the final AP II text] reflects the most fundamental rules.").

34 ICRC, Draft Additional Protocols to the Geneva Conventions of 12 August 1949, supra note 27 at art. 24.2.

35 Id. at art. 13 (emphasis added).

36 Id. at art. 26, §3b.

37 Protection of War Victims: Protocol 1 to the 1949 Geneva Conventions, Vol. III (Howard Levie ed. 1980) (edited transcripts of Geneva Convention deliberations, 1980), Arab proposal at 129, support from East German, Romanian, and North Korean delegates at 138, western advocacy for accepting "proportional" civilian harm at 140, 142, 165.

38 Georges Abi-Saab, Proceedings of the 1976 and 1977 Conferences in The New Humanitarian Law of Armed Conflict 250 (Antonio Cassese ed. 1979).

39 See Protocol Additional to the Geneva Conventions of 12 August 1949 (AP I) at art. 52, ¶2. By contrast, the 1973 Red Cross draft spoke of "objects designed for civilian use, such as houses, dwellings, installations and means of transportation"—which might imply a special concern with places where large numbers of civilians were likely to be present—and even then allowed such places to be attacked "if they are used mainly in support of the military effort." ICRC, Draft Additional Protocols to the Geneva Conventions of 12 August 1949, supra note 27 at art. 47, ¶2.

40 AP I, supra note 39 at art. 52, ¶3.

41 Id. at art. 51, ¶1.

42 L. Oppenheim, International Law: A Treatise §§247, 250 at 305, 308 (2d ed. 1912).

43 ICRC, Draft Additional Protocols to the Geneva Conventions of 12 August 1949, supra note 27 at art. 46, ¶5.

44 AP I, supra note 39 at art. 51, ¶8.

45 Id. at art. 85, ¶3.

46 ICRC, Draft Additional Protocols to the Geneva Conventions of 12 August 1949, supra note 27 at art. 42, ¶1.

47 AP I, supra note 39 at art. 44, ¶2.

48 Id. at art. 44, ¶3.

49 Id. at art. 44, ¶4.

50 Id. at art. 44, ¶7.

51 For general background on pre-World War I debates about the participation of "civilian volunteers" in combat, see Karma Nabulsi, Traditions of War: Occupation, Resistance, and the Law 5-12 (1999). For earlier treaty provisions see Convention (IV) Respecting the Laws and Customs of War on Land and its Annex: Regulations concerning the Laws and Customs of War on Land, art. 1, The Hague, Oct. 18, 1907, and Geneva Convention Relative to the Treatment of Prisoners of War, art. 4, Aug. 12, 1949.

52 AP I, supra note 39 at art. 47.

53 Stuart Jeffries, France Forced to Confront Betrayal, The Guardian (UK), Aug. 18, 2001. For background on de Gaulle's decision to abandon Arab fighters assisting the French army (so-called Harkis) in 1962, see Martin Evans, Algeria: France's Undeclared War 325-28 (2012).

54 R.R. Baxter, Humanitarian Law or Humanitarian Politics? The 1974 Diplomatic Conference on Humanitarian Law, 16 Harv. Int'l L.J. 1, 9-11 (1975); G.I.A.D. Draper, Wars of National Liberation and War Criminality in Restraints on War 147 (Michael Howard ed. 1979) (protesting AP I criteria for legitimate involvement in war as "racial" and "a fatal conflux of jus ad bellum and jus in bello"—focusing on special treatment of participants in "national liberation" struggles).

55 AP I, supra note 39 at art. 1, ¶4.

56 See David Galula, Counterinsurgency Warfare: Theory and Practice 17-23 (2006) (1964) (emphasizing terror as means of control over surrounding population).

57 See list of ratifications of Hague Conventions on land warfare in The Laws of Armed Conflicts, supra note 9 at 83-84: Of forty-seven parties to the 1899 convention, all had ratified within less than a decade, other than Fiji and South Africa which were not independent at the time and both ratified in the early 1970s. Of forty-nine parties to the 1907 convention, all but five had ratified by 1910 (the hold-outs—Ethiopia, Fiji, Finland, Poland, South Africa—had not participated at the time). Id. at 85-86. For ratifications of the four 1949 Geneva Conventions see id. at 635-49: Almost all states which failed to ratify by 1958 were not independent in the 1950s.

58 Id. at 785-91.

59 Id. at 792-818.

60 ICRC, Commentary on the Additional Protocols of 8 June 1977 to the Geneva Conventions of 12 August 1949, supra note 33 at 1335.

61 Jean-Marie Henckaerts & Louise Doswald-Beck, Customary International

Humanitarian Law, Vol. II: Practice, Part I 336-39, 1069 (Cambridge University Press 2005).

62 Id. at 76, 78, 326.

63 An ICRC analyst has even argued that IHL should be understood as a branch of international human rights law and international human rights law must continue to apply, even in war zones. Louise Doswald-Beck, The Right to Life in Armed Conflict: Does International Humanitarian Law Provide All the Answers?, International Review of the Red Cross, Vol. 88, 2006 at 881 (arguing for primacy of IHL by analogy with human rights law).

64 Mark Osiel, The End of Reciprocity: Terror, Torture, and the Law of War (2009).

65 Michael W. Doyle, Liberalism and World Politics, 80 Am. Pol. Sci. Rev. 1151 (1986); Amanda Perreau-Saussine, Immanuel Kant on International Law in The Philosophy of International Law (Samantha Besson & John Tasioulas eds. 2010) (of twenty-nine essays in the volume, this is the only one to focus on a single philosopher—but Kant fascinates contemporary thinking in this field as no other classical thinker).

66 Jean-Claude Favez, The Red Cross and the Holocaust 282 (John Fletcher & Beryl Fletcher trans., 1999) (1988): "In its way of working, in its methods of analysis, in its political perspective, the ICRC was by then out of phase with the ideological struggle that was what World War II was really about." More precisely: "Humanity" had less claim on the ICRC than its own very parochial interests as a Swiss organization committed to neutrality.

67 ICRC, Commentary on the Additional Protocols of 8 June 1977 to the Geneva Conventions of 12 August 1949, supra note 33 §1980 at 626.

68 On Amnesty International's reluctance to associate itself with "conservative opinions" warning of genocide in Cambodia (as late as 1977), see Samantha Power, A Problem from Hell: America and the Age of Genocide 113-14 (2002). See also William Korey, NGOs and the Universal Declaration of Human Rights: A Curious Grapevine 169 (1998), noting that Amnesty International, founded in 1961, did not issue a long report on political prisoners in the Soviet Union until 1975 and the organization's "non-involvement" in human rights advocacy for Soviet victims in the 1970s and early 1980s "was striking."

69 Moorehead, Dunant's Dream, supra note 1 at 643 (noting that ICRC regarded silence as necessary to retain cooperation with local authorities, which in this instance they did try to exercise to save civilian victims, in contrast with the organization's World War II practice).

70 L. Oppenheim, International Law, supra note 42, §274 at 334 ("one of the effects of every peace treaty is so-called amnesty—that is, an immunity for all wrongful act. . . . War crimes which were not punished before the conclusion of peace may no longer be punished after it conclusion.").

71 S.C. Res. 687, U.N. Doc. S/RES/687 (Apr. 3, 1991).

72 For an overview of criticism of the ad hoc tribunals for Yugoslavia and Rwanda, see Jeremy Rabkin, Global Criminal Justice: An Idea Whose Time Has Passed, 38 Cornell Int'l L.J. 753 (2005).

73 For an extremely detailed collection of relevant legal and diplomatic landmarks on the path to the Rome Statute, see The Legislative History of the International Criminal Court (M. Cherif Bassiouni & William A. Schabas eds. 2005).

74 Rome Statute of the International Criminal Court, art. 8, ¶2b(ii) defining "war

crimes" to include "intentionally directing attacks against civilian objects, that is, objects which are not military objectives" and ¶2b(iv) "launching an attack which will cause incidental...damage to civilian objects...which would be clearly excessive in relation to the concrete and direct overall military advantage anticipated," reprinted in Laws of Armed Conflicts, supra note 9 at 1317-18.

75 Id. at art. 12, ¶2, ¶3.

76 Id. at art. 17, ¶1: Cases are declared "inadmissible" if already considered by national authorities "unless the State [involved] is unwilling or unable to genuinely carry out the investigation or prosecution...[or] the State has decided not to prosecute...[due to] the unwillingness or inability of the State genuinely to prosecute."

77 Fanny Benedetti & John L. Washburn, Drafting the International Criminal Court Treaty: Two Years to Rome and an Afterword on the Rome Diplomatic Conference, Global Governance, Vol. 5, No. 1 at 26 (1999).

78 Al-Skeini and Others v. the United Kingdom, App. No. 55721/07 Eur. Ct. H.R. (2011).

79 Richard Ekins, What the Strasbourg Court Has Wrought—and What to Do About It, Reaction (UK), Sept. 23, 2016, available at http://reaction.life/strasbourg-court-wrought/.

80 Jaloud v. the Netherlands, App. No. 47708/08 Eur. Ct. H.R. (2014).

81 Maj. General Capewell, Statements to H.C. Def. Comm., Apr. 27, 2011, available at http://www.publications.parliament.uk/pa/cm201012/cmselect/cmdfence/950/11042701.htm.

82 High Level Military Group, Our Military Forces' Struggle Against Lawless, Media Savvy Terrorist Adversaries: A Comparative Study 7 (Feb. 2016), available at http://www.high-level-military-group.org/pdf/hlmg-lawless-media-savvy-terrorist-adversaries.pdf.

83 ICRC, Commentary on the Additional Protocols of 8 June 1977 to the Geneva Conventions of 12 August 1949, supra note 33 §1980 at 626.

84 See, e.g., Latest Developments From the Mideast, N.Y. Times (Jul. 18, 2006), available at http://www.nytimes.com/2006/07/18/world/middleast/18cnd-latest.html (reporting estimates of some 200 civilian deaths and denunciations of Israeli actions as "beyond any reasonable proportion," as the Italian foreign minister put it—evidently assuming that removing Hezbollah rockets should be achieved without hurting more Lebanese civilians than the rockets had managed to kill in Israel, with its better air raid protection facilities). For general survey of U.N. and European reactions, see Jan Kittrich, The Right of Individual Self-Defense in Public International Law 79-83 (2008).

85 For a sample of European reactions, see Joint Statement by the President of the European Council, Herman Van Rompuy, and the President of the European Commission, José Manuel Barroso in the name of the European Union on the Situation in Gaza, Aug. 3, 2014, available at http://www.consilium.europa.eu/uedocs/cms_data/docs/pressdata/en/ec/144223.pdf: "We strongly condemn continued rocket fire over Israel" as "an unacceptable threat to its citizens" but "legitimate defence needs to maintain proportionality." For critical analysis of the Goldstone Report for the Human Rights Council, see Peter Berkowitz, Israel and the Struggle Over International Laws of War (2012).

86 Anshel Pfeffer, Hezbollah 'Refused Hamas Request to Bomb Israel in Gaza

War," Haaretz, Nov. 10, 2010, available at http://www.haaretz.com/print-edition/news/hezbollah-refused-hamas-request-to-bomb-israel-in-gaza-war-1.323862.

87 Andreas Zimmermann, The Second Lebanon War: Jus ad Bellum, Jus in Bello and the Issue of Proportionality, 11 Max Planck Yearbook of United Nations Law 99-141 (2007).

88 Leila Nadya Sadat, International Legal Issues Surrounding the Mistreatment of Iraqi Detainees by American Forces, American Society of International Law, Vol. 8, Issue 10, May 21, 2004.

89 Robert Marquand, Dutch Still Wincing at Bush-era 'Invasion of The Hague Act,' CSMonitor (Feb. 13, 2009), available at http://www.csmonitor.com/World/Europe/2009/0213/p05s01-woeu.html.

90 EU: Use National Courts to Fight Impunity, Human Rights Watch (May 19, 2016), available at https://www.hrw.org/news/2016/05/19/eu-use-national-courts-fight-impunity.

91 See John Yoo, War by Other Means: An Insider's Account of the War on Terror 128-64 (2006).

92 Commander's Handbook on the Law of Naval Operations, reprinted in appendix to International Law: The Law of Naval Operations, Vol. 64 at 474 (Horace Robertson ed. 1991).

93 Id. at 475. See criticism by Dutch military lawyer, Frits Kalshoven, A Comment to Chapter II of the Commander's Handbook. Id. at 310 ("'war sustaining effort'...might easily be interpreted to encompass virtually every activity in the enemy country").

94 Law of War Manual, §§5.7, 13.5.

95 Preamble to Hague Convention (II) on the Laws and Customs of War on Land (1899), repeated in Hague Convention (IV) on the Laws and Customs of War on Land and its Annex (1907).

96 Lee A. Casey & David B. Rivkin, Jr., Rethinking the Geneva Conventions, in The Torture Debate in America 206 (Karen J. Greenberg ed. 2005).

97 Vienna Convention on the Law of Treaties, art. 60, ¶2b, May 23, 1969: "Material breach of a multilateral treaty...entitles...a party specially affected by the breach to invoke it as a ground for suspending the operation of the treaty...in the relations between itself and the defaulting State."

98 Id. at art. 31, ¶3b: Treaty "shall be interpreted in good faith," but interpretations may have "taken into account...any subsequent practice in the application of the treaty" indicating understandings of the parties.

99 See Reports of International Arbitral Awards: Eritrea-Ethiopia Claims Commission Vol. XXVI at 335, ¶121 (Dec. 19, 2005), available at http://legal.un.org/riaa/cases/vol_XXVI/291-349.pdf.

100 Mark J. Osiel, Obeying Orders: Atrocity, Military Discipline, and the Law of War 110 (1998). If Pictet did not actually say it, the attribution is understandable: It is much in the spirit of the Red Cross project.

CHAPTER 5

1 See U.S. Air Force, MQ-9 Reaper Fact Sheet (Sep. 23, 2015), available at http://www.af.mil/AboutUs/FactSheets/Display/tabid/224/Article/104470/mq-9-reaper.aspx; U.S. Air Force, MQ-1B Predator Fact Sheet (Sep. 23, 2015), available at http://www.af.mil/AboutUs/FactSheets/Display/tabid/224/Article/104469/mq-1b-predator.aspx; Lockheed Martin, Producing, Operating and Supporting

a 5th Generation Fighter, available at https://www.f35.com/about/fast-facts/cost (last visited Dec. 30, 2016).

2 FDD's Long War Journal, Pakistan Strikes, available at http://www. longwarjournal.org/pakistan-strikes/ (last visited Dec. 30, 2016).

3 See National Highway Traffic Safety Administration, Fatality Analysis Reporting System Encyclopedia, National Statistics, available at http://www-fars.nhtsa.dot.gov/Main/index.aspx (last visited Dec. 30, 2016); Insurance Institute for Highway Safety, Highway Loss Data Institute, General Statistics, available at http://www.iihs.org/iihs/topics/t/general-statistics/fatalityfacts/ state-by-state-overview (last visited Dec. 30, 2016).

4 Seth Robson, Maritime Drones Make Waves Among Navies Worldwide, Stars and Stripes (Aug. 3, 2011), available at http://www.stripes.com/news/ maritime-drones-make-waves-among-navies-worldwide-1.151087.

5 The U.S. Navy successfully conducted a test of swarming USVs at Newport News, VA, in late 2014. Jon Harper, Navy Debuts Unmanned Robotic Boats with New Swarm Capability, Stars and Stripes (Oct. 6, 2014), available at http://www.stripes.com/news/navy/navy-debuts-unmanned-robotic-boats-with-new-swarm-capability-1.306741.

6 See John Yoo, Assassination or Targeted Killings After 9/11, 56 N.Y.L. Sch. L. Rev. 57, 58 (2012).

7 Quoted in P.W. Singer, Robots at War: The New Battlefield, The Wilson Quarterly (Winter 2009), available at http://wilsonquarterly.com/quarterly/ winter-2009-robots-at-war/robots-at-war-the-new-battlefield/ (last visited Dec. 30, 2016).

8 Id.

9 For early discussion of some of these types of robotic weapons systems, see Ronald C. Arkin, Governing Lethal Behavior in Autonomous Robots (2009); Armin Krishnan, Killer Robots: Legality and Ethicality of Autonomous Weapons (2009). A more colorful journalistic account can be found in P.W. Singer, Wired for War: The Robotics Revolution and Conflict in the 21st Century (2009).

10 Michael W. Lewis, Drones and the Boundaries of the Battlefield, 47 Tex. Int'l L.J. 293, 296-98 (2012).

11 These virtues have led the United States to devote large resources to UAVs. From 2015-2017, the Pentagon plans to spend between $4.2–4.8 billion per year on unmanned air drones and their support systems. As of 2013, it had 147 MQ-9 Reapers and RQ-4 Global Hawks that can operate at high-altitude, loiter over areas for hours, and launch multiple weapons to destroy enemy targets. Entered into service in 2007, the Reaper can fly for more than 20 hours, has a range of 1,150 miles, and can carry a mixed payload of bombs and missiles. The U.S. also operates about 300 medium-altitude UAVs, such as the MQ-1 Predator, that can fire munitions, about 500 drones designed purely for long-range reconnaissance, and more than 9,000 for tactical surveillance. Even while U.S. spending will remain constant, industry estimates project that the global market in UAVs will rise to $89 billion over the next 10 years. Department of Defense, Unmanned Systems Integrated Roadmap FY2013-2038, available at http://www.acq.osd.mil/sts/docs/DoD%20USRM%202013. pdf.

12 See John Yoo, Assassination or Targeted Killings After 9/11, 56 N.Y.L. Sch. L. Rev. 57, 58 (2012).

13 See Bill Roggio, Charting the Data for US Airstrikes in Pakistan, 2004-2016, FDD's Long War Journal, available at http://www.longwarjournal.org/pakistan-strikes (last viewed Dec. 30, 2016).

14 See Chris Jenks, Law From Above: Unmanned Aerial Systems, Use of Force, and the Law of Armed Conflict, 85 N.D. L. Rev. 649, 650 (2010).

15 See, e.g., Chris Downes, 'Targeted Killings' in an Age of Terror: The Legality of the Yemen Strike, 9 J. Conflict & Sec. L. 277 (2004); Mary Ellen O'Connell, To Kill or Capture Suspects in the Global War on Terror, 35 Case W. Res. J. Int'l L. 325, 331-32 (2003); Sikander Ahmed Shah, War on Terrorism: Self Defense, Operation Enduring Freedom, and the Legality of U.S. Drone Attacks in Pakistan, 9 Wash. U. Global Stud. L. Rev. 77, 115 (2010); Gary Solis, Targeted Killing and the Law of Armed Conflict, 60 Naval War C. Rev. 127, 129, 133-35 (2007)

16 See Jacquelyn Schneider, Digitally-Enabled Warfare: The Capability-Vulnerability Paradox, Center for a New American Security (Aug. 29, 2016), available at https://www.cnas.org/publications/reports/digitally-enabled-warfare-the-capability-vulnerability-paradox.

17 Defense Advanced Research Projects Agency, Faster, More Precise Airstrikes Within Reach (Jun. 14, 2013), available at http://www.darpa.mil/news-events/2013-06-14.

18 See, e.g., Department of Defense Inspector General, Spider XM-7 Network Command Munition, Report No. D-2008-127 (Aug. 29, 2008), available at http://www.dodig.mil/audit/reports/fy08/08-127.pdf.

19 Unmanned Systems Integrated Roadmap FY2013-2038, supra note 11, at 6-7.

20 See Drones of the Seas, Global Defence Technology (Apr. 2014), available at http://www.nridigital.com/global-defence-technology.html?wv=s%2FGlobal%2520Defence%2520Technology%2F3adead8f-dcd8-5ed1-849a-2e4cab33b0ce%2FGDT1404Special%2Fseas.html.

21 Id.

22 Daniel Klaidman, Kill or Capture: The War on Terror and the Soul of the Obama Presidency 117-18 (2012).

23 See Get the Data: Drone Wars, The Bureau of Investigative Journalism, available at https://www.thebureauinvestigates.com/category/projects/drones/drones-graphs/ (last visited Dec. 30, 2016); Scott Shane, Drone Strikes Reveal Uncomfortable Truth: U.S. Is Often Unsure About Who Will Die, N.Y. Times, Apr. 23, 2015, available at http://nyti.ms/1PrJJN5.

24 Report of the Special Rapporteur on Extrajudicial, Summary or Arbitrary Executions, Study on Targeted Killings, Human Rights Council, 9-11, U.N. Doc. A/HRC/14/24/Add.6 (May 28, 2010) (by Philip Alston), available at http://www2.ohchr.org/english/bodies/hrcouncil/docs/14session/A.HRC.14.24.Add6.pdf.

25 Mary Ellen O'Connell, Unlawful Killing with Combat Drones, A Case Study of Pakistan, 2004-2009, in Shooting to Kill: Socio-Legal Perspectives on the Use of Lethal Force 263, 278 (Simon Bronitt et al. eds. 2012).

26 Id.

27 Chris Downes, 'Targeted Killings' in an Age of Terror: The Legality of the Yemen Strike, 9 J. Conflict & Sec. L. 277 (2004).

28 On this point, see Michael Walzer, Just and Unjust Wars: A Moral Argument with Historical Illustrations (4th ed. 2006). Walzer's view, which defends the

common understanding of the laws of war, has come under recent challenge from Jeff McMahan, Killing in War (2009).

29 Brief of Louis Henkin, Harold Hongju Koh, and Michael H. Posner as Amici Curiae in Support of Respondents, Rumsfeld v. Padilla, 542 U.S. 426 (2004), 2003 U.S. Briefs 1027, 2004 U.S. S. Ct. Briefs Lexis 299.

30 Tennessee v. Garner, 471 U.S. 1, 3 (1985).

31 For an effort to reconstruct the imminence standard in the context of terrorism and weapons of mass destruction, see John Yoo, Point of Attack: Preventive War, International Law, and Global Welfare 97-105 (2014).

32 Harold Koh, Legal Adviser, Department of State, The Obama Administration and International Law, Keynote Address at the Annual Meeting of the American Soc'y of Int'l Law (Mar. 25, 2010), available at http://www.cfr.org/international-law/legal-adviser-kohs-speech-obama-administration international-law-march-2010/p22300.

33 Id.

34 Special Rapporteur on Extrajudicial, Summary or Arbitrary Executions, Report of the Special Rapporteur on Extrajudicial, Summary or Arbitrary Executions, Human Rights Council, U.N. Doc. A/68/382 (Sept. 13, 2013) (by Christof Heyns), available at http://www.un.org/en/ga/search/view_doc.asp?symbol=A/68/382.

35 Id.

36 Robert Pape argues that coercive air power against economic or political targets has not succeeded, but that it can cripple an opponent's military operations. See Robert A. Pape, Bombing to Win: Air Power and Coercion in War (1996).

37 For a discussion of intelligence analysis of pattern of life, see Michael V. Hayden, Playing to the Edge: American Intelligence in the Age of Terror (2016).

38 Clifford J. Rogers, The Battle of Agincourt, in L.J. Andrew Villalon & Donald J. Kagay eds. The Hundred Years War (Part II): Different Vistas 37, 76 (2008).

39 See M16A2 5.56mm Semiautomatic Rifle M4/M4A1 5.56mm Carbine, Federation of American Scientists, available at https://fas.org/man/dod-101/sys/land/m16.htm (last visited Dec. 30, 2016).

40 For a similar conclusion, though somewhat different moral logic, see Bradley Jay Strawser, Moral Predators: The Duty to Employ Uninhabited Aerial Vehicles, 9 J. Military Ethics 342 (2010). Strawser proposes a "principle of unnecessary risk" which requires nations to reduce unnecessary risks to combatants, all other things being equal, in choosing a weapon.

41 Amy F. Woolf, Congressional Research Service, Conventional Prompt Global Strike and Long-Range Ballistic Missiles: Background and Issues (Feb. 24, 2016), available at https://www.fas.org/sgp/crs/nuke/R41464.pdf.

42 See Ronald C. Arkin, Governing Lethal Behavior in Autonomous Robots 71-91 (2009).

43 For a discussion of the use of air power in the Kosovo War, see Daniel L. Byman & Matthew C. Waxman, Kosovo and the Great Air Power Debate, 24 Int'l Security 5 (2000), and on the legal issues, see John Yoo, Kosovo, War Powers, and the Multilateral Future, 148 U. Pa. L. Rev. 1673 (2000).

44 See Lord Robertson of Port Ellen, Secretary General of NATO, Kosovo One Year On: Achievement and Challenge 13-15 (2000), available at www.nato.int/kosovo/repo2000/report-en.pdf.

45 For claims that NATO air forces violated the laws of war, see Amnesty International, Federal Republic of Yugoslavia (FRY)/NATO: "Collateral Damage" or Unlawful Killings? Violations of the Laws of War by NATO During Operation Allied Force (2000), available at https://www.amnesty.org/en/documents/EUR70/018/2000/en/. Critics argued that NATO pilots should have flown at lower altitudes to visually confirm whether targets were military or civilian. The prosecutor for the International Criminal Tribunal for the former Yugoslavia rejected these claims in 2000. See Committee Established to Review the NATO Bombing Campaign Against the Federal Republic of Yugoslavia, Final Report to the Prosecutor by the Committee Established to Review the NATO Bombing Campaign Against the Federal Republic of Yugoslavia, available at http://www.icty.org/x/file/Press/nato061300.pdf.

46 U.S. Department of Defense Directive 3000.09, Autonomy in Weapon Systems 13 (2012). The United Nation's special rapporteur on the issue announced an identical definition of lethal autonomous robotics. See Report of the Special Rapporteur on Extrajudicial, Summary or Arbitrary Executions, Human Rights Council, U.N. Doc. A/HRC/23/47, 7-8 (Apr. 9, 2013) (by Christof Heyns), available at http://www.un.org/ga/search/view_doc.asp?symbol=A/HRC/23/47.

47 U.S. Navy Fact File, MK 15—Phalanx Close-In Weapons System (CIWS), available at http://www.navy.mil/navydata/fact_display. asp?cid=2100&tid=487&ct=2 (last visited Dec. 30, 2016).

48 See Raytheon, Global Patriot Solutions, available at http://www.raytheon.com/capabilities/products/patriot/ (last visited Dec. 30, 2016); Raytheon, Iron Dome Weapon System, available at http://www.raytheon.com/capabilities/products/irondome/ (last visited Dec. 30, 2016).

49 Human Rights Watch & International Human Rights Clinic at Harvard Law School, Losing Humanity: The Case Against Killer Robots (Nov. 19, 2012), available at http://www.hrw.org/reports/2012/11/19/losing-humanity.

50 Wendell Wallach, Terminating the Terminator: What to do About Autonomous Weapons, Science Progress (Jan. 29, 2013), available at https://scienceprogress.org/2013/01/terminating-the-terminator-what to-do-about-autonomous-weapons/.

51 See Heyns, supra note 46, at 21-22; Jakob Kellenberger, Keynote Address, International Humanitarian Law and New Weapon Technologies, 34th Round Table on Current Issues of Humanitarian Law, San Remo, Italy, Sept. 8-10, 2011, quoted in Peter Asaro, On Banning Autonomous Weapon Systems: Human Rights, Automation, and the Dehumanization of Lethal Decision-making, 94 Int'l Rev. Red Cross 687, 691 (2012), available at https://www.icrc.org/eng/assets/files/review/2012/irrc-886-asaro.pdf.

52 Id.

53 Paul Scharre, Why Unmanned?, 61 Joint Force Q. 92 (2011).

54 See, e.g., Ryan Calo, Robotics and the Lessons of Cyberlaw, 103 Cal. L. Rev. 513, 538-49 (2015).

55 W.J. Hennigan, Drone Pilots Go to War in the Nevada Desert, Staring at Video Screens, L.A. Times (Jun. 17, 2015), available at http://www.latimes.com/nation/la-na-drone-pilots-20150617-story.html.

56 Asaro, supra note 51, at 692. See also Paul W. Kahn, The Paradox of Riskless Warfare, 22 Philosophy & Public Pol'y Q. 2 (2002), available at http://digitalcommons.law.yale.edu/fss_papers/326; Singer, supra note 9, at 431-33.

57 Id.

58 Asaro, supra note 51, at 694.

59 Additional Protocol I to the Geneva Conventions, art. 36 (Jun. 8, 1977), available at https://app.icrc.org/e-briefing/new-tech-modern-battlefield/media/documents/11-Article-36-of-Additional-Protocol-I.pdf.

60 Wilson D. Miscamble, The Most Controversial Decision: Truman, the Atomic Bombs, and the Defeat of Japan (2011).

61 Human Rights Watch, Losing Humanity: The Case Against Killer Robots (Nov. 19, 2012), available at https://www.hrw.org/report/2012/11/19/losing-humanity/case-against-killer-robots.

62 Asaro, supra note 51, at 695.

63 Mary Ellen O'Connell, Banning Autonomous Killing: The Legal and Ethical Requirement that Humans Make Near-Time Lethal Decisions, in The American Way of Bombing: Changing Ethical and Legal Norms, From Flying Fortresses to Drones 232 (Matthew Evangelista & Henry Shue eds. 2014).

64 For a recent argument in this direction, see generally Jens David Ohlin, The Combatant's Stance: Autonomous Weapons on the Battlefield, 92 Int'l L. Stud. 1 (2016). See also Peter Margulies, Making Autonomous Weapons Accountable: Command Responsibility for Computer-Guided Lethal Force in Armed Conflicts, in Research Handbook on Remote Warfare (Jens David Ohlin ed. 2016).

65 See, e.g., William H. Boothby, Conflict Law: The Influence of New Weapons Technology, Human Rights and Emerging Actors 146 (2014).

66 John Rawls, The Law of Peoples (2001); Michael Walzer, Just and Unjust Wars: A Moral Argument with Historical Illustrations (5th ed. 2015).

67 On Syria, see Leonard S. Spector & Avner Cohen, Israel's Airstrike on Syria's Reactor: Implications for the Nonproliferation Regime, 38 Arms Control Today 15 (2008).

68 See Chaim D. Kaufmann & Robert A. Pape, Explaining Costly International Moral Action: Britain's Sixty-Year Campaign Against the Atlantic Slave Trade, 53 Int'l Org. 651 (1999).

69 Sean M. Condron, Justification for Unilateral Action in Response to the Iraqi Threat: A Critical Analysis of Operation Desert Fox, 161 Mil. L. Rev. 115, 148-49 (1999).

70 Operation Desert Fox, Department of Defense, available at http://www.defense.gov/specials/desert_fox.

71 Gabriella Blum, The Crime and Punishment of States, 38 Yale J. Int'l L. at 73, 83, 94, 98 (2013).

72 See Marc Weller, Forcible Humanitarian Action: The Case of Kosovo, in Redefining Sovereignty: The Use of Force After the Cold War, at 277, 300 (Michael Bothe et al. eds. 2005).

73 Craig R. Whitney, Crisis in the Balkans: The Commander; Air Wars Won't Stay Risk Free, General Says, N.Y. Times, Jun. 18, 1999, at A22. Two years later, Short insisted that each air strike was "targeting a valid military target," while morale effects were "a peripheral result"—without denying his awareness that air strikes could "make the Serb population unhappy with their senior leadership because they allowed this to happen." Michael Short, Operation Allied Force from the Perspective of the NATO Air Commander, 78 Int'l L. Stud. 19, 25 (2002).

74 See, e.g., Isabel Kershner & Fares Akram, Israeli Strike Destroys Apartment Tower in Gaza, N.Y. Times, Aug. 23, 2014, at A4.

75 U.S. Department of Defense, Law of War Manual 241 (Jun. 2015).

76 See, e.g., Aaron Xavier Fellmeth, Questioning Civilian Immunity, 43 Tex. Int'l L.J. 453, 489 (2008); Stefan Oeter, Methods and Means of Combat, in The Handbook of Humanitarian Law in Armed Conflict 178-79 (Dieter Fleck ed. 1995); Charles P. Trumbull IV, Re-Thinking the Principle of Proportionality Outside of Hot Battlefields, 55 Va. J. Int'l L. 521, 542 (2015).

77 W. Hays Parks, Air War and the Law of War, 32 A.F. L. Rev. 1, 174 (1990).

78 In its report on the Persian Gulf War, for example, the United States declared "balancing may be done on a target-by-target basis, as frequently was the case during Operation Desert Storm, but also may be weighed in overall terms against campaign objectives." U.S. Department of Defense, Final Report to Congress on the Persian Gulf War 611 (1992).

79 Compare Eric A. Posner & Cass R. Sunstein, Dollars and Death, U. Chi. L. R. 537 (2005) with Michael Newton & Larry May, Proportionality in International Law 113 (2014).

80 Boothby, supra note 65, at 96-97.

81 Law of War Manual, supra note 75, at 245.

82 For an example, see discussion in U.S. Department of Defense, Law of War Manual, supra note 75, at 245 n.319.

83 Christopher M. Centner, Ignorance Is Risk: The Big Lesson From Desert Storm Air Base Attacks, Airpower Journal, Winter 1992, available at http://www.au.af. mil/au/afri/aspj/airchronicles/apj/apj92/win92/centner.htm.

84 Statement of Rear Admiral Thomas Wilson, DoD News Briefing, Apr. 22, 1999, quoted in U.S. Department of Defense, Law of War Manual, supra note 75, at 242 n.307.

85 The Nagasaki and Hiroshima bombs, for example, exploded with forces of about 15 and 20 kilotons. Today's U.S. Minuteman III carries 3 warheads of 300-500 kilotons each; earlier versions carried warheads of about 1 megaton in destructive power. United States Air Force, LGM-30 Minuteman III, available at http://www.af.mil/AboutUs/FactSheets/Display/tabid/224/Article/104466/ lgm 30g-minuteman-iii.aspx. The United States still maintains a fleet of 14 Ohio-class ballistic missile submarines, each with 24 ballistic missiles delivering up to 8 warheads of about 475 kilotons each—a total of 2,688 nuclear warheads that are 24 times more destructive than Hiroshima. United States Navy Fact File, Fleet Ballistic Missile Submarines—SSBN, available at http:// www.navy.mil/navydata/fact_display.asp?cid=4100&tid=200&ct=4.

86 Final Report to Congress on the Persian Gulf War, supra note 78, at 147.

87 Id.

88 Id. at 149.

89 Id. at 202-04.

90 U.S. Air Force, Air Superiority 2030 Flight Plan: Enterprise Capability Collaboration Team (May 2016), available at http://www.af.mil/Portals/1/ documents/airpower/Air%20Superiority%202030%20Flight%20Plan.pdf.

CHAPTER 6

1 Lee Kennett, A History of Strategic Bombing 12-13 (1982). Tellingly, this first use of aerial bombardment—"hardly more than a gesture"—was hailed by the Italian press as a great success for its psychological effect. "Terrorized Turks Scatter upon Unexpected Celestial Assault," ran one headline.

2 The Royal Air Force was established as an independent force in 1918 precisely

to devise attacks on distant targets, apart from supporting land attacks in the manner of artillery. A six-fold increase in such distant bombing operations was planned for the spring of 1919. For a contemporary account, taking this potential very seriously, see Morton William Royse, Aerial Bombardment and the International Regulation of Warfare 184-85 (1928).

3   John Arquilla & David Ronfeldt, Cyberwar is Coming!, 12 Comp. Strategy 141 (1993).

4   Adam Segal, The Hacked World Order: How Nations Fight, Trade, Maneuver, and Manipulate in the Digital Age 16, 44 (2016).

5   Compare Iran Buys Kamikaze Dolphins, BBC, Mar. 8, 2000, available at http://news.bbc.co.uk/2/hi/world/middle_east/670551.stm, with Peter Singer, Dolphins have no part in this dispute with Iran, The Guardian (UK), Jan. 19, 2012, available at https://www.theguardian.com/commentisfree/cifamerica/2012/jan/19/dolphins-no-part-in-dispute-with-iran, and Shaun Walker, Ukraine demanding return of combat dolphins from Russia, The Guardian (UK), Jul. 6, 2014, available at https://www.theguardian.com/world/shortcuts/2014/jul/06/ukraine-combat-dolphins-russia-give-back.

6   The website of the U.S. Navy Marine Mammal Program insists the animals are used to sniff out sea mines, as dogs are used to detect land mines. See FAQ, No. 4: "Does the Navy train its dolphins for offensive warfare, including attacks on ships, human swimmers or divers? No. The Navy does not now train, nor has it ever trained, its marine mammals to harm or injure humans in any fashion or to carry weapons to destroy ships." U.S. Navy Marine Mammal Program Frequently Asked Questions, available at http://www.public.navy.mil/spawar/Pacific/71500/Pages/faqs.aspx (last visited Jan. 4, 2017).

7   Testimony on Jun. 27, 1991, cited with other examples from that era in Andrew Jones & Gerald L. Kovacich, Global Information Warfare: The New Digital Battlefield (2d ed. 2016) at xxi.

8   Bruce Berkowitz, The New Face of War: How War Will Be Fought in the 21st Century (2003).

9   Elisabeth Bumiller & Thom Shanker, Panetta Warns of Dire Threat of Cyberattack on U.S., N.Y. Times, Oct. 11, 2012, available at http://www.nytimes.com/2012/10/12/world/panetta-warns-of-dire-threat-of-cyberattack.html.

10 Senators Joseph I. Lieberman & Susan Collins, At Dawn We Sleep, N.Y. Times, Dec. 6, 2012, available at http://nyti.ms/2j6n3XQ. A recent book—Fred Kaplan, Dark Territory, The Secret History of Cyber War (2016)—has an entire chapter entitled "A Cyber Pearl Harbor" (pp. 39-56), describing concerns about the possibility during the late 1990s.

11 One of the earliest analysts to raise that concern was Richard Clarke in 1998, when as a White House advisor he was already tasked with monitoring terrorist threats. Kaplan, supra note 10, at 97-99.

12 See, e.g., Scott J. Shackelford, From Nuclear War to Net War: Analogizing Cyber Attacks in International Law, 27 Berkeley J. Int'l L. 192 (2009); Dominic Basulto, Is Cyberwarfare the Nuclear Warfare of Our Generation?, Big Think, available at http://bigthink.com/endless-innovation/is-cyberwarfare-the-nuclear-warfare-of-our-generation; Russ Wellen, Cyberwar and Nuclear War: the Most Dangerous of All Conflations, Foreign Policy in Focus, Jul. 16, 2013, available at http://fpif.org/cyberwar-and-nuclear-war-the-most-dangerous-of-all-conflations/.

13 See Department of Defense Cyber Strategy (Apr. 2015), available at https://www.defense.gov/Portals/1/features/2015/0415_cyber-strategy/ Final_2015_DoD_CYBER_STRATEGY_for_web.pdf with background in Kaplan, supra note 10, at 283.

14 Richard A. Clarke & Robert K. Knake, Cyber War: The Next Threat to National Security and What to Do About It 67 (2010).

15 Kaplan, supra note 10, at 140-41, 240, 254-55, describes this episode—along with Clarke's somewhat flamboyant role as a member of President Obama's commission to study surveillance abuses by the NSA.

16 Michael Schrage, "A Stuxnetted Future," in Adam Segal, Cyber Conflict After Stuxnet: Essays from the Other Bank of the Rubicon 171 (Hannah Pitts ed. 2016).

17 Paulo Shakarian, Jana Shakarian, & Andrew Ruef, Introduction to Cyber-Warfare: A Multidisciplinary Approach, 16-21 (2013); Segal, supra note 4, at 60-66.

18 Shakarian, supra note 17, at 58-59; Segal, supra note 4, at 5-6.

19 Segal, supra note 4, at 51-60.

20 Shakarian, supra note 17, at 213-16.

21 Kaplan, supra note 10, at 205-211. Nearly a quarter of Iranian centrifuges were damaged beyond repair before discovery by the Iranians, then another 1,000 thereafter (bringing the total to about one-third).

22 Kaplan, supra note 10, at 206.

23 Dong Wei et al., Protecting smart grid automation systems against cyberattacks, IEEE Trans Smart Grid 2011, cited in Shakarian, supra note 17, at 212.

24 Barack Obama, International Strategy for Cyberspace 14 (May 14, 2011): "When warranted, the United States will respond to hostile acts in cyberspace as we would to any other threat to our country." "We reserve the right to use all necessary means—diplomatic, informational, military, and economic—as appropriate...."

25 Thomas Rid, Cyber War Will Not Take Place 35-54 (2013). A thoughtful challenge to this view still accepts its underlying premises. David Whetham, Cyber Chevauchées: Cyberwar Can Happen in Fritz Allhoff et al., eds., Binary Bullets: The Ethics of Cyberwarfare (2016). Whetham reaches back to English raids on French villages during the Hundred Years War for a model of war in which intermittent and dispersed damage, rather than concentrated, catastrophic devastation, can still "weaken the moral and economic base of reprisals, undermining their political legitimacy by raising the cost of conflict." It may be a semantic question whether this sort of ongoing annoyance should be called war. The strategic question is whether it would really continue between major powers for an extended period without provoking a more destructive kinetic response.

26 Michael V. Hayden, The Future of Things "Cyber," 5 Strategic Studies Quarterly 3, 3-4 (2011).

27 P.W. Singer & Allan Friedman, Cybersecurity and Cyberwar, What Everyone Needs to Know 73 (2014).

28 Clarke and Knake, supra note 14, at 68.

29 See Segal, supra note 4, at 16, 44.

30 For simplified overview of Internet operations, see Singer & Friedman, supra note 27, at 12-33.

31 Ian Black & Benny Morris, Israel's Secret Wars: A History of Israel's Intelligence Services 272 (1991) (retaliation attacks on PLO operatives in Europe required "complete deniability").

32 Thomas Rid & Ben Buchanan, Attributing Cyber Attacks, 38 Journal of Strategic Studies 4, 4-37 (2015).

33 See id. See also Eric Lipton et al., The Perfect Weapon: How Russian Cyberpower Invaded the U.S., N.Y. Times, Dec. 13, 2016, available at http://nyti.ms/2hBZd9C.

34 The Tallinn Manual, discussed in the next section, though it generally takes a very cautious approach to what is allowed, does acknowledge that in the context of an ongoing conflict, "neutral states" are obligated to suppress "belligerent" use of their cyber infrastructure by parties to a conflict and failure to exercise this obligation may justify victim states to shut down such "belligerent" activities. Rules 152-153, in Tallinn Manual on the International Law Applicable to Cyber Warfare, 558-62 (Michael N. Schmitt ed. 2013). Rid puts the point in more practical terms, discussing a hypothetical attack which involved major destruction and seemed to have originated in China: "If Chinese authorities denied their authorship without aggressively cooperating with US investigators, providing detailed log-files and all available forensic evidence that can lead the investigation a step closer to the perpetrators, either inside or outside China, then such a refusal of cooperation may be understood as a tacit admission of authorship; *we won't tell you who did it* would simply translate into *we did it*." Rid, supra note 32, at 161-62.

35 Brandon Valeriano & Ryan C. Maness, Cyber War Versus Cyber Realities: Cyber Conflict in the International System 164-87 (2015) (describing episodes attributed to non-state actors).

36 Id. at 217.

37 Id. at 213.

38 Irving Lachow, Cyber Terrorism: Menace or Myth? in Cyberpower and National Security 447 (Franklin D. Kramer, Stuart H. Starr, & Larry Wentz eds. 2009).

39 Id.

40 See, e.g., Clark & Knake, supra note 14, at 10.

41 Kaplan, supra note 10, at 210-211.

42 Jim Gray, Why Do Computers Stop and What Can Be Done About It?, Tandem Technical Report 85.7 (1985), available at http://www.hpl.hp.com/techreports/tandem/TR-85.7.pdf. For the conceptual grounding, see J. von Neumann, Probabilistic Logics and the Synthesis of Reliable Organisms from Unreliable Components, Princeton Automata Studies (1956).

43 Lance E. Davis & Stanley L. Engerman, Naval Blockades in Peace and War: An Economic History Since 1750 387-90 (2006).

44 See Hague Convention (II) on the Laws and Customs of War on Land, Jul. 29, 1899; Hague Convention (VI) on The State of Enemy Merchant Ships at the Outbreak of Hostilities, Oct. 18, 1907; Hague Convention (IX) on Bombardment by Naval Forces in Time of War, Oct. 18, 1907.

45 Protocol Additional to the Geneva Conventions of 12 August 1949, and relating to the Protection of Victims of International Armed Conflicts (Protocol I),

art. 49, para. 3 (Jun. 8, 1977): Provisions do not "affect the rules of international law applicable in armed conflict at sea" unless they affect civilians on land.

46 Hague Regulations on Land Warfare (Convention II on the Laws and Customs of War on Land, Jul. 29, 1899, and Convention IV on War on Land and its Annexed Regulations, Oct. 18, 1907), art. 42-56, cover "military authority over the territory of the hostile state" (that is, rules for an occupying army); Geneva Convention IV relative to the Protection of Civilian Persons in Time of War, Aug. 12, 1949, regulates obligations of occupying powers in wartime—on land. The 1907 Hague Conference produced several conventions on naval war, but they have no precise counterpart in land war, such as Convention VI on Enemy Merchant Ships, Oct. 18, 1907 (allowing enemy merchant ships to depart at the opening of hostilities), and Convention VII on Conversion of Merchant Ships, Oct. 18, 1907 (limiting conversion of merchant ships to military use). The only one of the 1949 conventions that addresses issues of sea warfare covers crews of military vessels, not civilians in general. (See Convention II, For the Amelioration of the Condition of Wounded, Sick and Shipwrecked Members of the Armed Forces at Sea, art. 13, Aug. 12, 1949—on coverage).

47 United States Department of Defense, Law of War Manual 998 (2015).

48 Department of Defense, Office of General Counsel, An Assessment of International Legal Issues in Information Operations 8 (May 1999) ("Purely civilian infrastructures must not be attacked unless the attacking force can demonstrate that a definite military advantage is expected from the attack."); Thomas C. Wingfield, The Law of Information Conflict: National Security Law in Cyberspace 44-46 (2000) (rules of conventional warfare apply); Maj. Richard W. Aldrich, The International Legal Implications of Information Warfare, 10 Airpower Journal 99, 102-96 (1996) (same principles apply in cyber as in conventional warfare); Oona A. Hathaway et al., The Law of Cyber-Attack, 100 Cal. L. Rev. 817, 851-55 (2012) (emphasizing the need to respect the principle of distinction in cyber conflict); Eric Talbot Jensen, Unexpected Consequences From Knock-On Effects: A Different Standard for Computer Network Operations?, 18 Am. U. Int'l L. Rev. 1145, 1187-88 (2003) (answering title question in the negative).

49 NATO Cooperative Cyber Defence Centre of Excellence, Tallinn Manual 2.0 on the International Law Applicable to Cyber Warfare 2 (Michael N. Schmitt ed. 2013).

50 Id. Rule 80, para. 1, at 375.

51 Id. Rule 71, para. 6, at 341.

52 Heather Harrison Dinniss, Cyber Warfare and the Laws of War (2012); Marco Roscini, Cyber Operations and the Use of Force in International Law (2014).

53 See, e.g., D.W. Bowett, Self-Defence in International Law 187-92 (1958).

54 The Charter of the United Nations: A Commentary 1420 (Bruno Simma et al. eds. 3d ed. 2012) ("… the [cyber] attack must not be over but still ongoing. This will often be difficult to determine and the burden of establishing that the attack is still ongoing lies on the State that purports to exercise its right of self-defense.").

55 Tallinn Manual, supra note 34, Rule 69, para. 7, at 332-33.

56 Id. Rule 71, para. 11, at 342.

57 Id. Rule 73, para. 12, at 353.

58 Id. Rule 70, para. 3, at 338.

59 Id. Rule 71, para. 12, at 342-43.

60 Id. Rule 82, para. 15, at 384.

61 Roscini, supra note 52, at 53-54, 135.

62 Dinniss, supra note 52, at 57.

63 Tallinn Manual, supra note 34, Rule 66, para. 36, at 324. The original 2013 edition of the Tallinn Manual does not give notice at all to the claims of humanitarian intervention as a possible exception from the general rules.

64 Roscini, supra note 52, at 191.

65 Protocol Additional to the Geneva Conventions of 12 August 1949, and relating to the Protection of Victims of International Armed Conflicts (Protocol I), art. 52, para. 2, Jun. 8, 1977 (emphasis added).

66 Id., art. 52, para. 3.

67 Id., art. 51, para. 4, 5.

68 Tallinn Manual, supra note 34, Rule 112, para. 3, at 470. The comment addresses the situation in which "the individual military components...could have been attacked separately," but does not consider the likely scenario in which there is doubt about whether this scenario is feasible or would be as reliable as the more comprehensive approach.

69 Tallinn Manual, supra note 34, Rule 144, para. 2, at 539. The comment acknowledges that "a minority of the Experts disagreed, taking the position that the term 'punishment' does not encompass the imposition of mere inconvenience or annoyance"—a view likely associated with American participants, but overruled by European "experts."

70 U.N. Charter art. 41.

71 Tallinn Manual, supra note 34, Rules 108, 109, at 460-64.

72 Id. Rule 109, para. 2, at 464.

73 Roscini, supra note 52, at 244.

74 Clarke & Knake, supra note 14, at 1-8. Clarke and Knake begin the first chapter with an account of this episode, suggesting that Israel had learned the relevant techniques from prior U.S. preparations. See also Kaplan, supra note 10, at 160-61.

75 Protocol Additional to the Geneva Conventions of 12 August 1949, and relating to the Protection of Victims of International Armed Conflicts (Protocol I), art. 52, para. 2, Jun. 8, 1977.

76 Jennifer E. Sims, Icarus Restrained: An Intellectual History of Nuclear Arms Control, 1945-1960, at 30-33 (1990).

77 Philip Hammond, Chancellor of the Exchequer, Launching the National Cyber Security Strategy (Oct. 1, 2016), available at https://www.gov.uk/government/speeches/chancellor-speech-launching-the-national-cyber-security-strategy. In fact, Philip Hammond had made the same plea a few years earlier, when serving as Minister of Defence: James Blitz, UK Becomes First State to Admit to Offensive Cyber Attack Capability, Financial Times, Sept. 29, 2013, available at https://www.ft.com/content/9ac6ede6-28fd-11e3-ab62-00144feab7de.

78 Segal, supra note 4, at 92.

79 See, e.g., Clarke & Knake, supra note 14, at 11-16 (describing Russia's alleged DDoS attack on Estonia).

80 Kaplan, supra note 10, at 115.

81 Segal, supra note 4, at 44.

82 David E. Sanger, U.S. Cyberattacks Target ISIS in a New Line of Combat, N.Y. Times, Apr. 24, 2016, available at http://nyti.ms/1UbaWs3.

83 General James Cartwright, then vice chairman of the Joint Chiefs of Staff, acknowledged to a congressional hearing: "If it's O.K. to attack me, and I'm not going to do anything other than improve my defenses every time you attack me, it's very difficult to come up with a deterrent strategy." Thom Shanker & Elisabeth Bumiller, Hackers Gained Access to Sensitive Military Files, N.Y. Times, Jul. 14, 2011, available at https://nyti.ms/2n15w5u.

84 Segal, supra note 4, at 129.

85 Id. at 114-16.

86 Tallinn Manual, supra note 34, Rule 66, para. 33, at 323. The Manual also takes the trouble to point out that "neither non-destructive cyber psychological operations intended solely to undermine confidence in a government, nor a State's prohibition of e-commerce with another State designed to cause negative economic consequences, qualify as uses of force." Id., Rule 69, para. 3, at 331.

87 Tallinn Manual, supra note 34, Rule 89, para. 5-94, at 410-411.

88 Michael D. Shear & Matthew Rosenberg, Released Emails Suggest the D.N.C. Derided the Sanders Campaign, N.Y. Times, Jul. 22, 2016, available at http://nyti.ms/2aBWnvd; Alan Rappeport, New Documents Released From Hack of Democratic Party, N.Y. Times, Sept. 13, 2016, available at http://nyti.ms/2jY8Q2p.

89 Carol D. Leonnig & Rosalind S. Helderman, Clinton, using private server, wrote and sent e-mails now deemed classified, Wash. Post, Sept. 1, 2015, available at http://wpo.st/XUSQ2.

90 Segal, supra note 4, at 117.

91 Michael Burleigh, Small Wars, Faraway Places: Global Insurrection and the Making of the Modern World, 1945-1965 172-73 (2013).

92 See Sanger, supra note 82.

CHAPTER 7

1 U.S. Department of State, Conventional Prompt Global Strike Fact Sheet (Apr. 8, 2010), available at https://www.smdc.army.mil/2008/NST/ConventionalPromptGlobalStrike.pdf. See also Amy F. Woolf, Conventional Prompt Global Strike and Long-Range Ballistic Missiles: Background and Issues, Congressional Research Service 7-5700 (Feb. 3, 2017), available at https://fas.org/sgp/crs/nuke/R41464.pdf.

2 European Space Policy Institute, 61 Space Policies, Issues, and Trends in 2015-2016 1, 13 (Nov. 2016).

3 Committee on Nat'l Security Space Defense and Protection, National Space Defense and Protection: Public Report 9 (2016).

4 Id. at 15.

5 Treaty on Principles Governing the Activities of States in the Exploration and Use of Outer Space, Including the Moon and Other Celestial Bodies, art. X, Jan. 27, 1967, 18 U.S.T. 2410, 610 U.N.T.S. 206 (hereinafter "Outer Space Treaty").

6 Id., art. IV.

7 Bin Cheng, Studies in International Space Law, at 515-22 (1997).

8 See, e.g., G.A. Res. 36/97C, U.N. Doc. A/RES/36/97C (Dec. 9, 1981); G.A. Res. 59/65, U.N. Doc. A/RES/59/65 (Dec. 17, 2004).

9 See, e.g., Jackson Maogoto & Steven Freeland, The Final Frontier: The Laws of Armed Conflict and Space Warfare, 23 Conn. J. Int'l L. 165, 183-84 (2007).

10 Joan Johnson-Freese, Heavenly Ambitions: America's Quest to Dominate

Space, at x (2009). See also Michael Krepon & Christopher Clary, Space Assurance or Space Dominance?: The Case Against Weaponizing Space (2003).

11 Douglas MacMillan & Telis Demos, Uber Valued at More than $50 Billion, The Wall Street Journal, Jul. 31, 2015, available at http://www.wsj.com/articles/uber-valued-at-more-than-50-billion-1438367457.

12 See Thomas Gryta, "AT&T Closes $49 Billion DirecTV Buy," The Wall Street Journal, Jul. 24, 2015, available at http://www.wsj.com/articles/at-t-closes-49-billion-directv-acquisition-1437766932.

13 Cenan El-Akabi, Space Policies, Issues, and Trends in 2015-16, European Space Policy Institute Report 61 at 18 (Nov. 2016), available at http://www.espi.or.at/images/Reports/Rep61_online_161128_1459.pdf.

14 See, e.g., Jeffrey T. Richelson, America's Secret Eyes in Space: The U.S. Keyhole Satellite Program (1990); Jeffrey T. Richelson, America's Space Sentinels: The History of the DSP and SBIRS Satellite Systems (1999).

15 See, e.g., Thomas Graham Jr. & Keith Hansen, Spy Satellites and Other Intelligence Technologies that Changed History (2007).

16 See, e.g., Melvin R. Laird, Memorandum for Assistant to the President for National Security Affairs, Subject: Revelation of the Fact of Satellite Reconnaissance in Connection with the Submission of Arms Limitation Agreements to Congress, Jun. 8, 1972, available at http://nsarchive.gwu.edu/NSAEBB/NSAEBB231/doc02.pdf.

17 For a popular work, see Max Boot, War Made New: Technology, Warfare, and the Course of History, 1500 to Today (2006). A more specialist work is Michael C. Horowitz, The Diffusion of Military Power: Causes and Consequences for International Politics 214-25 (2010). The classic work on the link between economic innovation and war is William H. McNeill, The Pursuit of Power: Technology, Armed Force, and Society Since A.D. 1000 (1982).

18 Donald Rumsfeld, Remarks as Delivered by U.S. Secretary of Defense Donald Rumsfeld at National Defense University (Jan. 31, 2002) (transcript available at http://www.au.af.mil/au/awc/awcgate/dod/transformation-secdef-31jan02.htm).

19 Joan Johnson-Freese, Space as a Strategic Asset, at 96 (2007).

20 Michael E. O'Hanlon, Neither Star Wars Nor Sanctuary: Constraining the Military Uses of Space, at 3 (2004).

21 U.S. Senate Armed Services Committee, Strategic Forces Subcommittee, Hearings on FY 06 Defense Authorization Budget Request for Space Activities, 109th Cong., 1st Sess. (Mar. 16, 2005). See also Benjamin S. Lambeth, Mastering the Ultimate High Ground: Next Steps in the Military Uses of Space, at 105 (2003).

22 United States Department of Defense, Report of the Commission to Assess United States National Security Space Management and Organization, Jan. 11, 2001, available at http://www.dod.gov/pubs/space20010111.html. The Commission was headed by Donald Rumsfeld, who became Secretary of Defense shortly after the study's report and was no doubt supportive of its calls for a reform of U.S. space programs.

23 Johnson-Freese, Strategic Asset, supra note 19, at 91-93 (2007).

24 Lambeth, supra note 21, at 112-13; Bob Preston et al., Space Weapons, Earth Wars, RAND Project Air Force, at 23 (2002), available at http://www.rand.org/content/dam/rand/pubs/monograph_reports/2011/RAND_MR1209.pdf.

25 Quoted in O'Hanlon, supra note 20, at 1.

26 Johnson-Freese, Heavenly Ambitions, supra note 10, at 68.

27 Everett C. Dolman, Astropolitik: Classical Geopolitics in the Space Age, at 2 (2002).

28 See 2009 Space Almanac: The U.S. Military Space Operation in Facts and Figures, Air Force Magazine, Aug. 2009, at 54, available at http://www. airforcemag.com/MagazineArchive/Magazine%20Documents/2009/ August%202009/0809SpaceAlm.pdf.

29 See Missile Defense Agency, Fact Sheet, The Ballistic Missile Defense System, Jun. 2016, available at https://www.mda.mil/global/documents/pdf/bmds.pdf.

30 Johnson-Freese, Heavenly Ambitions, supra note 10, at 77-78. See generally Robert Powell, Nuclear Deterrence Theory, Nuclear Proliferation, and National Missile Defense, 27 Int'l Security 86 (2003).

31 Johnson-Freese, Strategic Asset, supra note 19, at 134.

32 See David C. Gompert & Phillip C. Saunders, The Paradox of Power: Sino-American Strategic Restraint in an Age of Vulnerability, at 59 (2011).

33 James Clay Moltz, The Politics of Space Security: Strategic Restraint and the Pursuit of National Interests, at 297 (2d ed. 2011).

34 Quoted in Johnson-Freese, Strategic Asset, supra note 19, at 197.

35 Moltz, supra note 33, at 100.

36 Id. at 156-57.

37 Id. at 300-01.

38 Johnson-Freese, Heavenly Ambitions, supra note 10, at 90-91.

39 Id. at 9-10.

40 See Jonathan Shainin, Rods from God, New York Times Magazine, Dec. 10, 2006, available at http://www.nytimes.com/2006/12/10/ magazine/10section3a.t-9.html.

41 Id.

42 Office of the Pres., U.S. National Space Policy (Aug. 31, 2006), available at https://fas.org/irp/offdocs/nspd/space.pdf.

43 Johnson-Freese, Heavenly Ambitions, supra note 10, at 90-91.

44 Id. at 102.

45 Johnson-Freese, Strategic Asset, supra note 19, at 243.

46 Walter A. McDougall, ...the Heavens and the Earth: A Political History of the Space Age (1985).

47 Treaty Banning Nuclear Weapon Tests in the Atmosphere, in Outer Space and Under Water, Aug. 5, 1963, 480 UNTS I-6964, available at https://treaties. un.org/doc/Publication/UNTS/Volume%20480/volume-480-I-6964-English. pdf.

48 Outer Space Treaty, supra note 5, art. IV.

49 Id.

50 Id., art. II.

51 Id., art. IV.

52 See, e.g., U.S. National Space Policy, supra note 42.

53 See, e.g., Ram Jakhu, Cassandra Steer, & Kuan-Wei Chen, Conflicts in Space and the Rule of Law, Space Policy, Jan. 2016, at 3, available at https://papers. ssrn.com/sol3/papers.cfm?abstract_id=2722245.

54 See Walter A. McDougall, Promised Land, Crusader State: The American Encounter with the World Since 1776 at 172-98 (1997); John Yoo, Point of

Attack: Preventive War, International Law, and Global Welfare, at 107-29 (2014).

55 Outer Space Treaty, supra note 5, art. I.

56 Cheng, supra note 7, at 513-22.

57 Prevention of an Arms Race in Outer Space, G.A. Res. 43/70, U.N. Doc. A/RES/43/70 (Dec. 7, 1988).

58 Antarctic Treaty, Dec. 1, 1959, 12 U.S.T. 794, 402 U.N.T.S. 71, 19 I.L.M. 860.

59 On the U.S. justification for the Vietnam War under international law, see John Norton Moore, Law and the Indo-China War (1972).

60 See John Yoo, Politics as Laws?: The Anti-Ballistic Missile Treaty, the Separation of Powers, and Treaty Interpretation, 89 Cal. L. Rev. 851 (2001).

61 The White House Nat'l Sci. & Tech. Council, Fact Sheet, U.S. National Space Policy (Sept. 19, 1996) at 1, available at http://history.nasa.gov/appf2.pdf.

62 Report of the Commission to Assess United States National Security Space Management and Organization, Jan. 11, 2001, available at http://www.dod.gov/pubs/space20010111.html.

63 Moltz, supra note 33, at 267-75.

64 Id. at 269.

65 Office of the Pres., U.S. National Space Policy (Aug. 31, 2006), at 2, available at http://www.au.af.mil/au/awc/awcgate/whitehouse/ostp_space_policy06.pdf.

66 Office of the Pres., U.S. National Space Policy (Jun. 28, 2010), at 3, available at http://www.au.af.mil/au/awc/awcgate/whitehouse/national_space_policy_28june2010.pdf.

67 Id. at 7.

68 Id. at 3.

69 Moltz, supra note 33, at 316-17.

70 Mike Wall, North Korea Launches Satellite to Space, Space.com (Feb. 8, 2016), available at http://www.space.com/31860-north-korea-satellite-launch.html.

71 United Nations Conference on Disarmament, U.N. Doc. CD/1839 (Feb. 29, 2008), available at https://documents-dds-ny.un.org/doc/UNDOC/GEN/G08/604/02/PDF/G0860402.pdf.

72 Letter dated 18 August 2009 from the Permanent Representative of China and the Permanent Representative of the Russian Federation to the Conference on Disarmament, U.N. Doc. CD/1872 (Aug. 18, 2009), available at https://documents-dds-ny.un.org/doc/UNDOC/GEN/G09/631/75/PDF/G0963175.pdf?; Moltz, supra note 33, at 310.

73 EU Proposal for an International Space Code of Conduct, Draft (Mar. 31, 2014), available at https://eeas.europa.eu/topics/election-observation-missions-eueoms/14715/eu-proposal-for-an-international-space-code-of-conduct-draft_en.

74 Dr. Steven Lambakis, Missile Defense From Space, Policy Review, No. 141 (Feb. 1, 2007), available at http://www.hoover.org/research/missile-defense-space.

75 Dr. Steven Lambakis, On the Edge of the Earth: The Future of American Space Power, at 137 (2001).

76 Everett C. Dolman, Astropolitik: Classical Geopolitics in the Space Age, at 8 (2002).

77 See, e.g., Bruce M. DeBlois et al., Space Weapons: Crossing the U.S. Rubicon, 29 Int'l Security 50 (2004).

78 Johnson-Freese, Heavenly Ambitions, supra note 10, at 119-32.

79 Moltz, supra note 33, at 42-65.

80 See M.J. Peterson, The Use of Analogies in Developing Outer Space Law, 51 Int'l Org. 245, 255 (1997).

81 Id. at 252-60.

82 For a criticism of these analogies, see Moltz, supra note 33, at 14-23.

83 Herman Kahn, On Thermonuclear War 486 (1960), quoted in Moltz, supra note 33, at 19.

84 See Moltz, supra note 33, at 20-23; Philip C. Jessup & Howard J. Taubenfeld, Controls for Outer Space and the Antarctic Analogy (1959).

85 Moltz, supra note 33, at 20-23.

86 Bob Preston, Plowshares and Power: The Military Use of Civil Space, at 132 (1994), cited by Nina Tannenwald, Law Versus Power on the High Frontier: The Case for a Rule-Based Regime for Outer Space, 29 Yale J. Int'l L. 363, 383 (2004).

87 Id.

88 See, e.g., Dale Stephens & Cassandra Steer, Conflicts in Space: International Humanitarian Law and Its Application to Space Warfare, 40 McGill Annals of Air and Space L. 1 (2015); Jackson Maogoto & Steven Freeland, From Star Wars to Space Wars—The Next Strategic Frontier: Paradigms to Anchor Space Security, 33 J. Air & Space L. 10 (2008); Jackson Maogoto & Steven Freeland, The Final Frontier: The Laws of Armed Conflict and Space Warfare, 23 Conn. J. Int'l L. 165 (2007); Maj. Robert A. Ramey, Armed Conflict on the Final Frontier: The Law of War in Space, 28 Air Force L. Rev. 1 (2000).

89 Stephens & Steer, supra note 88, at 11.

90 Id. at 9, 10.

91 Manfred Lachs, The Law of Outer Space: An Experience in Contemporary Law-Making (1972).

92 See John J. Klein, Space Warfare: Strategy, Principles and Policy, at 51-60 (2006).

93 Moltz, supra note 33, at 51-52.

94 Id. at 53; Johnson-Freese, Strategic Asset, supra note 19, at 110-11.

95 Kevin Pollpeter, China's Modernization Efforts and Activities in Outer Space, Cyberspace, and the Arctic, in Assessing China's Power at 116 (Jae Ho Chung ed. 2015).

96 Klein, supra note 92, at 94.

97 Johnson-Freese, Strategic Asset, supra note 19, at 138-39.

98 See generally Powell, supra note 30.

99 There are no official statistics on the size of China's nuclear arsenal. In 2016, the U.S. Department of Defense estimated that China possessed 75-100 ICBMs, some of which had MIRV capability, but had no estimates of the number of warheads. Office of the Secretary of Defense, Annual Report to Congress: Military and Security Developments Involving the People's Republic of China 2016, Apr. 26, 2016, available at http://www.defense.gov/Portals/1/Documents/pubs/2016%20China%20Military%20Power%20Report.pdf.

100 Treaty on Measures for the Further Reduction and Limitation of Strategic Offensive Arms, art. 2, Apr. 8, 2010, T.I.A.S. 11-205.

101 See Jeffrey T. Richelson, Space-Based Early Warning: From MIDAS to DSP to SBIRS, The National Security Archive, Jan. 8, 2013, available at: http://nsarchive.gwu.edu/NSAEBB/NSAEBB235/20130108.html.

102 Bob Preston et al., Space Weapons Earth Wars, RAND Project Air Force, 40-45 (2002).

103 SATCAT Boxscore, Dec. 29, 2016, available at http://www.celestrak.com/satcat/boxscore.asp.

CONCLUSION

1 Special Rapporteur on Extrajudicial, Summary or Arbitrary Executions, Study on Targeted Killings by Philip Alston, Human Rights Council, 9-11, U.N. Doc. A/HRC/14/24/Add.6 (May 28, 2010), available at http://www2.ohchr.org/english/bodies/hrcouncil/docs/14session/A.HRC.14.24.Add6.pdf.

2 Jeffrey T.G. Kelsey, Hacking into International Humanitarian Law: The Principles of Distinction and Neutrality in the Age of Cyber Warfare, 106 Mich. L. Rev. 1427, 1439 (2008).

3 Marie Isabelle Chevrier & Alex Spelling, The Traditional Tools of Biological Arms Control and Disarmament in Biological Threats in the 21st Century: The Politics, People, Science and Historical Roots 351 (Filippa Lentzos ed. 2016).

4 Convention (IV) Respecting the Laws and Customs of War on Land and its Annex: Regulations Concerning the Laws and Customs of War on Land, art. 27, The Hague, Oct. 18, 1907.

5 Department of Defense, Law of War Manual 210 (2015).

Index